Sweet Negotiations

Sweet Negotiations

SUGAR, SLAVERY, AND
PLANTATION AGRICULTURE
IN EARLY BARBADOS

Russell R. Menard

University of Virginia Press
Charlottesville and London

University of Virginia Press

© 2006 by the Rector and Visitors of the University of Virginia

All rights reserved

Printed in the United States of America on acid-free paper

First published 2006

1 3 5 7 9 8 6 4 2

LIBRARY OF CONGRESS CATALOGING-IN-PUBLICATION DATA

Menard, Russell R.

Sweet negotiations : sugar, slavery, and plantation agriculture in early Barbados /
Russell R. Menard

p.   cm.

Includes bibliographical references and index.

ISBN 0-8139-2540-1 (cloth : alk. paper)

1. Agriculture—Economic aspects—Barbados—History—17th century.
2. Sugar trade—Barbados—History—17th century. 3. Slavery—Barbados—History—
17th century. 4. Plantations—Barbados—History—17th century. I. Title.

HD1855.43.M46 2006

330.972981—dc22

2005029315

*First, for Kathleen, more than forty years my wife
and still the joy of my life*

*Next, for Julie Beth Kays, Grace Kathleen Kays,
John Michael Kays III, Michael James Menard,
and Macie Beth Menard, who give me hope*

*Finally, for the members of the Minnesota Early
American History Workshop, who
kept me focused*

Contents

Illustrations

Preface

IN THE EARLY 1990S, when I made my first extended research trip to Barbados, I had no intention of working on a project that would raise questions about the notion of a sugar revolution. Quite the contrary, just a few years previously John McCusker and I had published a book in which we used the idea of a sugar revolution, the notion that sugar had thoroughly transformed Barbados by bringing African slavery and plantation agriculture to the island, as a device around which to organize our discussion of the economic history of early Barbados. Indeed, initially I went to Barbados hoping to add precision to some of the central arguments of the sugar-revolution hypothesis, with an eye toward adding a comparative dimension to some of my work on the transition to slavery in the mainland colonies. In particular I was interested in dating as precisely as possible the transition from indentured servitude to African slavery on the island, a transition that advocates of the notion of a sugar revolution claimed had been driven by an increased demand for labor as sugar had come to dominate the island's economy. I was also especially interested in how the transition had been financed.

According to the idea of a sugar revolution, the financing had been provided by the Dutch, who were thought to have played a key role in bringing sugar to the island. I hoped to pin down the role of the Dutch by discovering how much capital they had provided and what form the loans had taken. My modest ambition was not to write a book challenging the idea of a sugar revolution, a notion that seemed so firmly rooted in empirical research as to be beyond question. However, as I worked through the material in the Barbados National Archives I encountered several surprises. I was unable to uncover any evidence that the Dutch had loaned Barbadians money or sold them slaves, although I found abundant evidence that a group of London merchants centered on Martin Noell, a group previously little noticed by historians, had supplied islanders with both capital and slaves. I also encountered several scraps of evidence suggesting that contrary to the arguments of advocates of a sugar revolution, the planters of Barbados had been quite prosperous in the immediate presugar era and their prosperity had played an important role in financing the rise of sugar. I also found various clues indicating that plantation agriculture and African slavery had preceded sugar to the island. In short, the notion of a sugar revolution seemed to have things backward. I was not yet ready to reject the idea of a sugar revolution.

My moment of epiphany, if I may be permitted so grand a phrase, occurred toward the end of my stay, when Hilary Beckles invited me to address the history seminar at the Cave Hill campus of the University of the West Indies. As I prepared some notes for the seminar while sitting on one of the island's many lovely beaches, I came to realize that collectively my various archival discoveries raised some important questions about the idea of a sugar revolution. I concluded my remarks at the seminar by arguing that the notion of a sugar revolution, while a handy device for conceptualizing changes in Barbados about the middle of the seventeenth century, obscured the extent to which the Barbadian plantation regime had grown out of a quarter-century of activities in the presugar era.

The seminar proved an ideal setting to try out some new ideas. Here I was trying to sort out the meaning of my archival research with a group of scholars deeply versed in Barbadian history, many of whom had worked through the archival material that led me to question the conventional wisdom regarding what happened in Barbados in the 1640s. The 1640s was a crucial decade in the history of Barbados, and in the history of all of British America, for it was in that decade that large-scale plantation agriculture and African slavery became central to the island's economy. Once established in Barbados, those institutions spread throughout the English Caribbean and later to the plantation districts of British North America. Conventional wisdom has it that sugar was responsible for the transformation of Barbados. My research in the Barbados National Archives indicated that this is an oversimplification. By the end of the seminar I was arguing that Barbados had been well on its way to becoming a plantation colony and a slave society in response to the activities of men raising cotton, tobacco, and indigo before sugar came to dominate the island's economy. Sugar did not bring plantation agriculture and African slavery to Barbados; rather, it quickened, deepened, and drove to a conclusion a transformation already under way when sugar emerged as the island's major crop. If this book is successful in persuading some scholars to look at the idea of a sugar revolution more critically, its success should be attributed in large part to the conversation I had with Beckles and his colleagues at Cave Hill some fifteen years ago.

When I returned to Minnesota, I was anxious to get some of my new ideas and evidence into print. My first thought was to summarize the main points as an article. But the article I drafted turned out to be more than one hundred pages long, and I could see that it could be longer still. I considered breaking it into several articles but rejected that notion because the persuasiveness of my case depended on the collective impact of several arguments and new pieces of evidence; division, I feared, would lessen the power of my argument. So I settled on a book, reasoning that what had happened in Barbados during the 1640s was sufficiently important to early American history to warrant a book devoted to it. Once I made that fundamental choice, the project flowed smoothly, and despite occasional detours on my part to publish bits and pieces of the argument in other forms, the book moved rapidly to completion, always remaining rooted in that first research trip to Barbados and the conversations I had there at that time.

Early on in this project I realized that my task was more to raise questions then to settle them. Perhaps the most important question concerns the concept of a sugar revolution. While I doubt that the notion will disappear from the literature as a result of this book, I do hope that I will at least provoke a debate and persuade historians of the sugar islands to examine the notion more critically than they have in the recent past. Another important question concerns the organization of production in the sugar industry. Some historians have assumed that the integrated plantation and the gang system arrived in Barbados simultaneously with sugar. I hope I have managed to show that this is not true and that the creation of the Barbadian sugar complex was a complicated process whose history merits careful research. A third question concerns the economy of Barbados before the sugar boom. I hope my comments on that economy persuade some scholars that close attention to the presugar era in Barbadian history might yield rich rewards. Fourth, I hope this book persuades someone to pay close attention to the English merchants who played so important a role in the Barbadian sugar boom. I suspect they formed an interest group centered on the Noell brothers, a group that played a key role in organizing Britain's American empire. I also hope that this book persuades someone that the English merchants who helped build the sugar boom merit a collective biography. Finally, this book raises an important question about the relationship between African and American slavery. The tendency in the literature has been to stress their differences. The Barbadian experience, however, suggests that we ought to think about their similarities. Many of the persons who came to America as slaves had been slaves in Africa. It strikes me that once they reached America, they may have struggled to shape their experience to make it resemble what they had known before. If it manages to provoke some new scholarship on these and other questions, this book will have done its work. Finally, this book makes a contribution to the emerging field of Atlantic history by showing the extent to which developments in Barbados had a powerful impact throughout the English Atlantic world. In a related fashion it builds a strong case for including the English Caribbean, especially Barbados, in the curriculum of the colonial portion of U.S. history courses, since what happened on the island proved critical to the development of slavery, plantation agriculture, and racial ideologies in British mainland North America.

Acknowledgments

IN 1993 I SUFFERED a severe stroke while on a research trip to London. Recovering from a stroke is a collective enterprise, and I am most grateful to all who helped me along. My family played the key role. My wife, Kathleen, supervised and coordinated the effort. As one observer who watched the process closely noted, she was awesome through it all. Were it not for Kathleen's fierce commitment to my recovery, this book would not have been written. Mike and Tara helped out in ways too numerous to list. They always found time for me. Elizabeth and John, who lived far away, still managed to be enthusiastic participants in the process. They also became the parents of three of the children to whom this book is dedicated, thus giving me all the incentive I needed to work at recovery. And they provided me a home where I could make the final revisions of the manuscript.

I count myself most fortunate in having been able to pursue the business of relearning the historian's craft as a member of the history department at the University of Minnesota, certainly one of the most humane, collegial, and supportive environments one could find. My colleagues were extraordinarily helpful and encouraging as I worked at the task of getting better. I thank them all. I would also like to thank the therapists both in England and in Minnesota, but especially those at the St. Paul Jewish Community Center, for pointing me in the right directions. Another benefit of working at Minnesota has been the opportunity to work with some terrific students, several of whom—John Campbell, Sean Condon, David Hacker, Ginny Jelatis, Mat Mulcahy, J. Eliott Russo, and Dave Ryden—shared my interest in slavery and plantation agriculture. I learned as much from them as they did from me.

In developing the arguments of this book I presented portions at various venues, including the economic history seminar at the University of Chicago, the history seminar at the University of the West Indies, Cave

Hill, meetings of the Social Science History Association, and the annual conference of the Institute of Early American History and Culture. I thank the participants in all those events, especially S. H. H. Carrington, David Galenson, Farley Grubb, and Emily Melchner, for their kind and useful comments.

The most useful setting for testing arguments was close to home. During the years that I worked on this book the members of the Minnesota Early American History Workshop—Sarah Crabtree, Jason Eden, Kirsten Fischer, Ed Griffen, Joel Helfrich, John Howe, Brad Jarvis, Ken Mitchell, Lisa Norling, Jean O'Brien-Kehoe, Walter Sargent, Brie Swenson, Kate Thomas, and Serena Zabin—perhaps heard more about the economic history of early Barbados than they cared to. Nevertheless, they listened with patience and argued with me respectfully and helped make this a better book, for which I thank them all. My good friend and neighbor Leon Webster read the entire manuscript. By demanding that I express myself clearly, he did subsequent readers a major service. Leon also helped with various word-processing problems and prepared the book's graphs.

I also had help from scholars outside of Minnesota. My good friend and collaborator John McCusker, who knows more about the sugar industry than anyone else, saved me from many mistakes. Those that remain can be attributed to my stubborn refusal to listen. Jacob Price shared his unparalleled knowledge of London colonial merchants during daily visits while I was in the hospital in London. Stan Engerman provided the kind of detailed commentary that those of us who do economic history have come to expect of him. Richard Holway, of the University of Virginia Press, proved an outstanding editor. His enthusiasm for this project, prompt responses, and sage advice were critical in bringing the manuscript to completion.

I also owe a substantial debt to the staffs of the several libraries where I conducted research, particularly to the always helpful archivists at the Barbados National Archives and to the librarians at the several British repositories in which I worked, the British Library and the Public Records Offices at Chancery Lane and Kew. Again, I must return to my home institution. I have the good fortune of working within a few minutes' walk of the James Ford Bell Library, where first Carroll Urness and later Susan Hilliard and their staff proved most helpful.

I also want to thank Richard Dunn and Hilary Beckles, whose support and enthusiasm at an early stage in this project were critical in persuading me to stay the course. Unfortunately, Richard Sheridan died before I began this project, so I missed the opportunity to discuss early Caribbean economic history with him. Sheridan did, however, leave a substantial body of scholarship behind, from which I learned much and upon which I relied heavily.

I would be remiss if I did not thank the office staff at the University of Minnesota Department of History, where Sue Haskins and her crew, especially Amanda Nelson, who prepared the final version of the manuscript, provided the support I needed to return to work. Finally, I want to thank K.G., the Minnesota Timberwolves, and the NBA for providing necessary diversions. I love this game!

Sweet Negotiations

Introduction

BARBADOS, A SMALL ISLAND of only 166 square miles on the eastern fringe of the Caribbean, had an importance in England's American empire that far exceeded its size. Indeed, if one accepts Eric Williams's contention that the first British empire was organized around the trade in slaves and in products produced by slaves, it could be argued that Barbados was the empire's core, or at least its hub, to use a term from Williams.[1] Certainly it was the colony most thoroughly dominated by slavery and most heavily committed to export agriculture. There is considerable archaeological evidence that Arawak and later Carib Indians inhabited the island in pre-Columbian times, but it seems that the Indians, decimated by diseases and pummeled by slave raiders seeking workers for the mines of Hispaniola, deserted the island. Although Indians from neighboring islands may have visited Barbados in the early seventeenth century, by the time the first English colonists arrived in 1627, Barbados apparently was uninhabited.[2]

Barbados played an important role in the history of the British American mainland. It provided colonies whose markets were too small to be served directly from Africa with a source of slaves.[3] It provided a market for farmers unable to raise a staple that could find a purchase in the metropolis and thus became the terminus of a small but important trade that played a major role in the development of the continental economy, most evident in the rise of several of the mainland's larger port cities.[4] Its slave code became a model for those of several of the plantation colonies, while its central institution, the large, integrated plantation on which gangs of slaves produced crops for export, was widely copied, as was the slave-economy system, by which slaves were made responsible for growing much of their own food. The commission system by which those crops were marketed also emerged first in Barbados and later spread throughout England's American empire. Racial ideologies initially developed on the island, especially the notion that whiteness could provide a crucial source of solidarity, spread quickly to the plantation colonies on the mainland.

While the main outlines of what is usually referred to as the Barbadian sugar revolution, which has dominated the historiography of the island for three and a half centuries,[5] seem firmly established, close inspection of the records in the Barbados National Archives reveals major difficulties with the generally accepted account.[6] Usually, the sugar boom is explained as a result of a conjuncture between a failure in the Barbadian economy and the interests of the Dutch. In the years surrounding 1640 the island economy was thoroughly depressed as bad times in the tobacco industry hit the low-grade leaf grown in Barbados especially hard and as cotton failed to live up to its initial promise. The Barbadians, so the argument runs, had either to find another export or to abandon their pursuit of riches and accept a future much like New England's as small farmers at the edge of empire. Dutch merchants, their control of the sugar industry at Pernambuco in Brazil threatened, proved to be the island's salvation. They taught the Barbadians how to grow, harvest, and process sugarcane,

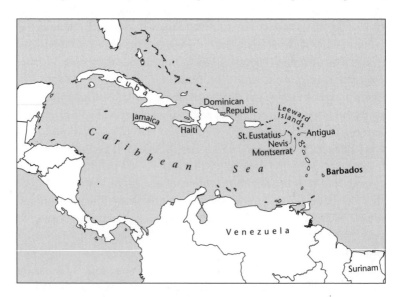

FIG. 1. The modern Caribbean. (Cartography Lab, University of Minnesota)

loaned them the capital to build plantations, sold them the slaves to do the work, shipped the product across the Atlantic, and marketed it in the major European trading centers. The results of this intervention were awesome and dreadful. The Barbadian sugar revolution, or as Richard Ligon called it, "the sweet Negotiation of Sugar,"[7] transformed the island in the decades surrounding 1650. Sugar monoculture drove out diversified farming; large plantations consumed small farms; blacks arrived by the thousands, and whites left; destructive demographic patterns took root; the island began to import food and fuel; and the great planters rose to wealth and power—all within the twenty years following 1640. The critical changes were the shift from English indentured servants to African slavery and the rise of great plantations, the explanation for which seems straightforward. Sugar, because of its substantial scale economies and handsome profits, was most efficiently produced on big units and greatly increased demand for labor. Growing demand for labor pushed wages and indenture prices up, stretched the capacity of the servant trade to the breaking point, and forced planters to look elsewhere for workers. African slaves, available in large numbers through the century-old Atlantic trade, were the most attractive alternative. Other islands in the British and French West Indies witnessed similar changes in the size of plantations and the composition of the labor force as sugar came to dominate their economies. Nowhere, however, did the sugar revolution strike with the speed and power apparent in Barbados.[8]

This is a compelling story, but it is incorrect in many of its details. In particular it underestimates the performance of the economy in the pre-sugar era and distorts the relationship between sugar and slavery in the crucial early years of the transformation of the workforce. It also overestimates the role of the Dutch and underestimates the accomplishments of the English both in the Atlantic economy as a whole and in Barbados and thus fails to appreciate the key role the English played in bringing sugar to Barbados.

The sugar revolution needs to be revisited. In taking up the task I begin this book with a description of the Barbadian economy in the 1630s and 1640s, contending that sugar emerged, not out of a depression, but out of what is best described as a diversified export boom.[9] Then, in chapter 2, I offer a description of the reorganization of land and labor during the middle decades of the seventeenth century that is more precise than what has been available previously and that suggests some revision in the usual account of that process by showing that the shift to African slavery and the growth of large plantations was a process well under way before sugar emerged as a major crop on the island.

Since this is the center of my case against the notion of a sugar revolution, I want to make my argument clear. I do not contending that Barbados was not changed profoundly in the middle decades of the seventeenth century;[10] however, I do contend that it is an error to attribute those changes solely and entirely to sugar, as Barbados was already on its way to becoming a plantation colony and a slave society in response to the decisions of planters who grew tobacco, indigo, and cotton before sugar emerged as the dominant crop on the island. Sugar did not transform Barbados on its own; rather, it sped up and intensified a process already under way in response to the activities of planters who grew what are usually considered minor crops. Thus it seems wrong to describe what happened in Barbados in the mid-seventeenth century as a sugar revolution. I prefer the more prosaic term *sugar boom*. My argument is not simply that other crops started Barbados down the road to slavery and plantation agriculture and that sugar then came along to complete the task but that success with tobacco, cotton, and indigo was essential to the rise of sugar because that success allowed planters to generate the incomes and build estates that would help finance the rise of sugar and established their competence as planters, as men who could be trusted with loans of the size needed to build sugar estates. Chapter 2 next focuses on the labor force, especially on the question whether there was a distinct Barbadian path toward slavery.

In chapter 3 I ask how the sugar boom was paid for, arguing that the role of the Dutch in financing it has been greatly exaggerated in previous scholarship.[11] I do this by focusing first on a group of English merchants who made a crucial intervention in the island's economy in the 1640s and then on planters on the island who used capital accumulated through farm building during the export boom and income from the minor exports to purchase slaves and build sugar estates. I then suggest that what might be called "the myth of the Dutch" was part of an ideology fashioned by planters who were unhappy with the restrictions imposed on them by the Navigation Acts of the 1660s. While the idea of a sugar revolution has gained general acceptance among students of the Caribbean, I am not the only scholar who is uneasy about the concept. Recently Michael Craton argued that there was no such revolution because the plantation system that flourished in Barbados "was not qualitatively new. It differed from its forerunners only in its scale and intensity, and it was not even, by any means, a culmination of a process."[12] While I am persuaded that Craton is wrong on this point and that the plantation complex that emerged in Barbados during the sugar boom was a largely new development, I am pleased not to be tilting against the windmill of the sugar revolution on my own.

Chapter 4 explores the Barbadian sugar industry in the aftermath of what I label the "sugar boom," rather than the "sugar revolution," contending that the dynamics of the industry's late-seventeenth-century expansion have usually been misunderstood. In the years after 1650 Barbadian sugar production increased substantially, while prices fell. The decline in sugar prices has usually been explained as a simple consequence of overproduction. I argue that this explanation misrepresents the dynamics of the industry. Sugar was a very competitive industry in the early modern era. Furthermore, prices in Europe were sufficiently high to restrict consumption to the relatively prosperous.[13] Thus there were considerable advantages to those producers who could afford to sell their sugars at lower prices. To capture those advantages, growers worked hard to improve efficiency. As they did so, prices tumbled and consumption increased. Sugar prices did not fall because production rose; rather, production rose and consumption increased because prices fell.[14]

Chapter 5 explores the changing organization of the Barbadian sugar industry through a focus on the development of four key institutions: the large-scale, integrated plantation; the gang system; the slave-economy system; and the commission system. In my first draft of chapter 5 I argued that there was a sugar revolution in Barbados in the mid-seventeenth century but that historians have misunderstood the direction of change. Sugar did not revolutionize Barbados; rather, Barbados revolutionized the sugar industry by replacing the earlier system in which small farmers grew cane for a big man's mill, with the large-scale, integrated plantation, in which growing and processing were brought together under a single owner. Although the integrated plantation would eventually transform the sugar industry, its rise to dominance was gradual, altogether too slow to constitute a revolution. This led me to conclude that the notion of a sugar revolution could not be salvaged and that we were better off consigning it to the historiographic dustbin. Both the integrated plantation and the gang system, which are sometimes interpreted as reflecting the physical requirements of the crop,[15] can be understood as a result of the efforts of planters to respond to the pressures of falling prices and to increase productivity and are thus particular examples of the more general process described in chapter 4.

Under the slave-economy system slaves were allocated plots of ground on which to grow their own food and allowed to market their products. Since the publication of Sidney Mintz and David Hall's classic article on the Jamaican internal marketing system, historians have tended to assume that the slave-economy system did not develop in Barbados because it is generally flat and gently sloping, entirely suitable for sugar cultivation and thus affording no space where slaves might grow provisions.[16] Despite its geography, the island had a vibrant slave economy by the late seventeenth century. Under the commission system, "which in the eighteenth century was to become an outstanding characteristic of the West India trade,"[17] planters became entrepreneurs and sold their sugars not on the island but in England through commission agents. Taken together, these four institutions, all products of the Barbadian sugar boom, defined the character of the Caribbean sugar industry throughout most of the colonial era, until abolition changed everything.

In a concluding chapter I explore the expansion of Barbados, arguing that what happened on the island during the sugar boom was influential well beyond the shores of that small island. In the aftermath of the sugar boom Barbadians scattered throughout the British Caribbean and the plantation districts of British mainland North America, bringing with them ideas, institutions, and ideologies first developed in Barbados during the sugar boom. Thus Barbados was a "cultural hearth" for the British colonies in America. A brief epilogue provides a reassessment of the idea of a sugar revolution. It also offers reflections on the notion of socioeconomic revolutions as used by historians, particularly by commenting on Ira Berlin's recent effort to extend the ideas of the sugar revolution to the mainland by means of the idea of a "plantation revolution."[18] Finally, a short appendix reproduces several contemporary estimates of the cost of establishing Caribbean sugar plantations, documents that reveal a good deal about the changing structure of those institutions. I hope that these documents, which can be used in various research exercises to explore the character of plantation agriculture, will enhance the usefulness of this book in the classroom.

Historiographically, this book is rooted in what has become known as the Chesapeake school, the tradition in which I earned my spurs as a historian. I have tried to extend the methods and approaches developed by historians of Maryland and Virginia to Barbados.[19] Indeed, when pressed for a quick summary of the book, I have sometimes described it as "a Chesapeaker goes to the islands"; I hope readers do not think it should be described as "a Chesapeaker goes on vacation."[20] While the particular historiographic roots of this book are in the Chesapeake school, it is also part of a more general expansion of the field of early American history, still in progress.[21]

Questions of currency bedevil students of the economies of all the American colonies, and Barbados proved no exception. By the middle decades of the seventeenth century Barbadians priced most transactions in terms of an imaginary money, or money of account, known as Barbados currency. Unfortunately, owing to the lack of legislation governing exchange rates, the value of Barbados currency relative to British sterling or to any other well-established money during the crucial years from 1640 to 1660 is unclear. The best guess is that it took £133.0.0 Barbados currency to purchase £100 sterling. After 1660 the exchange rate improved, doubtless a function of the successes of the sugar industry, reaching £110 Barbados currency per £100 sterling by the late 1680s. I generally note the currency in use whenever citing a value, but where I have failed to do so it should be assumed that Barbados currency is meant. The data indicate that Barbadians also used various local commodities as money in transactions, but whether this was an accounting device or whether the commodities actually changed hands is not clear. Fortunately, for our purposes here it does not matter.[22] In quoting freely from contemporary sources I have reproduced the original material as closely as possible. Those who built the Barbadian sugar industry had ideas about race that most readers today find nasty and wrongheaded. Nevertheless, in order to understand their behavior we must be familiar with those ideas.

Researching and writing this book took a long time. As noted in the acknowledgments, it was finished under extraordinary circumstances that resulted in an imbalance. Initially I intended to view the Barbadian sugar boom from the vantage point of both the island and the metropolis; however, I ended up relying more heavily on the island archives than on those in the metropolis. Since most of the literature relies more heavily on metropolitan sources to the neglect of those housed on the island, this might be regarded as a blessing in disguise. Indeed, it may help explain why my reading of what happened in Barbados during the middle decades of the seventeenth century so often diverges from the prevailing consensus.[23]

After reading through an early draft of this book I became dismayed at how reactive it seemed. Chapter after chapter reported a consensus in the existing historiography and then went on to argue that the consensus was wrong. Most historians agree that the Barbadian economy was depressed in the immediate presugar era, but my evidence suggests that sugar emerged out of a boom rather than a depression. The usual argument is that sugar brought slavery and plantation agriculture to the island, but my evidence indicates that Barbados was moving down that road well before sugar emerged as the dominant crop. While most historians argue that the Dutch financed the sugar boom, I could find no evidence of Dutch capital on the island as planters converted to sugar. Finally, Barbados, with its flat or gently sloping land, was not supposed to support the emergence of a system in which slaves grew much of their own food, yet I found evidence that they did so soon after the sugar boom had run its course. While I remained persuaded that each of my arguments is correct, and while this structure reflects my understanding of the discipline as a continuous conversation among scholars, I was concerned that the book was structured around refuting other historians' arguments rather than advancing an argument of its own. Upon reflection, however, it became clear to me that there was an important argument buried in my several refutations, an argument with implications for students not only of the British West Indies but also of European America in general.

As I have already mentioned, much of the prevailing consensus regarding the Barbadian sugar revolution was developed out of metropolitan sources, while my arguments are rooted in documents housed on the island. There is an important difference between the two types of source material. To use the language of Marc Bloch, the sources in metropolitan archives tend to be "intentional" or "narrative" sources, written to influence someone's understanding of events. The sources on the island, by contrast, are more often what Bloch called "witnesses in spite of themselves," sources constructed not to shape understanding but for some other purpose, to keep titles to land straight, to control inheritances, or to see that debts were repaid.[24] These sources do not tell a story on their own but can be made to tell one only after careful manipulation by historians.[25] As Josephine Tey put it, "Truth isn't to be found in accounts but in account books."[26] My larger point is that historians of European America need to be careful of metropolitan, intentional sources, which are often misleading, and put their trust more firmly in the "witnesses in spite of themselves found in colonial archives."[27] At the very least, we historians of European America must check the validity of the stories we find in metropolitan archives against at times seemingly intransigent sources housed in the colonies. One might argue that the narrative sources interpreting Barbados that one finds in metropolitan libraries and archives are unusually distorted because they are so often products of the great political struggles of the day, the controversy over the Navigation Acts in the mid-seventeenth century or the battle over the Royal African Company's monopoly at century's end. However, I would contend that such circumstances are part of the normal course of metropolitan–colonial relations and that those who commented on colonial affairs usually had an axe to grind. This book is focused on the Barbadian sugar industry and the men who built. While the great planters of Barbados dominated the building of the sugar industry, they did not build it alone, nor was their work unconstrained. Rather, as the title of this book implies, the planters built (or "tore violently," as Miss Rosa Coldfield would have put it)[28] their industry through a process of negotiation—with the merchants, who supplied much of the capital they needed; with the administrators of the emerging empire, who provided an institutional framework as well as defense against enemies both foreign and domestic; with the servants and slaves who did the work; and, finally, with the small planters, whose loyalty was necessary to the survival of their regime.

Despite its centrality to the creation of European America, sugar was indigenous to neither Europe nor America, although some observers, noting the presence of wild canes on various islands and reflecting on the importance of sugar to Caribbean life, claimed that the plant had a pre-Columbian history in the region. Nevertheless, the best evidence is that sugarcane (*Saccharum officinarum* L. was domesticated in New Guinea several millennia ago. From New Guinea there were several diffusions, the first, occurring about 800 BC, to India, the Philippines, and Indonesia, followed by a long, gradual westerly migration. From India the cane was carried westward by the Arabs, reaching Persia in the sixth century BC. As its westward migration continued, new centers of production flourished, while the older centers to the east went into decline. By the tenth century Arabs had carried sugar to the Mediterranean, where first Crete and then Sicily became major producers. (Sugar, it has been said, followed the Koran.) In the fifteenth century it spread to Madeira, the Azores, and the Canaries in the Atlantic, stepping-stones to the Americas. Columbus took cane from the Canaries to the Caribbean on his second voyage. Although the crop did well there, the Spanish, for reasons that remain unclear, muffed the chance to become the first major sugar producers in the Americas. That honor instead fell to the Portuguese, who had established a flourishing sugar industry in Brazil by the late sixteenth century. From Brazil, as we shall see, sugar migrated to the English Caribbean, where Barbados emerged as the world's largest sugar producer by the end of the seventeenth century, and the westward drift of sugar halted at least temporarily.[29]

1

The Export Boom in Barbados

THERE IS A LONG-STANDING scholarly consensus in Barbadian historiography that the island's economy was a failure before commercial sugarcane cultivation and that sugar emerged out of a severe depression. Carl and Roberta Bridenbaugh captured the view of most historians when they said that Barbadian planters found "their first truly profitable staple only with sugar. . . . To maintain that the white men made a success of their colonies prior to 1645 is to press the evidence too hard."[1] This chapter interrogates this consensus from the perspective provided by local records now in the Barbados National Archives and finds it wanting in two respects: first, the Barbados economy had some successes before sugar; and second, sugar emerged in the context of a boom and not a depression.

There is more to this argument than the simple inversion of an existing consensus. As we will see in chapter 3, the successes of the presugar era would prove critical to the emergence of sugar as the island's dominant staple. Those successes were important in four ways. First, Barbadians were able to use the estates they built in the 1630s to help finance the building of sugar plantations. Second, those successes permitted some Barbadians to show that they were capable of managing plantations and thus could be trusted with substantial loans, capital that could be used to purchase the slaves and equipment needed to enter the sugar industry. Third, it was during the export boom that Barbadians began to develop the legal infrastructure necessary to the success of African slavery on a large scale.[2] Although the details are now lost, Barbadians began to develop a law of slavery before the island legislature wrote the emerging English empire's first comprehensive slave code in 1661.[3] The essential issue was settled early, in 1636, at about the time that islanders were just beginning to ex-

periment with plantation agriculture, when the governor and council resolved "that Negroes and Indians, that came here to be sold should serve
for Life, unless a Contract was made before to the contrary."[4] Although the
preamble to the 1661 Act for the better ordering and governing of Negroes
taunts us with a reference to "many good Laws and ordinances . . . made
for the governing, and regulating and ordering the Negroes, Slaves in this
isle.,"[5] these have since been lost, and we will never know the full extent to
which legislation passed before the rise of sugar paved the way for the Barbadian sugar boom. Fourth and finally, in preparing the ground for tobacco, cotton, and indigo, planters also prepared the ground for sugarcane
cultivation. When the English reached Barbados, they found it densely
forested, thick with trees and underbrush that had to be cleared away before crops could be planted. According to John Oldmixon, "The Woods
were so thick, and most of the Trees so large and massy, that t'was not a
few Hands could fell them; which was another Discouragement to them."[6]
Planters did much of the clearing in the 1630s and early 1640s. Thus, when
they turned to sugar, some of the essential preliminary work had already
been done. Quite literally, the "minor staples" cleared the way for sugar.[7]

Contemporaries, and historians after them, told several stories about
the beginnings of sugarcane cultivation in Barbados, some of them conflicting. One tradition credits the Dutch and the Sephardic Jews. An anonymous note of about 1663 in Sir Robert Harley's papers is typical: "Barbados did not thrive at first, until it happen'd that the Dutch loosing Brasille,
many Dutch and Jews repairing to Barbados began the making of sugar."[8]
More persuasive accounts, if only because more detailed, assign a more active role to English planters, suggesting a long process of learning by doing, experimentation, and borrowing as Barbadians gradually acquired
the complex skills needed to grow and process sugarcane.

The plant reached the island shortly after the first English and Africans
in 1627. After depositing the settlers, Captain Henry Powell set off almost
immediately for the Dutch colony on the Essequibo River. He soon returned with provisions and several plant varieties, including sugarcane.
Since there are several recent, detailed accounts of sugar making in the literature, I will highlight only the most important points here.[9] First, sugar
plantations were large and complex institutions by the standards of early
modern agriculture, and careful management and close coordination
were necessary to produce a crop that would earn a profit. As the Jamaican
planter Bryan Edwards, writing at the end of the eighteenth century, put

it: "A plantation . . . ought to be considered as a well-constructed machine, compounded of various wheels turning different ways, yet all contributing to the great end proposed; but if any one part runs too fast or too slow, in proportion to the rest, the main purpose is defeated."[10] Second, it took a long time to produce a crop, process it, and ship it to market. Planting typically began in summer, during the rainy season, and crops were not harvested until the dry season some sixteen months later between January and May. Once harvested, the cane had to be processed. First the juice was extracted by milling, which had to be done soon after the cane was cut or it would lose its sweetness; next the juice was heated to crystallize it, which had to be done within hours of milling or the juice would ferment; and then the juice was drained of molasses in a curing house. There was work to be done on sugar plantations throughout the year, which some would argue explains the close association between sugar and slavery.[11]

The process began when slaves dug holes or trenches and inserted two-foot-long cuttings of old cane endwise in the holes or lengthwise in the trenches. Covered lightly with soil, these cuttings would sprout new plants within two weeks. Within a month the plants would reach a height of two feet, and the laborious weeding process would begin. Weeding was an almost continuous task for the slaves until the canes grew tall enough to suppress weeds on their own. Planters quickly learned to stagger planting in order to spread the harvest over several months. During the weeding process the canes were thinned, cuttings that failed to sprout were grubbed up and replanted, and several applications of dung were made.

Given the long growing season, the additional months it took to turn the harvested cane into marketable sugar, and the time required to ship the crop across the Atlantic and arrange for sale, nearly two and one-half years were likely to elapse between first planting and the day the planter saw any income from the crop, which left growers heavily dependent upon credit supplied by merchants. Some fourteen to eighteen months after planting, the canes would reach their full height of eight feet, and the harvest would begin. Slaves armed with curved knives known as "bills" would move into the fields, cut the canes, strip them of their leaves, tie them into bundles, and cart them to the mill. What happened to the cane once it reached the mill is ably described by Richard Ligon's diagram of a sugar works (fig. 2).

Once harvested, a cane field would yield a second crop, known as ratoons. Ratoon cane required less labor than fresh plantings and reached maturity in only a year. While new fields would yield several crops, despite heavy dunging, the land's fertility gradually declined, and along with it, the cane's saccharine content. Eventually the old cuttings would have to be grubbed up after each harvest, and the field allowed to lie fallow for a time before replanting with fresh cuttings. By the 1680s the land in Barbados was so exhausted that planters no longer harvested ratoons. Since processing had to occur soon after the cane was cut, it was best done on site, and the timing of work in the field and at the mill needed to be closely coordinated, which accounts for the advantage of the integrated plantation.

Historians impressed by the size of sugar plantations have usually assumed that sugar yielded substantial returns to scale. Sugar plantations were large: Richard Sheridan's analysis of probate inventories concludes that a typical Jamaican sugar estate in 1774 consisted of 266 acres worked by more than two hundred slaves and was worth about £19,000 sterling.[12] However, size alone does not establish that there were scale economies in the industry, and the best evidence is that beyond certain minimums— the first occurring at the point where it became possible to operate an integrated plantation, a second when the work force became large enough to be organized into gangs—there were no further advantages to size in sugar production.[13] The size of West Indian plantations is probably ex-

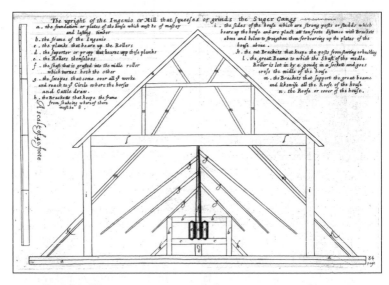

FIG. 2. Upright of the *ingenio,* or sugar mill, from Ligon, *True and Exact History of Barbados,* 84. (Courtesy of James Ford Bell Library, Minneapolis)

plained by their profitability rather than by the efficiencies of big operations. Investing in additional land and slaves to make more sugar was apparently the most profitable use of the capital planters had on hand.[14] Planters increased the size of their plantations to raise their income, not to increase their efficiency. Since sugar plantations often earned profits of 7 to 8 percent and higher in the seventeenth century, we should not be surprised to learn that planters thought that "capital put to sugar cane would make a sweet business" and often reinvested their profits in enlarging their plantation.[15]

Work in a sugar mill was hard and dangerous and required considerable skill. Thomas Tryon, a Barbadian with firsthand knowledge of sugar making, has left a rare seventeenth-century description of a mill that is worth quoting in full as it captures some of the flavor of the place:

> [To work in a sugar mill is] to live in a perpetual Noise and Hurry, and the only way to render a person Angry and Tyrannical, too; since the Climate is so hot and the labor so constant, that the Servants (we would say slaves) night and day stand in great Boyling Houses, where there are six or seven large Coppers or Furnaces kept perpetually boyling; and from which with heavy Ladles and Skimmers they Skim off the excrementitious parts of the Canes, till it comes to its perfection and cleans, while others as Stoakers, Broil as it were alive, in managing the Fires, and one part is constantly at the mill to supply it with canes, night and day, during the whole season of making sugar, which is about six months of the year.[16]

The work was especially dangerous because the workers were pushed to the point of exhaustion. Planters were reluctant to shut down the mill once it began to operate, forcing slaves to work around the clock. Most mills were equipped with fireplaces for burning straw to provide light so that operations could continue after sunset. It is not surprising that the folklore figure of the zombie emerged from sugar plantations. Slaves faced not only the danger of scalding but also that of getting their fingers caught in the mill's rollers. Since the arm was invariably drawn in, as Edward Littleton reports, "if a mill feeder be catch't by the finger, his whole body is drawn in, and he is squeez'd to pieces."[17] All mills were equipped with an axe, and maimed watchmen were common on Caribbean sugar plantations. Since the harvest season could last ten months, during which the mill ran constantly, shutting down only to clean or repair the machinery when rain prevented harvesting cane or on Sundays, the slaves were almost always exhausted. They are often described as sleeping on their feet, while in Brazil "sleepy like a sugar-mill slave" was a common expression.[18]

"Boiling and striking,—transferring the liquid, and arresting its boiling when ready," Sidney Mintz explains, "required great skill, and sugar boilers were artisans who worked under difficult conditions."[19] Mistakes at this stage—striking too soon or too late—could ruin the sugar and wipe out the fruits of months of hard labor in a moment. The skills exhibited by slaves in the sugar industry constitute a strong challenge to the persistent tradition, which maintains that slavery and skilled labor are incompatible. As Immanuel Wallerstein argues in a recent, but typical assertion of this tradition, "Slaves . . . are not useful . . . whenever skill is involved" because "slaves cannot be expected to do more than they are forced to do." Once skilled labor is involved, Wallerstein continues, "it is more economic to find alternative means of labor control, since the relatively low cost of slave labor is more than matched by low productivity."[20] The key role of skilled slaves in the Caribbean sugar industry is powerful evidence that this tradition is simply wrong.

Planters at first ignored sugar, concentrating instead on tobacco. But in the late 1630s, as tobacco prices began to slip, interest in sugarcane rose, and the plant was reintroduced to the island. Who reintroduced the crop and from where is uncertain. Some sources credit Pieter Brower, a Dutchman who later became a sugar planter at Essequibo River; others credit James Holdip, once a London merchant, who had been on the island as a planter and factor since 1629. Some sources say the plants came from Brazil; others say Madeira; still others, Guinea, although I suspect that the latter is a mistake for Guiana. Whoever introduced it and wherever it came from initially, it is clear that several planters, led by James Drax, were actively experimenting with sugar by the early 1640s.[21]

In 1647, when Richard Ligon arrived in Barbados, "the great work of Sugar-making, was but newly practiced by the inhabitants there." Although planters had managed to export some sugars as early as 1643, Ligon found the quality poor, "so moist, and full of molasses, and so ill cur'd, as they were hardly worth the bringing to England." Barbadian growers were learning quickly, however, "finding their errours by their daily practice" and "with new directions from Brazil," often brought back by planters who visited Pernambuco to master "the secrets of that mystery." Ligon mentions three specific things the first planters needed to learn before they could produce a satisfactory crop: (1) the proper time of planting and harvesting the cane: "They lacked the skill to know when the canes were ripe, which was not until they were fifteen months old, but they gathered them at twelve, which was a main disadvantage to the making of good sugar; for the liquor wanting of the sweetness it ought to have caused the Sugars to be lean, and unfit to keep"; (2) where to place the coppers in their furnaces; and (3) to plant canes lengthwise in trenches rather than endwise in holes, as that improved anchorage and reduced the need for weeding.[22]

By 1650, when Ligon returned to England, the industry had "grown to a high perfection." By then the planters "were greater proficients, both in boyling and curing [sugars], and they had learned the knowledge of making them white, such as your lump sugars here in England."[23] Sugars, although still "not so excellent as those they made in Brazil," had "gotten so much the start of all the rest of those, that were held the staple Commodities of the land, and so much overtop't them, as they are for the most part slighted and neglected."[24]

While contemporaries credited a variety of ethnic groups and several individuals with teaching Barbadians how to make sugar, they are strangely silent about Africans. It is likely, however, that Africans played a key role in the process of bringing sugar to the island. Ligon provides a valuable clue when he mentions some blacks "bred up amongst the Portugals at James Drax's plantation," apparently the site of the most advanced techniques on the island. These "Portugal Negroes," as Ligon calls them, were perhaps Afro-Brazilians who had worked in the fields and mills at Pernambuco or Bahia. If one were determined to master the complexities of cane culture and processing, how better to proceed than by buying workers who knew its "secrets" and "mystery."[25]

Ligon's chronology is confirmed by table 1, which reports the distribution of commodities used in more than twenty-five hundred transactions on the island over the period 1639–52 and thus should provide a rough index to the relative importance of the major exports. Sugar was first used as a means of payment in Barbados in 1644. It rivaled tobacco, its main competitor, by 1647. By 1648 it was the means of payment in 60 percent of the transactions on the island, and by 1649 it was clearly the dominant export, a position it has not surrendered to this day.[26] Sugar may have driven other crops out of transactions, but it did not drive them entirely out of production. In the mid-1660s islanders still exported a substantial cotton crop, most of it grown in St. Philip's Parish; a small amount of tobacco, grown by "the poor Catholics" in St. Lucy's; and small amounts of ginger, indigo, and fustic woods."[27]

Once commercial sugar production was established on the island it expanded rapidly, quickly turning the small island into one of the world's major sugar producers. By the early 1660s, a mere twenty years after the beginnings of commercial sugar production on the island, roughly 60 percent of the island was planted in sugarcane.[28] By the mid-1660s sugar and its by-products accounted for 90 percent of the value of Barbadian exports, while the Barbadian sugar crop of 1665–66 was worth more than that of Bahia in 1700. Also by the mid-1660s, contemporaries who attended to such matters were arguing that the Barbadian sugar crop was worth more than the exports of all the Spanish colonies in the Americas combined.[29] Small wonder that historians impressed by the speed with which the Barbadian sugar industry grew once it found its legs began to speak of a "sugar revolution." My critique of the concept of a sugar revolution does not challenge the point that the rise of sugar on the island occurred rapidly. Responding to my argument that there was no sugar revolution in Barbados by pointing to the rapid expansion of the industry, a tact taken by several scholars, is beside the point. My interest is not in denying the rapid expansion of the sugar industry but in another aspect of the sugar-revolution hypothesis. A central contention of those who advocate the idea of a sugar revolution is that sugar transformed Barbados about the middle of the seventeenth century because it brought plantation agriculture and African slavery in its wake. My point is that attributing

TABLE 1
Commodities used in transactions in Barbados, 1639–1652 (percent)

Year	Cotton	Tobacco	Indigo	Sugar
1639	43	57	0	0
1640	79	21	0	0
1641	74	26	0	0
1642	72	28	0	0
1643	43	47	6	0
1644	26	43	23	8
1645	16	64	5	16
1646	22	47	4	27
1647	12	47	0	41
1648	8	32	0	60
1649	0	0	0	100
1650	10	10	0	80
1651	0	0	0	100
1652	0	0	0	100

Source: Recopied Deed Books, RB 3/1, 3/2, 3/3, Barbados National Archives.

the transformation of Barbados entirely and solely to sugar oversimplifies a more complex process. Barbados was already on the way to becoming a plantation colony and a slave society before the rise of sugar. At most, sugar sped up and intensified an ongoing process.

What is surprising about the data reported in table 1 is not what they tell about sugar but what they tell about tobacco. Tobacco, the mainstay of the islands economy during the 1630s, was on the way out by the end of that decade. Growers in Europe and throughout the Americas had

FIG. 3. Eighteenth-century map of Barbados by Bryan Edwards, from Edwards, *History, Civil and Commercial*, 1:320. (Courtesy James Ford Bell Library, Minneapolis)

responded too robustly to a sharp run-up in prices during the mid-1630s, generating an "international crisis of over supply" as increased production glutted the major European markets. European prices broke in the early summer of 1637, and planters throughout the colonies soon felt the impact of a steadily worsening depression as farm prices fell by nearly half from 1636 to 1638 and by nearly a third by 1641.[30]

Unfortunately, there is no price series available for Barbadian tobacco. Nicholas Posthumus, whose work on prices in Holland is the source of most of the price data reported in this chapter, provides no tobacco prices. His principal sources were account books and purchase records of hospitals and orphanages, whose managers apparently did not provide their charges with tobacco. In the absence of a Barbadian price series, we must rely on prices from the Chesapeake colonies (see table 2). While Chesapeake tobacco probably commanded higher prices than did the Barbados leaf, it seems likely that the short-term fluctuations and long-term trends were similar for both varieties. At any rate, until someone constructs an island price series, Chesapeake prices will have to serve as a proxy.

Barbadians, who produced a poor-quality leaf for the low end of the market, were especially hard hit by the depression of the late 1630s. By 1640 their "tobacco was a very dead commodity and would yield little or nothing." Some expected that the leaf would be abandoned altogether (an ex-

TABLE 2

Farm-gate prices of Chesapeake tobacco, 1620–1650 (pence sterling per pound)

Year	Price	Year	Price	Year	Price
1620	12.00	1631	4.00	1642	4.20
1621	20.00	1632	2.90	1643	1.80
1622	17.80	1633	5.00	1644	2.30
1623	16.40	1634	5.00	1645	2.00
1624	12.90	1635	5.00	1646	3.00
1625	11.60	1636	5.50	1647	1.90
1626	10.40	1637	3.25	1648	2.40
1627	9.10	1638	2.80	1649	2.70
1628	7.80	1639	3.00	1650	2.55
1629	6.50	1640	2.50		
1630	5.30	1641	2.00		

Source: Menard, "Tobacco Industry in the Chesapeake Colonies," 157–58.

pectation apparent in table 1), and a few made provision for alternative methods of payment "in case there be not Tobacco generally planted" on the island when bills came due.[31]

While Barbados tobacco clearly had a poor reputation and earned only a low price, the source of its troubles is not fully clear. Some scholars blame the poor quality on the island's soil and climate.[32] My reading of the evidence suggests that it was a function of decisions made by planters. Barbadian planters, perhaps trading quantity for quality or perhaps because they had other export crops to work, apparently decided not to take the trouble to clean their tobacco carefully and make it presentable.[33] Planters were so casual about the quality of their crops that they often shipped tobacco to London in rolls, not even bothering to pack it in casks to protect it during the Atlantic crossing. Unfortunately, the kind of detailed evidence that might permit one to unravel their decision-making process does not seem to have survived.

Whatever the cause, there was widespread agreement that Barbadian tobacco was bad—so bad, according to one report, so "illconditioned, fowle, full of stalkes and evillcoloured" that Barbadians themselves refused to smoke it.[34] If tobacco, the island's mainstay, was so thoroughly depressed in the late 1630s, why did planters wait so long to turn to sugar? The answer has to do in part with technique and capital requirements. As we have seen, sugar was a complex crop. Although some planters "studied hard," they were "long learning" how to make a marketable product.[35] Sugar was also an expensive crop to produce, requiring a substantial investment in labor, equipment, and livestock, commitments that investors must have been reluctant to make until it was clear that Barbadians could master sugar's mysteries. The islanders' inability to produce a reputable tobacco crop may have raised doubts regarding their ability to master sugar, a much more difficult product to produce. Further, sugar prices also fell in the late 1630s and early 1640s, from .67 guilders per Dutch pound at Amsterdam in 1637 to a low of .31 in 1643 (see table 3).

Planters might experiment with sugarcane, but few would plunge into so difficult a commodity in a big way when prices were declining so quickly.[36] Finally, and perhaps most important, there were alternatives to sugar in the early and mid-1640s that were more attractive than historians have usually allowed, as the prices reported in tables 2 and 3 suggest. Tobacco was one alternative, perhaps the most important. As table 1 suggests, its importance to the island's economy fell off dramatically about

1640, but the leaf made an impressive recovery in the middle of the decade. From 1644 to 1647 it was again the island's dominant crop, at least if the transactions data provide a reliable guide. Tobacco's recovery is not hard to explain. It was a familiar crop with a known market that could be grown by small farmers alone or helped by a few servants, and it required only the simplest of tools. Prices recovered throughout the Atlantic economy in the mid-1640s (see table 2), and Barbados was no exception. After falling to a penny a pound in 1639, island prices fluctuated between 2P and 2.7P in the middle to late 1640s. Higher prices brought better returns, and with them came a powerful revitalization of the Barbadian tobacco industry.[37] While tobacco was apparently the major alternative to sugar, it was not the only one. Cotton, like tobacco a crop that could be grown by small farmers with simple tools and little in the way of start-up costs, was an attractive option throughout the 1630s and 1640s. In contrast to tobacco, Barbadian cotton had the reputation of being better "than any place in the world."[38]

This complicates the puzzle regarding Barbadian tobacco. Why did Island planters take pains with one crop and not the other?[39] From 1640 to 1642, the transactions data suggest, cotton eclipsed tobacco as the island's

TABLE 3
Prices of sugar, cotton, and indigo in Amsterdam, 1624–1650 (guilders per Dutch pound)

Year	Sugar	Cotton	Indigo	Year	Sugar	Cotton	Indigo
1624	0.3	0.81	4.13	1637	0.67	0.47	3.90
1625	0.38	0.84	3.85	1638	0.54	0.38	4.43
1626	0.42		3.76	1639			
1627				1640	0.49	0.34	8.10
1628	0.44	0.60	3.90	1641	0.38	0.33	4.95
1629				1642	0.34	0.29	5.25
1630	0.57	0.53	3.72	1643	0.31	0.29	4.58
1631	0.59	0.48	3.55	1645	0.39	0.56	3.15
1632	0.54	0.50	3.45	1646	0.57	0.61	2.78
1633	0.54	0.48	3.83	1647			
1634	0.50	0.48	3.75	1648	0.43	0.28	2.31
1635	0.51	0.56	3.90	1649	0.52	0.29	2.57
1636	0.52	0.50	1.83	1650	0.49	0.28	2.79

Source: Nicholas Posthumus, *History of Prices in Holland*, 1:119, 281, 415–16, reported in Batie, "Why Sugar?"

major crop. It soon lost that position, though since cotton prices rose sharply from 1643 to 1646, its initial relative decline was probably due more to a revival of tobacco production than to a declining interest in cotton.[40]

There was a cotton boom in Barbados in the 1630s, but it has gone largely unrecognized because the subsequent sugar boom overshadowed it. Nevertheless, it was important and merits our attention if only because it helped pave the way for sugar, in part by demonstrating that, despite the reputation of their tobacco crops, there were some competent planters on the island whose enterprises might reward investors.[41] When Henry Colt visited Barbados in 1635, he reported that the "trade in cotton fills them all with hope."[42] Father Andrew White, who visited Barbados on his way to Maryland in 1634, offered some brief observations on the island's cotton industry that are worth quoting in full because they provide rare detail:

> Their trade is chiefely in corne and cotton, which cotton it delighted us much to see grow upon trees in such plenty. The cotton tree is not much higher than a Barbara bush, but more treelike. It beares a little bude in bignesse like a walnut, which at full time opening in the middle into fower quarters their appears a knot of cotton white as snow, with six seede in the middle of the bignesse of vetches which with an invention of wheeles they take out and soe keep it till the merchants come to fetch it from them.[43]

These high hopes for cotton were doubtless buoyed by the sharp increase in prices during the early 1630s and then dashed by their collapse at decade's end (see table 3). Indeed, there is evidence that hopes were so high while prices were rising that the process of land consolidation, of building larger plantations by buying up small farms, a process usually associated with the sugar boom, actually got under way in anticipation of profits to be made in cotton.[44] One planter expected those profits to be so high that he suggested erecting "a cotton manufacture on Barbados so the profits realized on the sale of cotton might be reinvested in the island's economy."[45]

Cotton, or "cotton-wool," as it was known in the seventeenth century, is a vegetable fiber attached to the seeds of several varieties of *Gossypiem*. The variety grown on the island, and the apparent ancestor of the crop familiar to American historians as "Sea Island" or "long-staple" cotton, yields a long fiber easily separated from the smooth seeds. It is apparently related to and perhaps descended from *G. aboreum* L., a tree cotton indigenous to the Spanish Main, where the Arawaks, who probably introduced the plant to Barbados, domesticated it. If Awaraks did introduce the

plant to the island, Anglo-Barbadians repaid the helpfulness of some Indians by enslaving others to be certain they could command their skills
at spinning the fiber into yarn and then weaving the yarn into cloth. The
crop was relatively simple to cultivate, although its processing, that is, the
separation of the fiber from the seed, was complex as it took some skill to
operate the gin. This gin was a roller mill, or *chakra,* developed in India,
that perhaps reached Barbados by way of Brazil. There are several stories
about how cotton came to the island. One of them is of course that the
Dutch introduced it, although I find this no more credible than the tradition that credits the Dutch with bringing sugar to the island. My sense
from the admittedly thin evidence is that the plant was brought to the island by Awaraks who came to the island with Captain Henry Powell in
the 1620s but that the roller gin was brought to Barbados by one of the
many planters who visited Brazil in search of agricultural knowledge.
The actual transfer of the technology may have been accomplished by
purchasing a slave familiar with the roller gin.[46] Unfortunately, the only
detailed descriptions of cotton cultivation on the island during the colonial era, those provided by Hans Sloane and Dalby Thomas, date from
1725 and 1690, respectively, and it will not do to assume that the methods
they describe were those of the cotton boom.[47] Nor will it do to reproduce,
as historians have occasionally done, Sloane's drawing of a roller gin as an
example of the gins in use during the 1660s, which I suspect were much
simpler devices.[48]

Planters also made indigo in the middle 1640s, a crop that demanded
more capital and labor than cotton or tobacco and was complicated to
process.[49] In addition, they experimented briefly with ginger. Given that
cotton and tobacco prices remained strong, it seems unlikely that adding
indigo and ginger involved cutting back production on the primary
staples. Instead Barbados seems to have experienced a diversified export
boom in the mid-1640s, which must have reassured planters, who had
seen prices for cotton and tobacco swing sharply and alternatively swell
and shrink their incomes, for it offered an opportunity to plant more than
one export crop at a time or to switch from one to another in response
to shifting returns. Some planters did just that. William Hilliard, for example, although on the road to sugar monoculture, had seventy acres in
tobacco, five in cotton, and five in ginger in 1648.[50] An account of a plantation sale in 1647 captures the enthusiasm this diversity generated: the
land is described "as fit to bear sugar canes, indigo, ginger, cotton & to-

bacco as any on the island."[51] The description also suggests some uncertainty about the future, for although sugar would soon dominate island exports, it had not yet done so, and it was not clear to all Barbadians that it would. The key point, however, is that sugar emerged as the major staple of the island, not during a depression but in the context of an impressive boom in exports characterized both by the diversity of its products and by the prosperity it brought to those planters able to seize its opportunities. Further evidence of the positive performance of the island's economy in the immediate pre-sugar era comes from demographic data (see table 4). Richard Dunn provides an efficient summary of the pattern of population growth on the island: "Barbados started slowly, but grew rapidly during the late 1630s, and reached about the same population as Massachusetts or Virginia by 1640."[52] Given what we know about island sex ratios and what we suspect about mortality, this growth must have been largely a function of immigration, not of reproductive increase.

If the island's economy was depressed, why did so many people move there in the 1630s and 1640s? Indeed, fully 20 percent of the people who left London in the mid-1630s for the colonies headed for Barbados.[53] One reason that so many headed for Barbados was the opportunities available there. Servants who completed their terms in Barbados in the 1630s were more likely to become landowners than those who went to other colonies or those who went to Barbados after the sugar boom.[54]

The issue of Barbadian sex ratios merits further discussion. Among those who left London for the island in 1635 males outnumbered females by about sixteen to one.[55] This extreme imbalance did not persist through-

TABLE 4
Estimated population of whites and blacks in Barbados, 1630–1690 (thousands)

Year	Whites	Blacks	Total
1630	1.8		1.8
1640	14.0		14.0
1650	30.0	12.8	42.8
1660	26.2	27.1	53.3
1670	22.4	40.4	62.8
1680	20.5	44.9	65.4
1690	17.9	47.8	65.7

Source: McCusker and Menard, *Economy of British America,* 153.

out the seventeenth century, and according to a report provided by John Scott, the numbers of males and females were roughly equal in the early 1680s.[56] Despite some improvement, females were in short supply in the 1630s and 1640s. The shortage of women may explain the frequency of partnerships on the island. Small farmers, finding that the work of running a farm was too much for one person but unable to find a wife, often went into partnership with another small farmer as a way of coping with the demands of running a farm.

The question of mortality is more problematic than that of the sex ratio, in part because historians think they know more about death rates on the island than the evidence supports. No one has yet managed to measure life expectancy on the island in the seventeenth century, nor is it likely that such an estimate is possible given the available evidence, so we will have to make do with the observations of contemporaries, remembering that it will not suffice to generalize from the postsugar era to the years before sugar dominated the economy, or from the experience of Africans to that of Europeans. With those warnings in mind, it seems safe to say that death rates on the island were high by mainland standards in the early seventeenth century. Beyond that, the evidence does not permit us to venture.[57] However, as Gary Puckrein has noted, the shortage of freshwater on the island and the steady ocean breezes offered inhabitants some protection against mosquitoes and the diseases they carried and may have made the island a healthier place than the southern mainland colonies.[58]

Around midcentury, evidence of the diversified export boom and the prosperity it brought began to appear in contemporary commentaries on the island. In 1650, for example, Nicholas Foster, an island planter, reported "the number of Ships that come yearly to that Island" as "not lessse than a hundred Sayle; the commodities (being not onely Sugar) but also Indico, Ginger, with Cotton-wools and some small quantities of tobacco."[59] In the next year George Gardyner reported that Barbados "flourisheth so much, that it hath more people and Commerce then all the Islands of the Indies."[60] In 1646, according to John Oldmixon, Barbados was looked upon as a "flourishing Colony."[61] The optimism the export boom generated is conveyed in Richard Ligon's report of a conversation with James Drax. Drax had come to Barbados with £300 sterling. He told Ligon that he would not return to England, where he planned to live out his life, until he could purchase an estate that would yield an annual income of £10,000 sterling, something he expected to accomplish in a few years.[62] Further evidence of prosperity in the years just prior to the sugar boom is provided by Alison Games's study of opportunities among those who came to the island as servants in 1635. Many former servants, Games reports, were able to acquire land and set up as independent planters during the late 1630s and early 1640s. Merchants who were willing to provide credit to promising young men facilitated land acquisition. This is strong testimony to the island's prosperity and to the expectations of profits during the diversified export boom. Merchants would not have been so willing to loan money if they had not expected their creditors to make sufficient profits growing tobacco, cotton, and indigo to pay off their debts.[63]

I might conclude this discussion of prosperity in the presugar era by noting that land prices increased sharply on the island during the 1640s (see table 5), from £1.2 Barbados currency per acre in 1638 to £5.4 Barbados currency per acre in 1648, which suggest significant productivity gains in island agriculture of the sort one might expect during a diversified export boom. At the very least this evidence is incompatible with the notion that the Barbadian economy was depressed when sugar emerged as the dominant crop.[64] Given that there is so much evidence of prosperity in the presugar era, why have historians missed it? I suspect they were both blinded and misled: blinded by the dazzling fortunes accumulated on the island during the sugar boom and thus unable to see the accomplishments of those who had come before; misled by the occasional visitors to early Barbados who were so struck by the island's lack of elegance that they missed the evidence of comfortable, if crude, prosperity;[65] and misled as

TABLE 5
Land prices in Barbados, 1638–1650 (per acre in Barbados currency)

Year	Price (£)	Year	Price (£)
1638	1.20	1645	4.70
1639	1.60	1646	5.20
1640	1.30	1647	5.40
1641	1.80	1648	5.40
1642	2.30	1649	5.50
1643	3.20	1650	5.50
1644	4.20		

Source: Beckles, *White Servitude and Black Slavery,* 156.
Note: Beckles gives the prices in Barbados cotton currency. They have been reduced to Barbados money currency by the procedure described in McCusker and Menard, "Sugar Industry in the Seventeenth Century," 299.

well by the idea of a sugar revolution, which encouraged scholars to stress the contrast on the island before and after sugar. Since by some measures the island was rich and successful after sugar, since sugar had revolutionized the island, it followed that it must have been poor and a failure before sugar.

2

Land and Labor during the Export Boom

THE CENTRAL ARGUMENT of the sugar-revolution hypothesis is that sugar brought slavery and plantation agriculture to Barbados. As Eric Williams put it with his usual clarity and forcefulness, the origins of African slavery "can be expressed in three words: in the Caribbean, Sugar; on the mainland, Tobacco and Cotton."[1] The explanation for why sugar brought slavery in its wake is straightforward. Because it earned substantial returns to scale and large profits, sugar both increased labor productivity and required large numbers of workers. Therefore, with the introduction of sugar, demand for labor in Barbados increased sharply. Given the supply elasticities of servants and slaves, growing demand for labor meant that the price of servants rose relative to that of slaves, and planters, who always had their eye on the bottom line, bought more slaves and fewer servants.

While this argument seems persuasive at first glance, it is not without difficulties. It seems to assume, for example, that the large, integrated plantation, in which cane was processed on the plantation where it was grown, worked by large gangs of slaves, appeared on the island simultaneously with commercial sugar production. As we will see, however, initially small farmers, who took their crop to a large farmer's mill for processing, grew much of the sugar produced in Barbados. Not until the 1660s did it become clear that there were economies to be captured by growing and processing cane on the same unit, and it was not until the 1680s that the large, integrated plantation dominated production. Further, it was not until the eighteenth century that gang labor came to dominate the way in which the work of slaves was organized. Finally, it is not entirely clear that there were economies of scale in sugar production beyond certain minimums. Given these difficulties with the usual argument, that is, the apparent lack of a need for large workforces in the early days of the Barbadian sugar industry, it might be worth our while to probe the relationship between sugar and slavery on the island more closely. We can begin by recalling the timing of sugar's rise to dominance of the island economy, described in chapter 1 (see table 1).

During the 1630s and early 1640s cotton, tobacco, and indigo seem to have dominated Barbadian exports. It was not until 1644 or 1645 that sugar became a commercially important crop on the island, and not until mid-century did it dominate the Barbadian export sector. A variety of evidence suggests that slavery was expanding rapidly on the island before sugar became the dominant crop, while planters still devoted most of their attention to what we have come to call the minor staples.

Before going into detail about the growth of slavery in Barbados, it is important to note that it was part of a more general process in which all the plantation colonies of British America were Africanized during the seventeenth century. We will be better able to understand the process on the island if we first look at the broad context in which it occurred and pay some attention to British indentured servitude, the chief alternative to African slavery on the island in the seventeenth century.[2]

With the advantage of hindsight, the rise of African slavery in the Americas seems almost inevitable. By the mid-eighteenth century African slavery and Europe's American colonies had become so thoroughly intertwined as to seem inseparable. Much of European America was made up of Africanized slave societies. Before 1750, or even as late as 1820 or 1830, imported slaves from Africa far outnumbered colonists from Europe among migrants to America.[3] "From Brazil and the Caribbean to Chesapeake Bay," David Brion Davis reminds us, "the richest and most coveted colonies—in terms of large scale capital investment, output and value of exports and imports—ultimately became dependent upon black labor."[4] The association of blacks and bondage was eventually so central a feature of American history that it takes a major effort of imagination to entertain other outcomes.

Such an effort is essential. There was nothing inevitable about the Africanization of slavery or its entrenchment in the Americas. Several well-known facts establish the point: White slavery, an old and well-established institution in much of the West, persisted in the early modern era around the Mediterranean and in eastern Europe and did not disappear—at some times and places it even flourished—with the rise of the Atlantic slave trade.[5] Several American colonies never depended on African slaves, while some did so only briefly before turning to other peoples and other methods of organizing labor. Finally, and most important for this chapter, many colonial societies that eventually became dependent on Africans did so only after an initial period of reliance on white indentured servants or native Americans. Again, a proposition from David Davis is helpful: "The Africanization of large parts of the New World was not the result of concerted planning, racial destiny, or immanent historical design, but of innumerable local and pragmatic choices made in four continents."[6]

This chapter examines one set of such local and pragmatic choices, looking at the transition to an African workforce in Barbados. Several propositions are useful in ordering the record, the most important being that transitions to African slavery in the several colonies of British America can be understood if England's emerging Atlantic world is approached as a single if imperfect labor market and if changes in the composition of the workforce are approached through a focus on the supply and demand for labor. Some historians contend that transitions to African slavery are more profitably approached through an examination of culture, especially of planter attitudes toward various types of workers, and by attending to emerging racial ideologies rather than through an analysis of labor markets.[7]

We can begin exploring the rise of slavery in Barbados with some demographic evidence, although the available demographic evidence for the island in the seventeenth century leaves much to be desired. While it is clear that some slaves were delivered to the island in the 1630s, it is impossible to assign a number to deliveries during that decade with any confidence, although a rough guess would be that at least one thousand slaves arrived on the island in the 1630s. For the early 1640s, fortunately, we are on firmer ground: from 1640 to 1644 the best estimate is that thirteen hundred slaves were delivered to Barbados each year.[8] As a result of all these imports, Barbados began to acquire a sizeable slave population. In 1643, at about the time that sugar was beginning to emerge as a commercially important crop, there were already about six thousand slaves in Barbados. In 1650, just after sugar was established as the island's dominant export, there were roughly thirteen thousand slaves, nearly a third of the island's total population.[9]

This evidence suggests that the notion of a sugar revolution has things backward: instead of being brought to the island by sugar, slaves seem to have reached the island in substantial numbers before it became a major sugar producer. The flimsy demographic evidence finds support in some more reliable data on the workforce on private estates gathered by Richard Dunn, Hilary Beckles, and Andrew Downes, presented in table 6. The data in table 6 suggest that Barbadian plantations had always been big and that they grew bigger as the export boom of the 1640s began to reorganize the island's economy. The most important change described by the table is in the composition of the unfree workforce: on the estates for which data are presented in the table at least, despite the increase in the servant population over the decade, there were twice as many slaves as servants in the late 1640s, just before sugar emerged as the dominant crop in the Barbadian export mix. Dunn, Beckles, and Downes were chiefly interested in the rise of the planter class and devoted their attention, sensibly enough, to compiling descriptions of estates owned by big planters.

Table 7, which attempts a description of the workforce of all Barbadian landowners during the 1640s and 1650s, provides a more comprehensive and I hope more precise view of the island's transformation. This table requires some explanation. The extant early records of the colony include a substantial number of deeds and mortgages. These records were recopied in the early nineteenth century, and both the originals and the copies are now housed in the Barbados National Archives at Lazaretto, St. Michael's. The records are a bit of a hodgepodge, and the proportion of the whole that survives is uncertain. Further, as legal forms were gradually elaborated, the documents became steadily more terse and less revealing, which accounts in large part for the decline in the number of estates apparent in the table. At any rate, it was common practice in early Barbados to sell or mortgage plantations as a whole, and often the workforce, housing, tools,

TABLE 6
Servants and slaves per estate in Barbados, 1635–1670

Year	Estates	Slaves per Estate	Slaves per Estate	Ratio of Servants to Slaves
1635–40	8	15.4	0.1	154.0
1641–43	9	12.0	3.4	3.8
1646–49	6	9.5	11.1	1.8
1650–57	7	18.4	24.0	0.8
1658–70	10	3.1	111.1	0

Sources: Dunn, *Sugar and Slaves*, 54, 68; Beckles and Downes, "Economics of the Transition to the Black Labor System," 228.

livestock, and the like were described in detail in the deed. Such estates are the source of section B of the table, which describes the workforce of plantations that had some unfree labor. Unfortunately, deeds of sale do not always make clear whether workers were sold with the land, so deeds of sale could not yield an estimate of the proportion of landowners who also owned labor. For that estimate, which appears in section A, I relied on mortgages, which seemed to be more complete in their descriptions than deeds of sale. Unfortunately, both the number of surviving mortgages and the detail they provide tail off sharply after the early 1640s. Section C combines the estimates of the proportion of landowners with unfree labor in section A and the workforce estimates among labor owners in section B to estimate the number of servants and slaves among all landowners. It must

TABLE 7
Barbadian plantations during the export boom, 1640–1657

Variable	1640– 1641	1642– 1643	1644– 1645	1646– 1649	1650– 1657
A. Proportion of landowners with servants or slaves					
N mortgages	69	40	28	22	
With labor	25 (36%)	16 (40%)	15 (54%)	13 (59%)	
Without labor	44 (64%)	24 (60%)	13 (46%)	9 (41%)	
B. Landowners with labor					
N	84	32	31	26	29
N servants	160	112	76	130	263
N slaves	1	55	78	199	477
Servants per estate	4.3	3.5	2.5	5.0	9.1
Slaves per estate	0	1.7	2.5	7.7	16.4
Workers per estate	4.3	5.2	5.0	12.7	25.5
Acres per estate	46	60	59	82	119
C. All landowners					
Servants per estate	1.5	1.4	1.3	3.0	5.0
Slaves per estate	0	0.7	1.4	4.5	10.6
Workers per estate	1.5	2.1	2.7	7.5	16.4
Acres per estate	37	42	41	55	83

Sources: Recopied Deed Books, RB 3/1, 3/2, 3/3, Barbados National Archives.

be emphasized that not enough mortgages survive to estimate the proportion of labor owners for the 1650s; the estimates in section C for that decade simply assume that the trend evident since 1640 continued by setting the proportion of labor owners at 65 percent.

In the early 1640s, the data in table 7 indicate, Barbados was a society of small farmers, although a handful of men owned substantial estates. Most plantations were owner operated, worked by an unmarried man (women were still in short supply on the island) or by two or three single men working in partnership, living in tiny, impermanent, sparsely furnished board houses on small farms of only twenty to thirty acres. They grew cotton, tobacco, and provisions, slowly cleared the land and sold off the lumber, and raised a bit of stock and a few chickens, usually without the help of servants and slaves. Just over one-third of the plantations were worked by unfree labor, most often one to three servants. Such estates were difficult to distinguish from those without servants except by their slightly larger scale. There were also a few big planters on the island, big at least by the standards of the day: seven of the eighty-four estates reported in table 7 for 1640–41 had ten or more servants, one had twenty, and two had twenty-six. Again, judging by the few inventories that survive, these bigger plantations were distinguished from smaller farms more by scale than by elegance.[10]

While table 7 demonstrates that Barbados was a society of small farmers in the early 1640s, it also shows that the 1640s witnessed substantial changes on the island. The pace of change was fairly slow during the first half of the decade, when tobacco and cotton remained the dominant commercial crops. The proportion of estates with labor and the average size of plantations rose modestly, from 37 acres and 1.5 unfree workers per unit in 1640–41 to 41 acres and 2.7 laborers in 1644–45, testimony to the prosperity that came with the island's export boom. The most important change was the growth of slavery. Slaves were rare at the beginning of the decade, but by the middle of the decade, when sugar was just beginning to emerge as a commercially important crop on the island, there were as many slaves as servants in Barbados, and slaves appeared on just half (sixteen of thirty-one) of the island's labor-owning plantations. By the late 1640s slaves were in the majority among unfree workers on the island.

Three points about this initial increase in slaves should be stressed. First, it occurred without a marked increase in inequality among property owners: the big plantations of 1644–45 were not much bigger, or more elegant, than those at the beginning of the decade. Apparently, the prosperity suggested by the increase in farm size and in slaves was broadly shared by the free population. Second, the initial growth of slavery preceded the emergence of sugar as the island's major crop. Commercial sugar cultivation apparently began in Barbados in 1643, but it was not until the end of the decade that sugar established itself as the dominant export. In 1644–45 sugar remained a commodity of the future; most of the first slaves were brought to the island to work cotton, tobacco, and indigo. Third, this early increase in slaves was not accompanied by a decline in servants. Indeed, the ratio of servants to estates rose across the 1640s, from 4.3 at the start of the decade to 5.0 at its end, falling just shy of keeping pace with the ratio of slaves to estates, which grew from 1.7 to 7.7 over the same years.

The pace of change picked up noticeably after 1645. The proportion of estates with labor continued to increase, as did the average acreage per plantation. Most important, the size of the unfree workforce nearly tripled between the middle and the end of the decade, from 2.7 workers per estate in 1644–45 to 7.5 in 1646–49. These trends continued into the 1650s, when the average plantation reported 83 acres, 6 servants, and 11 slaves. There are several things to emphasize about these post-1645 developments. Most important is the continued growth of slavery: slaves thoroughly dominated the unfree workforce by the 1650s, outnumbering servants by nearly two to one. However, their dominance did not reflect a decline in the number of servants: the ratio of servants to estates doubled from the middle to the late 1640s and doubled again in the 1650s. Second, the quickened pace of change clearly reflects the rise of sugar. Sugar did not bring slavery and plantation agriculture to Barbados. The island was in the process of becoming a plantation colony and slave society while sugar was still a relatively minor crop. While sugar did not transform Barbados on its own, it did quicken and intensify a process already under way. Second, the changes were accompanied by a marked increase in inequality among the free population and the appearance of truly large (and increasingly elegant) plantations. Before 1645 none of the estates described in table 7 reported a total of 30 servants and slaves. From 1650 to 1657 ten (14%) reported a total of 30, eight (28%) reported more than 40, three reported (10%) more than 50, and one reported more than 100.

Barbados, along with the other major plantation colonies of British America, experimented with other forms of labor before committing to African slavery. The developers of British America had several options in recruiting and organizing a workforce; they could draw on free workers and indentured servants from Britain, on Indians from the vast North American interior, and on slaves from Africa. With the exception of Africans, all of those workers moved in small markets, circumscribed by geography and political divisions and characterized by sharp, unpredictable shifts in volume and price. Africans, by contrast, were trapped in a much larger net; they were a commodity in a stable, large-scale international labor market, which made them the victims of choice in the rapidly expanding plantation colonies of European America.[11]

Since the main alternative to slaves in Barbados was indentured servants (as the data in tables 6 and 7 indicate), it will be useful to begin the process of trying to understand the growth of African slavery on the island with a brief look at indentured servitude.[12] Although the principle behind it was articulated as early as the 1580s, the Virginia Company devised indentured servitude late in the second decade of the seventeenth century to finance the recruitment and transport of workers to the colony. There is uncertainty concerning the institution's antecedents. While some historians view it as an entirely new development, most view it as an adaptation of the traditional institution of apprenticeship to a new set of circumstances. There were broad similarities between servitude and apprenticeship, but there were also major differences. Indentured servitude was largely a rural, agricultural institution, designed to move people into field work. Apprenticeship, by contrast, was urban, aimed toward trade, crafts, and professions. Servitude attracted those too poor to purchase passage across the Atlantic, while apprenticeship was for those prosperous enough to pay an entry fee in exchange for training. Servants could be sold from one master to another without their consent or even consultation, while apprentices could not. And despite occasional promises that servants would be instructed in "the mystery, art, and occupation of a planter," servitude was a labor system, not an educational institution.[13] These differences led David Galenson to suggest a different antecedent for indentured servitude, "service in husbandry." Farm servants were numerous in Stuart England, accounting for perhaps 10 percent of the wage-earning population, appearing in one-quarter to one-third of all rural households, and making up about half of all hired, full-time agricultural workers. Typically they were boys and girls from poor families who left home in their early teens to work for more prosperous farmers until they could marry and set up on their own. They usually lived in the master's household, agreed to annual contracts for wages, food, and lodging, and changed places frequently, often every year. Given the pervasiveness of this form of life-cycle service, it was a likely antecedent for indentured servitude and a major source of recruits for American plantations.[14]

There were important differences between indentured servitude and service in husbandry. According to Galenson, the major differences followed from the distances indentured servants traveled on leaving home. This proved "a sufficiently important economic difference to necessitate several modifications in the institution," changes in the length of term of service, the sale of contracts, and discipline, all of which made the indenture system more rigid and formal than its English counterpart.[15] Servants in husbandry served short terms, seldom remaining with a master for more than a year or two, and usually renegotiating their contracts annually. Indentured servants served for longer periods under fixed terms negotiated at departure. While four years was the usual term for servants who had reached maturity, the length of service varied with the time needed to repay the borrowed passage fare. Greater distance and longer terms led to transferable contracts. Planters would have been reluctant to lay out the substantial sum required to purchase a servant if it meant committing themselves to the entire term, without the possibility of sale, while the servant trade could not have functioned had ship captains, merchants, and recruiting agents been unable to transfer contracts to colonial masters.[16] To sell an English man or woman "like a damned slave" was at first shocking to some contemporaries, but it was essential to the success of the indenture system.[17]

These changes, Galenson notes, introduced "a new adversary status . . . into the relationship between master and servant."[18] Longer terms, together with the inability of servants to renegotiate contracts and change masters, produced tension and conflict, evident in the frequency with which servants ran away and were hauled before magistrates. Unlike servants in husbandry, who were often integrated into their masters' families and treated as added children or poor relations, colonial servants were simply workers and investments. While Galenson may be too optimistic about the treatment of servants in husbandry and may underestimate the potential for affection and mutual trust between indentured servants and their masters, many of whom had begun life in the colonies as servants themselves, colonial servitude was clearly a harsher institution than its English ancestor.

There were at least four distinct forms of indentured servitude in British America, three of them voluntary. Under the most common, servants signed a contract in Britain specifying the length of term and conditions of service, which was sold to a master when the servant reached the colonies. Perhaps 40 percent of those who migrated to the Chesapeake in the seventeenth century arrived without a written contract, however, to serve according to "the custom of the country," customs gradually specified in colonial legislation.[19] While customary servants were common in Maryland and Virginia, they were much less common in the other colonies. In the Chesapeake region at least, there were systematic differences between customary servants and those who arrived with a signed contract. Customary servants were younger, on average about sixteen years of age when they immigrated, in contrast to servants with contracts, who were usually in their early twenties. Customary servants also served longer terms than those who arrived with indentures, even if age is held constant, perhaps reflecting that planters expected customary servants to be less productive than those who arrived with contracts. Customary servants may also have been less likely to be skilled and more likely to be illiterate, without prior work experience, of lower social origins, without living parents or guardians to look out for their interests, easier marks for an unscrupulous "crimp," and generally less sophisticated about labor relations and opportunities in the colonies.[20] The third form of voluntary servitude appeared in the eighteenth century with the German migration to the middle colonies. German redemptioners promised to pay passage fare upon arriving in the colonies, a promise that shifted much of the risk in the servant trade from merchants and shippers to the migrants. If they proved unable to pay, they were sold as servants to satisfy the debt.[21] In addition to these voluntary systems, penal servitude, a minor institution in the seventeenth century, became an important source of labor later in the colonial period.[22] Although there is little evidence of a substantial flow of convicts to Barbados during the sugar boom, many political prisoners were shipped there during England's civil war. According to one estimate, some fifty-five thousand political prisoners had reached the island by 1655. While Sheridan thinks this is an exaggeration, it is clear that the number was substantial.[23]

Servants played a central role in the development of British America. During the seventeenth century roughly 350,000 indentured migrants reached the English colonies, the vast majority going to the West Indies and the tobacco coast. Perhaps half of the white migrants to the colonies before 1775 arrived as servants. Servants were especially important in the plantation colonies. Roughly 70 to 85 percent of the European migrants to the Chesapeake region in the seventeenth century arrived as servants, and their share in the Caribbean was probably even higher.[24]

Some historians object to my characterization of servants as voluntary migrants, especially to the implication that servants were able to choose among the several available destinations. One critic has gone so far as to call me an apologist for the institution.[25] Gary Nash, for example, maintains that servants "were not making the choices, for power in the commercial transactions that brought bound labor across the Atlantic resided in the hands of the supplier and the buyer."[26] Similarly, James Horn contends, "The servant's individual desires played little part in determining where he eventually ended up. Instead, it was the trading community that was responsible for directing and regulating migration in response to the needs of the colonies."[27] While there were doubtless instances of outright coercion, and uneducated rural youths must have been at a disadvantage in negotiations with shrewd, experienced merchants, servants were not simply passive victims of a process beyond their control. The best evidence on the issue is provided by David Galenson's analysis of indenture contracts. Older servants with skills and work experience who could read and write served shorter terms than younger, unskilled, illiterate boys and girls. Further, servants apparently discriminated among destinations. Those who went to Barbados, where death rates were high, opportunities slender, the work hard, and treatment severe, served shorter terms than those who went to the mainland.[28] The variations in term length were not trivial. Among servants who left London in the 1680s, for example, those who could write their names signed on for terms seven months shorter on average than the terms of those who could not; those who went to Maryland served nine months longer than those who went to Barbados. Given a typical term of five or six years, these are substantial differences. The patterns only make sense if it is assumed that migration was voluntary and that servants struck bargains and made choices among competing destinations.[29] Galenson's analysis also indicates that servants were fairly well informed about conditions in the several competing destinations, a subject that merits further study.

Evidence of another type permits a test of the proposition that the choices servants made helped shape the pattern of migration to the colonies. If servants made the decisions, one would expect that they would pay close attention to opportunities and incomes at home and that the size of the migrant stream would be inversely related to English real wages. If, on the other hand, the choices of merchants and planters controlled the volume of migration, there would be little relation between real wages and the number of migrants. A comparison of annual fluctuations in the number of servants who left Bristol in the seventeenth century with an English real-wage index shows a strong inverse relationship. Servants left in greater numbers when wages were low, strong evidence that they made the decision to move. A comparison of the volume of customary servants arriving in the Chesapeake colonies with English real wages shows the same pattern, indicating that even servants without contracts, whom one might assume were least likely to be in control of the situation, made decisions informed by an assessment of their prospects at home.[30]

Elsewhere I have suggested that there were two distinct paths toward an Africanized workforce in British America. In one, the Barbadian case, the shift was triggered by a sharp increase in the demand for labor associated with a new crop, sugar. In the other, the Virginia pattern, the change was gradual and not connected to a new crop, instead reflecting a decline in the supply of workers from other sources.[31] The description of what happened in the island's export sector and to its workforce offered above demonstrates that this argument needs revision. The early stages of the growth of slavery in Barbados were connected, not exclusively to the growth of sugar, but to a diversified export boom that witnessed increased production of tobacco, cotton, indigo, and ginger, as well as the beginnings of commercial cane cultivation. Clearly, Eric Williams's strong statement of the notion of a Barbadian path, which can be paraphrased as "no sugar, no slaves," will not stand. Does this mean we should abandon the idea altogether?

There is a persistent tradition that so argues, maintaining that growing demand for labor played no role in the replacement of servants by slaves in Barbados. Instead, this tradition contends, the transformation of the Barbadian workforce was a function of a decline in the supply of servants, leaving planters with a shortage of labor, which led them to turn to slaves.[32] This tradition asserts that there was no distinct Barbadian path toward slavery, that what I have called the Virginia pattern prevailed both on the island and along the tobacco coast. While the evidence presented in tables 6 and 7 showing that the number of servants increased while slavery was taking root on the island should be sufficient to put the supply-side explanation of the workforce transformation in Barbados to rest, its persistent appearance in the literature suggests that we ought to pay close attention to the pattern of servant migration both to British America as a whole and to Barbados. Unfortunately, there is little direct evidence on the volume of servant migration, as contemporaries rarely bothered to keep track of those who crossed the Atlantic under indentures during the seventeenth century. It is possible to develop estimates indirectly, however. Given birth and death rates and the size of colonial populations, net migration can be estimated as a residual, as that portion of change in population size that cannot be explained by the difference between births and deaths. H. A. Gemery has used such a method to derive estimates of migration to British America and its major subregions for the seventeenth century. Table 8 builds on his work to estimate the number of Europeans who arrived in British America and the British West Indies from 1630 to 1700.

It must be emphasized that these are net figures. The method cannot be used to identify return migration. For British America as a whole, these estimates should be read as minimums; the true volume of transatlantic migration was probably slightly higher. A further problem with the subregional figures is that the method does not make it possible to distinguish transatlantic migrants from those who moved between regions within the empire. Thus, the estimates for the last third of the century, when there was considerable movement from the islands to the mainland, probably exaggerate the share of the transatlantic migrant stream bound for the continent. Finally, these estimates are based on estimates of total population and vital rates; few of them, especially for the Caribbean, are firmly rooted in solid empirical work. They must therefore be used with caution.[33]

TABLE 8
Estimated European migration to British America and the West Indies, 1630–1700 (thousands)

Decade	British America	English Caribbean
1630–40	39.7	20.0 (50.4%)
1640–50	68.5	55.9 (81.6%)
1650–60	60.2	39.2 (65.1%)
1660–70	48.2	15.4 (32.0%)
1670–80	45.2	15.5 (24.3%)
1680–90	40.7	10.5 (42.4%)
1690–1700	40.1	17.0 (42.4%)

Sources: Gemery, "Emigration from the British Isles"; Menard, "British Migration," 105.

Despite these difficulties, most historians seem persuaded that these estimates provide a rough approximation of the pattern of migration; they are reliable enough for my purposes. These figures suggest that the number of European migrants to British America rose until about midcentury and then declined. I take some comfort from the appearance of a similar pattern in the Wrigley-Schofield estimates of migration from England (see fig. 4). These estimates exhibit the same pattern as do the estimates of European arrivals in British America, showing a steady rise to a peak in the mid-seventeenth century followed by a late-century decline.[34]

The estimates for migration to the West Indies in table 8 describe an exaggerated version of the pattern of migration to the colonies as a whole, with both a steeper rise and a sharper fall. Given the frequency of movement between islands, use of the indirect method to estimate migration to particular West Indian colonies is especially problematic. However, the several English departure lists assembled in table 9 suggest that just as migration to the islands exaggerates the pattern for British America as a whole, movement to Barbados exaggerates the West Indian pattern, showing an especially dramatic rise to a midcentury peak followed by a sharp drop to a late-century low.[35]

A similar pattern appears in estimates of net migration to Barbados provided by David Galenson, which show a peak of just fewer than seventeen thousand whites moving to Barbados in the 1650s, followed by a decline to a low of fewer than three thousand in the first decade of the eighteenth century.[36] During the 1630s, these data suggest, Barbadian

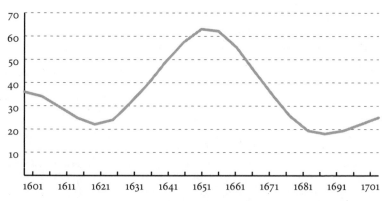

FIG. 4. Estimated net migration (thousands) from England, 1601–1701, from Wrigley and Schofield, *Population History of England,* 219

planters were able to get what labor they needed in the British-American market for indentured workers. At least a third of the English servants bound for the colonies went to the West Indies, a majority of those to Barbados. The export boom of the next decade (driven in its early stages by a mix of crops, later by sugar) drove up demand for labor and sent planters and merchants scrambling for workers. Planters bought slaves in increasing numbers, but there were also determined efforts to recruit more servants as planters offered higher prices and shorter terms in their attempt to divert a larger share of the migrant stream to the island.[37] Initially the efforts succeeded: the number of migrants to British America rose sharply, reaching its seventeenth-century peak in the 1640s, and the lion's share, more than 80 percent of the total, ended up in the West Indies. Despite an increase in the number of farms, Barbadian planters managed to increase the ratio of servants to estates over the 1640s. Slaves did not come to outnumber servants on Barbadian plantations in the late 1640s because of a fall in the number of indentured workers. As tables 6 and 7 show, the numbers of both servants and slaves increased over the 1640s; the number of slaves simply grew at a faster rate.

Signs of strain appeared almost immediately, however, as Barbadian planters stretched the servant trade to capacity during the export boom. Higher prices were one such sign. Few quotations of servant prices survive, but what data there are suggest a sharp increase, asserting that the

TABLE 9
Destinations of migrants to British America, 1635–1729

Departing From	Period	Barbados (%)	Other West Indies (%)	Mainland (%)	Total Migrants
London	1635	20.1	14.6	65.3	3,190
Bristol	1654–59	68.7	2.9	28.4	2,954
Bristol	1660–69	22.1	19.6	58.3	4,548
Bristol	1670–79	10.3	21.3	68.4	2,549
Bristol and London	1680–89	15.9	32.2	51.9	2,260
Liverpool	1697–1707	2.6	3.5	93.9	766
London	1718–29	1.7	31.3	67.0	1,416

Sources: Dunn, *Sugar and Slaves*, 56; Galenson, *White Servitude*, 220–27.

"price of servants" in Barbados "doubled what they were" between 1640 and 1660.[38] Shorter terms were another sign of strain. Strain was also evident in changing recruiting practices as merchants cast a wider net in efforts to meet the burgeoning demand for labor. Political prisoners became an important source of workers around midcentury as the Civil War worked "to make merchandise of men" and several prominent West Indian merchants used their close connections with the Protectorate to see that the merchandise went to the island.[39] Merchants also began shipping convicts to the island in the 1640s, and they took so many young workers from "spirits" that the colony's name became synonymous with kidnapping, as *barbadosed* acquired the meaning attached to *Shanghaied* in the early twentieth century.[40]

A final evidence of strain was a widening of the recruiting net to include Ireland and Scotland, which added ethnic diversity to the island's population and ethnic tension to its politics. Henry Whistler described the island's population following a visit there in 1655, when the export boom was in full swing, capturing the results of the scramble for workers in vivid language: "This Island is inhabited with all sortes: with English, French, Duch, Scotes, Irish, Spaniards thay being Jewes; with Ingones, and miserabell Negors borne to perpetuall slavery they and Thayer seed. . . . This island is the Dunghill wharone England doth cast forth its rubidg: Rodgs. Hors and such like peopel, which are generally brought heare."[41] Recruiting servants was doubtless made more difficult by the island's growing reputation as a place where servants were worked hard and mistreated. One servant described Barbados as a "miserable place of torment."[42] Martin Noell, a sugar merchant and major investor in the island, tried to defend Barbados, claiming that "the work done by servants there was no harder than that done by the common husbandman here." Since Noell was so obviously an interested party, I doubt that many found him persuasive.[43]

Merchants and planters thus pushed the Barbadian servant trade to its limits, increasing the number of servants brought to the island roughly fourfold during the 1640s. Even at its peak that market was simply too small to satisfy the export boom's seemingly insatiable demand for labor. Despite the great increase in the number of indentured workers, Barbadians complained of "a great want of servants,"[44] and they purchased even more slaves, so that black arrivals outnumbered white immigrants in the 1650s.

It soon became apparent that Barbadians would be unable to sustain the level of servant migration achieved in the 1640s. Migration from Britain to the colonies fell off after midcentury as England's population declined and opportunities at home improved. Barbados also faced growing competition for this dwindling supply of workers from the mainland colonies and from other islands, at first the Leewards, especially Nevis, later Jamaica.

As the competition increased, the export boom transformed Barbados in ways that made it progressively less attractive to young English men and women. Plantation agriculture changed working conditions on the island, turning Barbados into "a land of Misery and Beggary" by curtailing opportunities for poor whites, raising mortality and morbidity rates, and introducing a rigorous and degrading work regime.[45] As that happened, servant migration to the island fell off, slowly at first but dramatically after 1660. By the end of the century Barbados, which had once dominated the English-American migration stream, had become only a minor destination for indentured servants.

These data on migration are a significant challenge to the tradition that contends that the transformation of the Barbadian workforce had nothing to do with demand and was entirely a function of changing supplies of labor. That tradition implies a rapid decline in the number of servants in the 1640s as the workforce Africanized. In fact, servant migration to the island rose severalfold during the 1640s, and it remained well above its pre-export-boom level until the end of the 1650s. Servant migration to Barbados did eventually decline, but only in the 1660s, after the fact of Africanization and in part as a consequence of the changes brought by the export boom. Apparently, an increase in the demand for labor brought about by an export boom driven initially by a mix of crops, later by the growth of sugar cultivation, and not by a decline in the supply of servants, made Barbados a slave society. In short, there was a "Barbadian path."

The conditions that made Barbados unattractive to servants also shaped the supply of free labor, making it impossible for planters to recruit large numbers of wageworkers to their plantations. The export boom produced severe overcrowding and slim prospects for ex-servants, making Barbados the "worst poor man's country" in British America.[46] Servants "out of their time" found their progress blocked. Despite the lack of opportunities, few were willing to work as plantation laborers alongside African slaves. Some took supervisory jobs or positions as craftsmen on large plantations; others found work in Bridgetown; still others became tenants or small landowners, raising provisions, the minor staples or sugar for processing at a big man's mill. Many simply left to seek a new future elsewhere, making Barbados "a nursery for the planting of Jamaica, Surinam and other places" in the Caribbean and on the mainland.[47] The export boom made Barbados the source of the largest population movement within British America in the seventeenth century as some ten thousand people left the island and struck out for other colonies.[48]

The existence of a highly developed, large-scale Atlantic slave trade was essential to the Africanization process and to the success of the Barbadian export boom. During the first half of the seventeenth century that trade delivered on average more than seven thousand enslaved persons a year to European America, the bulk of them to Brazil and the Spanish colonies. Thus, when the increased demand for labor in Barbados stretched the capacity of the servant trade, planters had an alternative: they only had to persuade someone to divert a portion of the substantial slave traffic to the island. The Dutch, "those great encouragers of plantations," were eager to accommodate them. So too were a group of London merchants who were to play a key role in bringing plantation agriculture to the island.[49]

The Barbadian export boom coincided with and perhaps helped initiate a century-long expansion of the Atlantic slave trade as deliveries to European America rose from just over seven thousand persons a year in the mid-seventeenth century to more than sixty thousand a year by the mid-eighteenth century.[50] One striking feature of the expansion is that its early stages were not accompanied by rising prices. Indeed, prices initially fell and did not begin a sustained rise until 1700, powerful testimony to what must be recognized (despite the offensiveness of applying such analytic terms to so grisly a business) as the impressive productivity gains and high elasticity of supply that characterized the trade.[51] In Barbados, slave prices rose sharply about 1650, apparently reflecting the powerful increase in the demand for labor associated with the export boom and the need to divert slaves away from competing markets. Prices then fell, perhaps by half, until the 1660s and remained low until the outbreak of war pushed them higher during the last decade of the century.[52]

Slave deliveries rose rapidly to a peak in the 1650s, when more than three thousand persons per year were delivered to Barbados, and then tailed off somewhat, averaging, despite sharp, short-term fluctuations, from twenty-five hundred to three thousand persons annually for roughly a century (See table 10). Such high levels of slave imports, accompanied by white flight, transformed the demography of the island. Blacks were a majority of the population by 1660, two-thirds by 1680, and by 1710 fully 80 percent of the inhabitants of Barbados were enslaved.[53]

As Galenson has explained, the transition from servants to slaves in Barbados was a two-stage process in which slaves first replaced servants as field laborers and only later, toward the end of the seventeenth century, came to dominate in craft and supervisory positions as well.[54] Further, as Carole Shammas has noted for the Chesapeake region in an argument that probably holds for Barbados as well, there was an important gendered dimension to the replacement of servants by slaves: There were few female servants in early Barbados, so the transition was not simply a matter of slaves replacing servants; it is more accurately described as a process by which male servants were replaced by male and female slaves.[55]

It has become a commonplace to describe the transition from servants to slaves as the transformation of a society in which there were slaves into a slave society. Ira Berlin explains the difference between the two types of society as follows:

> What distinguished societies with slaves was the fact that slaves were marginal to the central productive processes. In societies with slaves, slavery was just one form of labor among many. Slave owners treated their slaves with extreme callousness and cruelty at times, because this was the way they treated all subordinates, be they indentured servants, debtors, prisoners of war, pawns, peasants, or perhaps simply poor folks. In societies with slaves, no one presumed the master-slave relationship to be the exemplar. In slave societies, by contrast,

TABLE 10
Estimated net slave imports to the British West Indies, 1630s–1690s

Decade	Barbadian Imports	Total Imports
1630s	1,000	1,500
1640s	18,000	21,000
1650s	31,364	19,394
1660s	28,650	37,568
1670s	22,219	53,435
1680s	21,885	59,078
1690s	35,027	94,572

Sources: For the 1630s and 1640s, population figures in McCusker, "Rum Trade," 694–97, 699; for the 1650s through 1690s, Galenson, *White Servitude*, 218.

slavery stood at the center of economic production, and the master slave relationship provided the model for all social relations.[56]

This is a useful conceptual device because it has permitted historians to
explore the social and cultural consequences of the transition. The dis-
tinction between a slave society and a society in which there are slaves is
not without difficulties. For one thing, scholarship on the issue is plagued
by a lack of precision on the difference between the two types of societies.
This lack of precision is rooted in the work of Moses Finley, the source of
the categories, who, when he introduced them, announced his refusal to
play what he contemptuously called the "numbers game" in distinguishing between them, thus leaving us without a precise standard to mark the
difference between the two types of society.[57] Further, dualism obscures
the continuity between the two and hides the extent to which slave societies grew out of and were shaped by societies in which there were slaves.
Finally, in some scholarship there seems to be a tendency to assume that
once the revolutionary transition from a society with slaves to a slave society occurred important development stopped. As Ira Berlin, taking his
cue from Edward Thompson's classic analysis of class, has pointed out,
slavery was constantly made and remade as slaves and masters renegoti-
ated its terms.[58]

While most would agree that Barbados was a slave society by at least
1680, when enslaved Africans accounted for nearly 70 percent of its population, there were clearly major changes in the institution following that
date, as the slaves' share of the population continued to rise, reaching 76
percent by 1700 and 84.2 percent by 1770 (see table 5); as slaves moved into
craft and supervisory positions; as plantations continued to increase in
size; as the gang system emerged as the primary way of organizing work;
and as planters developed an ideology of whiteness as a means of maintaining social control. Insofar as the dualism of the dichotomy of slave society and society with slaves obscures these developments, it does students
of the Barbadian slave regime a disservice.[59]

3

Who Financed the Sugar Boom?

THE BARBADIAN SUGAR BOOM was enormously expensive, as some quick, back-of-the-envelope calculations illustrate. Islanders spent more than £1 million sterling on slaves alone between 1640 and 1660, to which must be added expenditures on servants, processing equipment, land, and livestock, which must have come to at least half that spent on slaves. Barbadians, although they had done better during the 1630s than most historians allow, did not have those sorts of resources. Who supplied the capital?

The London Merchants

Plantation development in British America could be financed in several ways. One possibility was to purchase new workers and new land, livestock, equipment, and the like, out of savings or current income, but that would be a slow process, inadequate to account for the rapid pace of growth in Barbados during the sugar boom. Credit and capital transfers from abroad sped things up. One source of outside capital was short-term commercial credit supplied by merchants willing to defer payment until crops were in, a common practice in the slave trade. This was helpful, but financing economic development required more long-term investment. It was also possible to borrow funds on a local credit market, from neighboring merchants and planters, often secured by bond or mortgage, but in a still new colony such as Barbados at the start of the export boom such possibilities were limited. For the sort of money Barbadians needed it was necessary to look abroad, to relatives, friends, or big merchants in the colonial trades, again with loans secured by bonds and mortgages. Another source of capital was funds transferred to the colonies by immigrants who used inheritances or proceeds from the sale of property at home to make a start in America. Finally, sometimes residents of the metropolis invested directly in colonial enterprises, buying land and developing plantations on their own.[1]

One finds evidence of all these strategies in all the colonies, although one or another usually seems to have predominated. South Carolina, home to the large and prosperous Charleston merchant community, was able to finance the growth of slavery and plantation agriculture internally, with capital provided by the local merchants.[2] In the Chesapeake, by contrast, slavery seems to have been paid for in large part out of savings and current earnings, which may account for Chesapeake gradualism, the relatively slow growth of plantations in the region, and the near half-century it took the tobacco coast to commit to African slavery.[3] Barbados was no exception on either count; one finds evidence of capital coming from a variety of sources, but it is usually argued that the island's development in the early stages of the sugar boom was especially dependent on external sources of capital.

One tradition contends that the Dutch played the key role: "Hollanders," John Scott reported, "that are great encouragers of plantations . . . did at the first attempt of making sugar, give credit to the most sober inhabitants."[4] The Dutch successfully invaded northeastern Brazil in 1630, occupied it, and controlled its sugar industry from 1630 until 1654, when they were expelled by a successful revolt in what some regard as a Luso-Brazilian war of liberation.[5] For the argument advanced here it is worth noting that some Dutch merchants muttered that Brazilian sugar planters supported the revolt with enthusiasm because it seemed to be a way of escaping the debts they owed.[6]

Another tradition, which apparently began with Adam Smith, credits the English. In Smith's opinion, "the stock which has improved and cultivated the sugar colonies of England has, a great part of it, been sent out of England, and has by no means been altogether the produce of the soil and industry of the colonists. The prosperity of the English colonies has been, in great measure, owing to the great riches of England, of which a part has overflowed, if one may say so, upon those colonies."[7] John Stuart Mill, pushed Smith's argument to an extreme: "Our West Indian colonies, for example, cannot be regarded as countries with a productive capital of their own. . . . All the capital employed is English capital."[8]

The Dutch, if they did play a major role in financing the sugar boom, have left few tracks in the surviving records at the Barbados National Archives. While I would not go so far as to argue that Dutch merchants played no role in financing the sugar boom, it does seem clear that their importance has often been exaggerated. As Pieter Emmer has noted, "In view of the disastrous results of providing extended credit in Brazil, it seems unlikely that the WIC [the Dutch West-India Company] would have made the same mistake twice. Instead it probably hesitated to extend generous credit to foreign planters."[9]

Since there is so little evidence that Dutch merchants supplied the capital, it is worth asking where the notion that they did so came from and why it has lasted so long. What I have come to think of as the "myth of the Dutch," the idea that Dutch merchants dominated trade with the English colonies during the mid-seventeenth century, was created by colonial planters during the depression of the early 1660s as part of the ideology they were developing to combat the newly imposed Navigation Acts, which they blamed for the hard times they were suffering.[10]

If Dutch merchants did not get the sugar they needed from Barbados after their expulsion from Brazil, one wonders where they did get it, since substantial supplies of raw sugar were essential to the rapidly expanding Amsterdam refining industry. Most of the needed sugar came from Asia, especially South China and Taiwan, where the Dutch East-India Company (VOC) encouraged the development of a booming sugar industry in part to compensate for its loss of Brazil. These efforts were a success, for as Neils Steensgaard reports, as early as the 1640s the VOC was importing more than a million pounds of sugar annually from its Asian sources, which was more than adequate to meet the needs of Amsterdam refiners.[11] It is worth noting that Dutch historians of early modern expansion seem less likely to be persuaded by the myth of the Dutch than do those from other ethnic groups, perhaps because they are more interested in the emerging Dutch empire in Asia than in Dutch mercantile activities in the Americas.[12]

If the tradition regarding the Dutch is largely mythic, there is considerable evidence in support of Adam Smith's position. Some English gentlemen became absentee owners of Barbadian plantations in the early days of the sugar boom.[13] And some members of the English gentry, many of them royalists in search of a safe haven, moved to Barbados and put what was left of their fortunes in sugar.[14] Such investments pale in comparison with the activity of certain English merchants, many of them previously involved in importing sugar to England from the Mediterranean and Brazil and apparently interested in developing a more certain source of supply. In helping to finance the Barbadian sugar boom, these London merchants took a crucial first step in the construction of what one scholar has called England's "empire of credit."[15]

I have identified seventy-five English merchants who owned land in Barbados between 1640 and 1650. A few of these merchants were already prominent in colonial trade and are familiar to students of England's Atlantic economy during the first half of the seventeenth century: Maurice Thompson, William Pennoyer, Thomas Andrews, Richard Bateson. Some had long been active in West Indian trade, especially in tobacco and cotton, but others were obscure men with no previous Barbadian experience who saw an opportunity to make a big strike in sugar on the island and took the chance. In a few cases—Martin Noell is surely the best known—the results were spectacularly successful.[16]

While English merchants were active in buying land and developing plantations on the island throughout the 1740s and 1750s, their activity rose to a powerful crescendo in 1647. English merchants annually purchased one to two tracts from 1639 to 1642, four to five from 1643 to 1646, thirty in 1647, eleven in 1648, and two to three in 1649 and 1650.[17] That their efforts peaked in the late 1640s is not surprising. Sugar prices ran up to a sharp spike in 1646 and remained high for the rest of the decade as the revolt at Pernambuco disrupted production there, greatly reducing the available supply. We can gain some insight into the role of English merchants in financing the sugar boom by following them through the fairly full documentation that survives for 1647 (see table 11).

Twenty-two English merchants acting alone or in partnership purchased more than ten thousand acres in Barbados from March to December 1647. While some of the tracts were undeveloped, others were working plantations with servants, slaves, housing, livestock, tools, and crops in the ground, which accounts for the large variation in price per acre apparent in table 11. Merchant capital transformed these plantations, adding more workers and livestock, increasing the acreage, and purchasing the expensive equipment needed to process cane. Not all the deeds included prices, but the total value of the investments made from 1639 to 1650 must have been in the neighborhood of £25,000 sterling. All but two of these merchant investors were Londoners, and all but one of them were men. The sole female was the widow Beatrice Odiarne, who seems to have taken over her husband Thomas's interests on the island. The 1,654.5 acres the

London merchants purchased in 1647 does not seem like a lot of land in the abstract; however, Barbados is a small island of only 106,240 acres, so the merchants bought outright or acquired an interest in 1.5 percent of the island in 1647. If they had continued to purchase land at that rate they would have acquired the entire island in only sixty-five years. As it was, over the course of the sugar boom, from 1640 to 1660, English merchants acquired eighty-five tracts on the island. If we assume that those tracts that traded hands in deeds that failed to mention acreage contained the average of 65.2 acres of deeds in which acreage was reported, then by 1660 English merchants owned outright or had an interest in 5,444.2 acres on the island, just over 5 percent of the island's land and probably an even larger share of the land suitable for sugar.

TABLE 11
English merchants who bought land in Barbados in 1647

Merchants[a]	Acreage	Price (£)	Date
Martin Noell, James Noell, William Seeman	67.5	800	8 March
Colleton, John	80	250	14 March
Henry Quintyne	77		10 April
Martin, James, Stephen, and Thomas Noell	5	30	14 April
Thomas Walker, John Webster, Nathan Grafty, Philip Holman	10		17 April
Walker, Webster, Grafty, Holman	80		18 May
M., J., and T. Noell	21	160	29 May
Laurence Chambers	300	20,000	2 June
Walker, Webster, Grafty, Holman	30	300[b]	9 June
Richard Ellis	25	40	11 June
Thomas Mathew	184	5,000	13 June
Richard Batson	40		1 July
Walker, Webster, Grafty, Holman	18		1 July
M., J., S., and T. Noell	20	200	July
Nathaniel Starkey	23.5		7 August
M., J., S., and T. Noell	6.5	32.6	20 August
Beatrice Odiarne	60		9 September

Source: Recopied Deed Books, Barbados National Archives.

Note: All prices are in Barbados currency.

[a] Names reported as they appear in the documents.

[b] Price estimated based on a performance bond.

The biggest plungers were the four Noell brothers, James and Martin, who remained in London, and Stephen and Thomas, who came to Barbados in 1646 to develop and manage the firm's island investments. Their first recorded purchases were modest enough, four acres in June 1646 and again in December, although it could be that Thomas and Stephen were adding small parcels to fill out a plantation that the "four brethren" had acquired earlier.[18] The first big investment I found record of came in March 1647, when James and Martin joined William Seaman, another London merchant, to buy a quarter-share of the Spring Plantation, a 270-acre tract in St. Joseph's Parish already planted with 50 acres of cane, from Thomas Pead and James Worsum, also London merchants. Apparently, Worsum and Pead needed the £800 sterling the Noells and Seaman brought to the enterprise to build a sugar mill and supply the plantation with sixty servants and seven oxen or bulls to drive the mill by the following August.[19]

That partnership was only the beginning: Between April and August the brothers purchased four tracts, one of them a small plantation of 21 acres, the other three undeveloped parcels of 5, 6.5, and 25 acres, all of them in St. James's Parish and adjacent to land they had acquired in 1646. These several parcels formed the nucleus of their Black Rock Plantation.[20] In July they purchased a small plantation of 20 acres in St. Peter's Parish, soon adding to it an adjoining tract of 44 acres. They also bought a lot near the session's house in Bridgetown, where they perhaps planned to open a store and a warehouse. Again in July, Martin, this time in partnership with another London merchant, Mark Mortemore, bought another fully stocked plantation in Christ Church Parish for £2,400, to be paid within twenty-one years. Finally, in November the brothers bought yet another developed plantation, a 60-acre tract at the border of St. Peter's and St. James's, for £1,200.[21] By the end of the year the Noell brothers and their various partners were operating at least five plantations in Barbados on some 600 acres, representing an investment of from £9,000 to £10,000 sterling.[22]

Before moving on to other activities of these London merchants, it may help clarify why they invested so heavily to note that members of the London merchant community had been engaged with Barbados since its first settlement by the English. William Courteen, for example, helped fund the initial expedition to the island, while a syndicate of merchants led by Mathew Royden were major creditors of Lord Carlisle, the first proprietor of the island, and were given a 10,000-acre tract of land in partial settlement of the debts.[23] While I have not yet uncovered any direct connection between this early activity and the London merchants who invested in the sugar boom, there seems to have been a fairly continuous interest in the island on the part of the London merchant community during the first half of the seventeenth century.

As Jacob Price has pointed out, attention to the legal context within which debtors and creditors operated is essential to understanding the willingness of London merchants to invest in the Barbadian sugar boom. In Brazil and Spanish America what Price calls the "Latin Rule" prevailed.

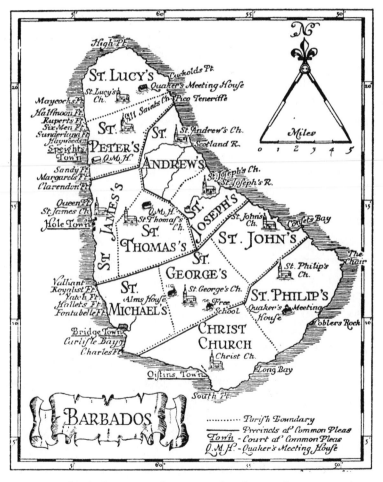

FIG. 5. Map of Barbados ca. 1720, showing parishes, from Harlow, *History of Barbados,* facing 335

That rule protected the integrity of the plantation as a working unit. Creditors could seize crops, but they could not use the courts to seize the non-landed accoutrements of the plantation or sugar mills, such as agricultural equipment, livestock, or slaves, and thus diminish the units' productive capacity. Price contrasts this with the Anglo-Saxon, or "creditor-defense," model, in which all of a debtor's assets could be seized to cover an outstanding obligation, which prevailed in Barbados and in most of British America. The consequence of this was that credit tended to be harder to come by, and interest rates higher, in Latin America than in the British colonies.[24]

Because Barbados did not take the extreme path and follow the Latin Rule, we should not jump to the conclusion that the island was a creditor's paradise. That was hardly the case, as the Royal African Company (RAC) and many independent English merchants discovered to their dismay. The Barbadian legislature and courts, both of them dominated by planters, many of whom were deeply in debt, proved quite creative in erecting obstacles to the easy collection of debts. The Barbadian legislature, along with many of the islands, put ceilings on interest rates that were lower than the market rate, although Barbados did not go as far as Nevis, which for a time prohibited interest altogether. The Barbadian legislature also proved adept at manipulating currency to promote inflation, which of course favored debtors. K. G. Davies calls this the "classic strategy of the colonial debtor."[25] One tactic of this sort especially favored by colonial legislatures was the use of paper currency, which the colonies often declared legal tender, meaning that it could be used to pay all debts owing in the colony. Legal-tender laws usually required inhabitants, or anyone doing business in the colony, to accept paper currency, whatever its value, in payment for debts formerly payable in hard cash. In this, as in so many other things, Barbados led the way.

The Barbados paper money act of 1706, ostensibly passed to address the shortage of money on the island, created a paper currency backed by a land bank, which enabled anyone who owned real estate on the island to obtain paper credit for one-quarter the value of their real property. Since paper currency often deflated rapidly, merchants thought such acts contrary to their interests and lobbied the home government to preserve the value of their outstanding debts. The Board of Trade, determined to protect the value of debts owed English merchants and worried that paper money would disrupt commerce, raise prices, and reduce royal revenues, recommended disallowance. The Privy Council supported the recommendation, and the queen vetoed the measure. Further, to prevent other colonies from following the Barbadian lead, the queen instructed her governors not to approve any paper-money measures without the prior approval of the crown unless they contained a clause suspending their operation until they received royal approval. This successful lobbying by the merchants against the Barbados legislation can be regarded as the first step in a long movement that culminated in the Currency Act of 1764. Since many colonists thought paper money essential to ensuring the money supply necessary to their domestic economies, they were outraged by the merchants' opposition and by their own inability to get their way within the empire on so crucial an issue.[26]

So successful were these various strategies that debtors were encouraged to make the RAC their selling agent in London, and they could do so without paying the usual commission of 2 percent. Nor did the RAC find relief when it turned to the courts. Judges and jurors, often debtors themselves, were reluctant to find in favor of a London merchant against their friends and neighbors. The Company of Royal Adventurers Trading to Africa, the RAC's predecessor, complained to the Privy Council in 1664 that judicial proceedings in Barbados "afford no remedy but what is worse than the disease."[27] Thomas Modyford, an ally of the London merchants who invested in the island, later governor of Jamaica and agent for the Company of Royal Adventurers in the early 1660s, registered a similar complaint.[28] Modyford explained that the laws of Barbados made debt collection by the company on the island close to impossible. Although the governor was willing to change procedures in favor of the company, no change was likely, as it would require the consent of the council, and "the old planters in the Council, cary it in favour of their brethren."[29] Apparently, what Governor Daniel Parke claimed was a maxim in Antigua—"never to give any cause, how just soever, on the behalf of a stranger, against an inhabitant"[30]—was the rule throughout the islands. Despite its best efforts, the Company of Royal Adventurers Trading to Africa was unable to collect what it was owed, and in 1701 it decided to offer its Caribbean debts for sale to the highest bidder.[31]

Given its difficulties with debt collection, one wonders why the RAC continued to allow planters to purchase slaves on credit. The answer seems to be that it had no choice. By its royal charter in 1672 the RAC was granted a trade monopoly on the west coast of Africa, which in effect was intended to give it a monopoly in the slave trade to the English Caribbean. However, as David Galenson has shown, the RAC was unable to enforce its monopoly. Instead of the powerful monopolist of contemporary imagination, the RAC is best understood as a regulated public utility. As such, it had to do what those in power in the government wanted or loose its charter. What those in power wanted was a steady supply of slaves to the islands sufficient to produce the sugar needed to keep revenues flowing to government coffers. Since planters were unable to pay cash for slaves, the RAC had to offer credit. So it struggled along, never producing much in the way of profits for its shareholders, accumulating a mounting debt. When the RAC lost its charter with the flight of James II in 1788, its role in the slave trade rapidly dwindled; it finally collapsed into bankruptcy in 1752.[32] If, as Dalby Thomas put it, the RAC was "wonderfully kinde in the credit they have given the plantations," this was because of the RAC's political position rather than because of the generosity of the men who ran it.[33] Since interest rates on the island fell over the colonial period, one must conclude that the complex and often tense negotiations surrounding debt collection in Barbados were resolved in a way that satisfied the concerns of the merchants, since if they were persuaded they could not collect on debts, interest rates probably would have risen to reflect the high risk of extending credit to sugar planters.[34]

These English merchants did not limit their activity in Barbados to investment and plantation development. They mobilized opposition to proprietary government on the island, almost succeeding in voiding Lord Carlisle's patent with a petition to Parliament in 1646–47.[35] The merchants had invested heavily in Barbados and were worried about protecting their investments from arbitrary proprietary exactions in the form of rents and taxes. This petition failed; however, they had more luck in 1651, when they raised the issue again with the enthusiastically antiroyalist Rump Parliament, which immediately called in Carlisle's patent. The Rump took another step in furthering the merchants' interests when it began to help them reassert their hegemony over the island's trade. During the English Civil War the Barbadians had taken the opportunity presented by metropolitan distractions to operate as a virtually independent polity. Independence included opening trade to all comers, including the Dutch. Although historians have clearly exaggerated the Dutch role in the sugar boom, there is no doubt that the Dutch became important traders to the island. There is considerable evidence in the Barbados National Archives of Dutch merchants active in Barbados during the boom, but that evidence shows Dutch merchants buying sugar and selling European manufactures, not extending long-term credit to sugar planters. Islanders were in fact persuaded that free trade was in large part responsible for the prosperity of the 1640s, and they were committed to do what they could to keep their ports open. This determination led them to flirt with royalism and defy Parliament.

The merchants were as determined to exclude foreigners from colonial trade as the islanders were to keep trade open. The merchant planters, especially Maurice Thompson and Martin Noell, were much better connected in Parliament than were the free traders, and the merchants got what they wanted. Maurice Thompson's influence rested on his position as the preeminent colonial merchant of the time.[36] Noell was the leading sugar merchant; furthermore, he had been a partner of Cromwell's personal secretary, Robert Spavin, in various Barbadian ventures.[37] Led by Thompson and Noell, the merchants were able to persuade Parliament to reduce Barbados to submission by force.[38] And they were able to secure the Navigation Act of 1651, which confined colonial trade to English ships. As this last accomplishment demonstrates, the merchants' influence extended beyond Barbados to the empire as a whole. For the Navigation Act, which Noell and Thompson are sometimes credited with writing, served as the cornerstone of commercial policy for the British Empire in America throughout the colonial period.[39] Furthermore, with Barbados back under their control and the commercial policy of the empire defined, they turned their attention to expanding the English presence in the Caribbean and were the driving force behind what came to be known as the "western design," which brought Jamaica into the empire and created major opportunities for investment and development of the sort of plantation regime they had created in Barbados.[40] It is not surprising that many of the merchant investors in Barbados, Martin Noell prominent among them, played a major role in the development of Jamaica, where they worked to build a close replica of the Barbadian plantation complex.[41]

In addition to these political accomplishments, the merchant investors saw that Barbadians had the horses and oxen to drive the mills and haul the sugar to port.[42] They recruited servants to the island and were in part responsible for the surge in indentured laborers evident in the late 1640s and 1650s.[43] And they moved into the African slave trade in a big way, trying both to challenge Dutch hegemony in that branch of commerce and to supply Barbados with the workers essential to the sugar industry they were intent on creating. There is evidence that they were successful on both counts. Ernst van den Boogaart and Pieter Emmer, leading students of the Dutch slave trade, concluded "that the English were ahead of the Dutch in bringing slaves to the Caribbean" from the start of the sugar boom, a conclusion supported by several other recent scholars.[44] Between February 1645 and January 1647 the Dutch governors at El Mina, on the Gold Coast of West Africa, observed nineteen English slave ships capable of carrying a total of perhaps two thousand blacks. At that time deliveries to Barbados averaged roughly eighteen hundred slaves per year; thus, at the height of the Civil War, when Dutch inroads into island trade should have peaked, English merchants had the capacity to supply a substantial share of the trade.[45] It would seem that assertions that the Dutch brought slavery and plantation agriculture to Barbados are greatly exaggerated. Conventional historiography claims that the English were only marginal participants in the slave trade until the organization of the Royal African Company in 1672. Clearly, that judgment requires revision. It is also clear that the history of the English slave trade in the seventeenth century, which has been neglected for a generation, would repay close reexamination.[46] There is also evidence, which I will present in chapter 5, that the merchant investors played an important role in shaping the changing organization of the sugar industry in Barbados. English merchants thus played a key role in the Barbadian sugar boom, providing a crucial infusion of funds that helped make possible the sugar boom of the late 1640s.

The merchants had a keen appreciation of their role in the sugar boom. In an undated document, probably from the 1650s, they put it as follows: "While the planters had dug the land, it had not yielded so much wealth if the merchants had not sowed it (as it were) with their gold."[47] Capital provided by English merchants would continue to play an important role in the Barbadian sugar industry for the remainder of the colonial period, but more in the form of short-term commercial credit or longer-term loans provided by commission agents serving as bankers to big planters than through direct investment. Running a complex sugar-making enterprise at the edge of empire from its metropolitan center was a difficult and troubling business. Many of the merchant investors found themselves in tiresome squabbles with the relatives and agents they sent out to manage their island affairs.[48] Given the prices sugar commanded in the 1640s, it was worth the difficulty, and the returns were high enough to cover the inefficiencies absentee management entailed and the headaches it brought. But as sugar prices fell after midcentury, merchants began to view their investments in a different light.[49] A few held on, still managing their Barbados plantations from London into the 1660s.[50] More moved to the island to run their operations directly, in the process founding some of the great

West Indian fortunes of the colonial era.[51] But most sold off their holdings, taking the sensible path of restricting their engagement in the sugar industry to finance and marketing.

The Local Planters

We could stop here and conclude that Adam Smith was right, that the sugar boom was the work of English merchants. Matters were more complex than that, however. Some of the great Barbados plantations were the result of England's riches overflowing, but many were not. Some of those who eventually acquired "very great and vast estates" "began upon small fortunes," building "according to Barbados custom" with crops that required little capital land and labor and reinvesting what they earned in workers, land, and equipment until they were big enough to make sugar.[52] "I have at present 16 acres of cotton planted at the least, as much corne for my provisions, bysides tobacco," Richard Vines reported in 1647. "The next yeare I intend for sugar."[53] The proportion who started small with cotton and tobacco and built great sugar plantations through savings out of current income is impossible to tell, but the diversified export boom of the mid-1640s brought that dream within reach for many ambitious farmers. It is worth noting that nearly 40 percent of the great planters who dominated the island in 1660 came from families established in the pre-sugar era.[54]

How the sugar boom was financed is illuminated by approaching the question through another mystery concerning the sugar boom: why Barbados? Why was that island the site of the first successful effort in the Caribbean to produce sugar on a grand scale? The usual answer, which is partly correct, has turned on security. Barbadians were fairly safe from attacks by Indians, the Spanish, and pirates, and despite the occasionally tumultuous politics on the island, they were even fairly safe from one another. And such security was essential if investors were to risk capital in the amounts necessary to fund the sugar boom. But historians have defined security too narrowly and attended only to its political and military dimensions. During the presugar era some Barbadians had accumulated estates through farm building and on the profits of the minor exports while demonstrating their competence as planters on the Caribbean frontier. Their properties and reputations doubtless gave investors in the first West Indian sugar adventure the sense of security that persuaded them to risk their funds.[55]

The importance of this accumulation of property and experience is suggested by the frequency with which the London merchants who invested in the island put their funds into established plantations and went into partnership with resident planters. It is also revealed in a remarkable set of documents in the Barbados National Archive that bring together several of the themes of this book. Over two and one-half weeks in July and August 1644 Captain George Richardson, master, and Richard Parr, merchant, sold 251 slaves brought to the island on the British ship *Marie Bonadventure*, of London (table 12). A similar set of documents for a much smaller sale, of 26 slaves to 8 purchasers from the *Mary*, also of London, by John Wadloe on 5–25 March 1645 (table 13), describes patterns similar to those discussed here. To begin with the obvious, both ships were English, not Dutch. The pace of sales was brisk, testimony to the island's prosperity and the demand for labor generated by the export boom. Most of the sales were in small lots of one to five slaves, evidence that this was still a society of small planters. However, there is evidence of the transformation just beginning to work through island society. The big purchasers were a mixture of established planters and new arrivals, one of whom, Christopher Thompson, may have been acting for a group of London merchants intent on building sugar plantations.[56]

The way in which the planters paid for these slaves is also suggestive. Seven slaves were given to Governor Philip Bell, apparently to ensure that the wheels of commerce and law would be well greased. Only thirty-three slaves were sold for "ready goods," seven for a lot and storehouse in Bridgetown, where Richardson and Parr set up shop, the rest for various country commodities, indigo, tobacco, cotton, and pork, but not sugar. The remaining slaves, 211 in all, 85 percent of the total, were sold on credit, all due in the next April, when crops would come in, some of them secured by mortgages, evidence of how farm building and the export boom helped finance the move toward slavery. While a few of the purchasers drew bills of exchange on London, most paid, or promised to pay, in commodities in a pattern that mirrored the diversity of the island's export boom and the initial use of slaves. The purchase of William Hilliard reflects the transformation under way on the island. Hilliard was a long-term resident who had made a fortune in cotton and tobacco and was about to go into sugar in a big way in partnership with Samuel Farmer, a Bristol merchant.[57] He purchased 30 slaves for £660 sterling due in April 1645, secured by a mortgage against his estate, promising to pay by shipping indigo,

TABLE 12
Sale of slaves from the *Marie Bonadventure,* of London, Captain George Richardson, master, and Richard Parr, merchant, in Barbados, 27 July–17 August 1644

A. SIZE OF SALES

Number of slaves	Number of purchasers	Total slaves
1	3 (7.1%)	3 (1.2%)
2	15 (35.7%)	30 (11.9%)
3	2 (4.8%)	6 (2.4%)
4	3 (7.1%)	12 (4.8%)
5	4 (9.5%)	20 (8.0%)
7	4 (9.5%)	28 (11.2%)
8	2 (4.8%)	16 (6.4%)
10	6 (14.3%)	60 (23.9%)
12	1 (2.4%)	12 (4.8%)
30	1 (2.4%)	30 (12.0%)
34	1 (2.4%)	34 (13.5%)
Total	42 *(100%)*	251 *(100%)*

B. FORM OF PAYMENT

Gift	7 (2.8%)
Ready goods	33 (13.1%)
Credit	211 (84.1%)
Total	251 *(100%)*

C. TYPE OF PAYMENT

Commodity paid or promised	Number of slaves
Tobacco	62 (25.4%)
Cotton	43 (17.6%)
Sugar	42 (17.2)
Bills of exchange	18 (15.6)
Indigo	26 (10.7)
Land	7 (2.9)
Pork	2 (0.8%)
Unspecified	24 (9.8%)
Total	224

Source: Recopied Deed Books, RB 3/1, 591–94, Barbados National Archives.
Note: Percentages may not add up to 100% because of rounding.

cotton, tobacco, and sugar, a list that describes the current state of the Barbadian economy and points toward its future. The documents do not describe the age and gender composition or the provenance of the slaves, but if they resembled those brought to the island in the second half of the seventeenth century, they were roughly 60 percent male, 13 percent children, and predominantly from the Senengambia and Gold Coast regions of West Africa.[58]

It would be useful to conclude this discussion of sources of funding for the sugar boom by allocating shares among the several contributors. While there is no evidence that would permit such an exercise, I do have some thoughts on the issue. First, I suspect that Barbados would have become a major sugar producer with or without the contribution of the London merchants, but if islanders had to rely on savings out of current earnings alone, it would have been a much slower process, and there would be no talk of a sugar revolution or even a sugar boom. While the intervention of the merchants was not necessary to the rise of the Barbadian sugar industry, it did speed it up and give it that special intensity that set it apart

TABLE 13
Sale of slaves from the *Mary*, of London, by John Wadloe, merchant, in Barbados, 5–25 March 1645

A. SIZE OF SALES

Number of slaves	Number of purchasers	Total slaves
2	5 (62.5%)	10 (38.5%)
3	2 (25.0%)	6 (23.1%)
10	1 (12.5%)	10 (38.5%)
Total	8 (100%)	26 (100%)

B. FORM OF PAYMENT

Credit	26 (100%)

C. COMMODITY *paid or promised*

Tobacco	20 (76.9%)
Ginger	5 (19.2%)
Cotton	1 (3.9%)
Total	26 (100%)

Source: Recopied Deed Books, RB 3/1, 591–94, Barbados National Archives.

and made it possible to speak of the sugar revolution or the sugar boom instead of a more prosaic rise or growth of the sugar industry.

However it was paid for, the Barbadian sugar boom had a noticeable impact on the island. As the boom wound down about 1680 Barbados was a much different place than it had been at its start in the early 1640s. While this transformation is familiar to most early Americanists through the work of Richard Dunn, it is useful to conclude this chapter with a quick summary of the major changes, if only to underscore the importance of the sugar boom in the island's history and to make clear the importance of paying attention to the details of the boom. While I am convinced that it is an error to speak of a "sugar revolution," since slavery and plantation agriculture were well on their way to Barbados before sugar became the dominant crop, there was still a sugar boom on the island, which changed life there considerably, as the following brief summary of Richard Dunn's work demonstrates.

In the 1630s, before the start of the diversified export boom, Barbados was an island of small planters who produced cotton, tobacco, and provisions on small, owner-operated plantations by themselves or with the help of a few servants or slaves. By 1680, by which time the export boom had almost run its course, things had changed considerably. There were still plenty of small planters on the island; in fact they were a majority of property owners. As Dunn notes, the often-repeated assertion that by 1680 big planters had bought up all the land on the island and squeezed the small men out is a "myth." Although the big planters were not the only planters on the island in 1680, they were clearly dominant. The 175 men whom Dunn classifies as big planters owned about 200 acres and more than sixty slaves each. These 175 big planters were only about 7 percent of the property owners, but they owned about half the land, 60 percent of the servants, and just over half the slaves. Furthermore, they thoroughly dominated the island's government, holding nearly all the major positions in both the civilian government and the militia. Perhaps the most important change was in the composition of the population. In the 1630s, before the export boom, the slave population was about equal to the free population. In 1680, by contrast, Barbados had a substantial black and slave majority, a majority that would soon become almost overwhelming (see table 5).[59]

These shifting demographic patterns, a rapidly growing black population, and the slow shrinkage of the number of whites, were cause for concern on the part of many planters. Barbados did not experience a slave revolt during the seventeenth century, but the planters were not foolish enough to conclude that the absence of a revolt meant that their slaves were content and they were safe. They had uncovered conspiracies among servants in 1634 and 1647 and among slaves in 1686 and 1692. The biggest fear among the planters was that the two groups would come together in a general rising that would turn Barbados upside down. They uncovered evidence that servants and slaves had conspired together in both the 1686 and 1692 plots, although given that the so-called evidence consists largely of "confessions" extracted by torture, one must ask how much of this fear reflects reality and how much reflects planters' apocalyptic fantasies. We will never know.[60]

Given the planters' fear of a slave-servant combination, one wonders whether they understood, as did their counterparts in the Chesapeake, the potential utility of racism, and especially of an ideology of whiteness, in ensuring that servants and poorer whites generally understood where their interests and loyalties lay should the day of reckoning arrive and Barbadians face a slave rebellion.[61]

4

The Growth of the Barbadian Sugar Industry over the Seventeenth Century

AFTER EMERGING AS a major commercial crop in the 1640s, sugar quickly expanded to become the center of the Barbadian economy. As early as 1645, 40 percent of the island was planted in sugar. By 1767 the proportion had risen to 80 percent, which meant that "virtually all the land useful for agriculture of any kind was devoted to this one crop."[1] One can also trace sugar's rise in the data available on exports, which are summarized in table 14. English imports of Barbadian sugar, which must serve as a proxy for exports in the absence of true export data, expanded mightily over the second half of the seventeenth century, from fewer than four thousand tons about 1650 to more than twelve thousand tons by 1700. According to contemporaries, the expansion of the sugar industry made Barbados a great success. By the late seventeenth century, David Eltis notes, "the exports of no other European colony approached the value of that of Barbados." Indeed, "Barbados was probably exporting more relative to its size and population than any other polity of its time or indeed any other time up to that point."[2]

One critical point about this expansion is that it occurred within a context of rapidly falling prices, as is clear the prices on the island presented in table 15. Prices in Europe, whether measured at the retail or the wholesale level, at London or at Amsterdam, the two leading markets, also show a steep decline over the last half of the seventeenth century.[3] As even casual inspection of the data in tables 14 and 15 indicates, prices and output in the sugar industry were inversely related, a relationship that held for much of the period from 1640 to 1775.[4]

In most accounts the relationship between falling prices and rapidly

expanding exports is straightforward: planters responded too enthusiastically to the high prices at the beginning of the sugar boom, made more
sugar than the market would bear, and drove the price down.[5]

According to the planters, the difficulties they faced because of falling
prices were compounded by metropolitan policy, especially by the exclu-
sion of the Dutch and other foreign merchants from trade with the island,
and by the high taxes sugar importers had to pay, which kept the English
price artificially much higher than it needed to be given what the planters
were getting on the island and thus restricted the market by keeping the
English price too high for many potential consumers.[6] Planters, the argument continues, responded to falling prices by making ever more sugar in
desperate attempts to maintain incomes, a response that of course compounded the problem by glutting markets and driving prices down even
further. At first inspection one would think the planters had a point. English colonial sugar paid a basic tax of 1s. 6d. sterling per hundredweight.
Foreign sugars, however, were taxed at a much higher rate (4s. 9d. sterling
per hundredweight on raw sugar, or muscavado). Furthermore, colonial
clayed, or semirefined, sugar paid 4s. 9d. sterling per hundredweight,
while foreign clayed sugar paid 7s. sterling. Thus, English colonial producers were given a virtual monopoly on the lucrative home market. An
attempt to raise the duty on colonial sugar in 1671 was defeated by the
planters and their supporters in Parliament, but four years later, in an
attempt to balance the national budget, James I doubled the rate in legislation that was not repealed until 1693.[7]

While planters gained a near monopoly of the English market, they
might have had an argument when they asserted that the Navigation Acts

TABLE 14
Estimated sugar exports from Barbados to London, 1651–1706 (tons)

Year	Sugar exported	Year	Sugar exported
1651	3,750	1697	5,154
1655	7,787	1698	15,587
1663	7,176	1699	9,140
1669	9,525	1700	12,170
1683	10,000	1705	9,419
1691	9,191	1706	10,236
1696	7,613		

Source: Dunn, *Sugar and Slaves*, 203.

and the high tariffs put their product at a disadvantage in the markets of the European continent. Under the Navigation Acts sugar was an enumerated commodity, which meant that no matter what its ultimate destination, it had to be first shipped to England, where it would pay the duties and be unloaded, then reloaded on another ship for shipment to its final destination, at which time some, but not all, of the tariff charged on sugar destined for the English domestic market was rebated. Despite this cumbersome system and the costs it imposed, sugar produced in the English Caribbean did well in the markets of Europe. During most of the seventeenth century between one-half and two-thirds of the colonial sugar shipped to England was reexported to the European continent.[8]

In addition, in 1663–64, as part of the settlement transferring governance of the colony from the proprietorship of Lord Carlisle to the crown, the Assembly of Barbados granted the king a 5 percent duty on all exports in exchange for the guarantee of cloudy and uncertain land titles and in consideration of the costs of defense and administration.[9] This 5 percent tax proved a source of tension between the planters of Barbados and the crown for as long as it was in force, and the planters did what they could to evade it.[10]

While there is perhaps some truth in the assertion that growing production and high taxes drove sugar prices down, the relationship between output and price in the seventeenth-century sugar industry was in fact more complex and more interesting than that argument allows. Since there were few major changes in the way sugar was processed between the invention of the three-roller vertical mill in Sicily during the seventeenth century and the conversion to steam power in the nineteenth century, it is often assumed that the technology of sugar making did not

TABLE 15
Sugar prices in Barbados, 1646–1694 (shillings per hundredweight)

Year	Price	Year	Price
1646	50s.	1655	25s.
1649	37s. 5d.	1661	15s.
1652	20s.	1673–84	12s.6d.
1653	25s.	1687	6s. 5d.
1654	16s. 7d.	1694	9–10s.

Sources: Starkey, *Economic Geography of Barbados*, 67; Recopied Deed Books, RB 3/2, 629–30, 659, 679, 718, Barbados National Archives.

change and that there was little improvement in the productivity of sugar plantations in the colonial era.[11] This may be true if we define technology narrowly as having to do with men, metal, and machines and confine our attention to processing. However, if we think of technology more broadly as encompassing how things were done and consider the organization of the industry, as well as what happened in the field and in shipping and marketing, we uncover many minor improvements that add up to some fairly impressive gains and reveal a classic new-industry pattern in which expansion of the market was led by improvements in productivity, which permitted planters to sell at lower prices, which, in turn, increased consumption of Barbadian sugar.[12] As Dalby Thomas reported, in the last half of the seventeenth century in Barbados "new Improvements and Experiments were dayly added to the Art of planting, making, and refining sugar."[13] Such improvements fueled the expansion of the island's sugar industry.

Stuart B. Schwartz has recently published a detailed description of the process of sugar production in seventeenth-century Brazil.[14] Barbadian planters learned much of what they knew about sugar making in Brazil. Further, as Schwartz notes, "the techniques of sugar production in all of the American colonies were essentially the same."[15] We can therefore rely heavily on Schwartz's account in trying to understand what happened in early Barbados, although we must take care to allow for local variation in some details. For example, it is likely that Catholic Brazil allowed more work stoppages for religious holidays than did Protestant Barbados. Further, Barbadians, because of their close connection to London merchants and a legal system that favored creditors, may have been able to pursue a somewhat more capital-intensive agriculture than were Brazilians.[16]

During the seventeenth century, planters faced steadily falling sugar prices and were thus under intense pressure to improve the efficiency of their operations. Perhaps the first major boost in productivity was achieved by shifting from English indentured servants to African slaves. As Lorena Walsh has noted in a Chesapeake context, this transition allowed owners to ignore the conventions that protected English servants from overwork and other forms of abuse.[17] Along the Chesapeake these conventions included a rest period in the heat of the day, many traditional holidays, and Saturday afternoons free of work. In the sugar industry, perhaps the most important of these conventions concerned the gender division of labor and the work deemed appropriate for women to perform. As long as English servants were the dominant form of unfree labor, planters seem to have been reluctant to assign women to work in the fields. With the shift to slaves that reluctance disappeared. Hilary Beckles contends that this differential treatment of white and black women was a key element in the great planters' project of building white solidarity and constructing an ideology of whiteness.[18]

While evidence is thin for the seventeenth century, by the eighteenth century the tradition of assigning black women to field labor was well established. On both the Newton and Codrington estates, the two best-documented Barbados properties for the eighteenth century, female slaves were more likely than male slaves to work in the field. Women also often worked as drivers, usually on one of the inferior gangs that contained large numbers of children and adolescents.[19] Further gains in labor productivity were captured in the seventeenth century as slave prices fell, reflecting increased efficiencies in the slave trade. David Eltis reports that by the 1680s "slave prices in Barbados had probably reached an all-time low for any market in the Caribbean."[20] Finally, we might note that African slaves were more likely than British servants to be familiar with the hoe-based agriculture practiced in Barbados, which perhaps raised their relative productivity.[21] At any rate, planters were quickly persuaded that African slaves were a better workforce than British indentured laborers. As Governor Jonathan Atkins explained in 1676, island planters "had found from experience that they could keepe three Blacks, who work better and cheaper than one white man."[22]

The emergence of the large-scale, integrated plantation, discussed in chapter 5, brought additional productivity gains. By bringing growing and processing under one planter's supervision, the integrated plantation allowed the mill owner to better control the supply of cane to the mill and thereby ensure that the sugar works was able to operate at maximum efficiency throughout the milling season. In addition, late in the seventeenth century planters shifted from planting in holes to planting in trenches, which improved root development and anchorage, thereby reducing the frequency with which plants were uprooted during storms. Trench culture also reduced erosion, an important effect given the planter's persistent struggle to maintain soil fertility. Related to this was a discovery that canes could be planted closer together, which reduced weeding.[23]

The drift toward sugar monoculture also increased the productivity of Barbadian agriculture. In the early stages of the sugar boom the island's economy as a whole, as well as particular plantations, was marked by diversity as planters continued to grow the minor staples as well as provisions.[24] As the boom proceeded, however, planters concentrated their resources on the most profitable option and quickly drove the economy toward sugar monoculture. As I noted at the beginning of this chapter, by 1667 an estimated 80 percent of the island, almost all the arable land on the island, was planted in cane.[25] So tenacious was sugar monoculture's grip on Barbados that in the 1970s, more than three hundred years after the sugar boom, Richard Sheridan could report that Barbados had seven-eighths of its cultivated land planted in sugarcane.[26] Finally, Otis Starkey suggests that the rise of the large-scale, integrated plantation and the related decline of the small producer had the effect of eliminating less efficient producers, thus increasing the overall productivity of the island's sugar industry.[27]

During the 1650s planters turned from horses to more efficient cattle to drive their mills, which doubtless led to considerable savings in feed and labor costs. The appearance of two camels on Richard Ligon's 1650 map of the island suggests that planters were willing to experiment broadly in their struggle to reduce costs (fig. 6). According to John Oldmixon, while

FIG. 6. Richard Ligon's map of Barbados, 1650, from Ligon, *True and Exact History of Barbados*. (Courtesy James Ford Bell Library, Minneapolis)

several camels were brought to the island, "they did not thrive, and for that reason no more were brought over."[28] Eventually the planters replaced animal-powered mills entirely, with water mills and windmills, which permitted considerable savings in livestock and related costs. I suspect that planters who converted to windmills maintained a few animals for a while until they were fully satisfied that the wind could be depended upon.[29]

Barbados is well situated to use wind power: its elevation is high, the land is relatively flat, and the island is favored by steady ocean breezes. Nevertheless, the conversion to windmills in the eighteenth century was a slow process, perhaps because they represented a substantial capital investment (the estimates we have put the cost of a windmill at just under £1,000 sterling), and planters had to be persuaded that the new technology was reliable. Mills powered by cattle persisted throughout the colonial era, but their numbers steadily diminished until in 1773 only 14 were still in operation, down from some 350 in the 1650s, when the conversion began.[30] Water and windmills turned faster and with more force than animal powered mills, which further increased their efficiency advantage as mills powered by water or wind extracted more juice from the cane than did mills driven by animals (fig. 7).

FIG. 7. Cattle-driven sugar mill, from Rochefort, *Histoire naturelle et mirale,* facing 332. (Courtesy James Ford Bell Library, Minneapolis)

Some other important changes at the sugar mill also improved productivity. Scholars disagree about the history of the three-roller vertical mill. Some attribute its invention to Pietro Speciale, prefect of Sicily in 1649. Others claim that it was invented in Peru. At any rate, the three-roller vertical mill was introduced to Brazil, between 1608 and 1612 and quickly became the standard throughout the sugar industry (fig. 8).[31] I do not

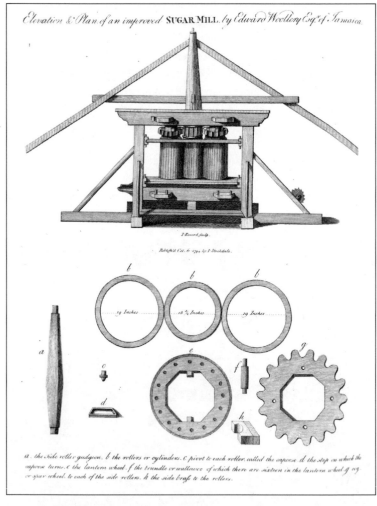

FIG. 8. Three-roller vertical mill, drawn by Bryan Edwards, from Edwards, *History, Civil and Commercial,* 2:222. (Courtesy James Ford Bell Library, Minneapolis)

know how canes were crushed in Barbados before the three-roller mill became the standard, but in Brazil a variety of devices were used, including an edge roller (initially developed in the Mediterranean to crush olives), in which canes were crushed by a large wheel rolled on a track, and various devices by which canes were crushed or ground between stones. All of these were much less efficient at extracting juice from the cane than the three-roller vertical mill, so its appearance made for a significant increase in productivity. In addition to being faster and more efficient, the three-roller vertical mill had other advantages over the devices it replaced. For one thing, with the earlier devices it was necessary to chop the cane into small pieces before milling them, while cane stalks could be fed whole into the three-roller mill, which greatly reduced labor time. Moreover, the cane trash left over from the three-roller mill, once dried in the sun, made an adequate fuel for the sugar boilers, an important consideration on small islands such as Barbados, where wood seems to have always been in short supply.[32]

It is likely that three-roller vertical mills were used on the large-scale, integrated plantations as soon as they appeared but that smaller operators used the less efficient devices, which would be another reason that productivity improved with the rise of large estates. Of lesser importance was the development of the Jamaican train, which, despite its name, appears to have been invented in Barbados, a system of flues that allowed a single furnace to heat a number of kettles and thus reduced fuel costs.[33]

Planters also began to further refine their sugars rather than shipping them in relatively raw form to England for refining there. Early in the growth of the sugar industry most of the sugar exported from Barbados was muscavado, whose name derived from the Portuguese word *mascavado,* meaning "unfinished" or "incomplete," and which Schwartz defines as "brown sugar considered of second quality after white sugar."[34] McCusker provides a fuller definition and along the way gives us a succinct description of the process of making sugar, which merits quoting in full: "The production of table sugar from sugar-cane juice involves a series of stages during which progressively greater quantities of liquid are purged from the crystallizing sugar. The initial boiling of the cane juice resulted in both a raw brown sugar called muscavado and a liquid by-product called molasses."[35]

Those planters who were satisfied to ship raw muscavado put the boiled juice into clay pots and let them drain for about a month. After the sugar was taken from the pots it was spread out in the sun for a day.

This process, known as sun drying, hardened the grain and kept the sugar from dissolving during shipment. As the century progressed, however, Barbadians exported an increasing proportion of their sugar in a semirefined form through a process known as claying, in which muscavado set in a sugar mold was smeared with clay moistened with water. "The water percolated through the mold, and as it drained carried off remaining impurities and molasses." This percolation process was repeated as many as six times, depending on the quality of the sugar. "The sugar at the top of the form became white, that in the middle somewhat darker, and that on the bottom very dark."[36] One commentator on claying in Brazil was moved to observe that it was a wonder that dirty mud turned sugar white, just as the mud of one's sins, when mixed with tears of repentance, cleansed one's soul of sin.[37] After several weeks, when the sugar had crystallized, it was removed from the molds. The white sugar at the top of the loaf was then separated from the brown sugar at the middle and bottom.[38] Barbadians usually classified their processed sugars into six categories, ranging from coarse clayed, which differed little from muscavado, to best whites, which competed successfully with European refined sugars.

The export records prepared by Barbadian naval officers do not reflect this increase in the export of clayed sugar, as they apparently classified clayed sugar with muscavado. Nevertheless, it is clear that as the seventeenth century progressed an increasing proportion of the sugar sent from Barbados to England was of the clayed variety.[39] Since clayed sugar paid a much higher tariff than muscavado (raw sugar paid 1s. 5d. sterling per hundredweight, whereas clayed paid 4s. 9d. sterling), one suspects that planters were in some way responsible for the failure of the naval officers to record the increase in clayed sugar among exports.[40] Not only did clayed sugar bring a higher price in England but shipping it in this form reduced bulk and thus saved shipping costs as well. Finally, claying sugar yielded more molasses, which could be distilled into rum. Planters in Barbados also began to export their molasses by-products and to use them to make rum, which they also exported. In the mid-1660s molasses and rum accounted for less than 7 percent of Barbadian exports by value, but by the end of the century they accounted for almost 30 percent.[41]

The seventeenth century also witnessed some important savings in shipping and marketing costs. Measuring freight costs in the sugar trade is complex. During the seventeenth century trade conventions dictated that sugar, like tobacco, paid freight on a customary ton of four hogsheads, without regard to the actual weight of those hogsheads. Sugar planters followed tobacco growers in pursuing the opportunity buried in those conventions by increasing the size and weight of the casks in which they shipped their sugar in order to lower freight charges. Since sugar was such a dense product, the increase in the size of casks forced merchants to abandon the trade convention by 1697 on most of the islands, somewhat later on Jamaica. Armed with this information, a series of hogshead weights, and a series of nominal freight charges, I concluded that freight costs in the Barbadian sugar trade were stable over the second half of the seventeenth century. James Shepherd and Gary Walton, using different assumptions about hogshead weights and the size of a ton, found a substantial decline in freight costs over the years 1678–1717.[42]

Constant freight costs do not mean that there were no improvements in shipping efficiency during the period. Seamen's wages rose slightly, while shipbuilding and victualing costs rose sharply. Apparently in the sugar trade the gains in efficiency were just adequate to hold off rising costs and keep freight charges from rising in the late seventeenth century.[43] While there is some uncertainty about the behavior of freight charges, the movement of insurance rates, another major component of shipping costs, is clear: wartime insurance rates on sugar shipped from the West Indies to London fell from 17 percent in 1689–97 to 10 percent in 1739–48, reflecting the development of the convoy system, improved information flows, and a gradual understanding of Caribbean weather patterns. Peacetime rates registered a similar decline.[44] Insurance charges continued to fall over the eighteenth century; insurance on shipments from America to England fell from 10 percent about 1700 to 4.5 percent by the 1780s.[45]

There is reason to think that the fees commission consignment merchants charged for handling planters' affairs also fell in the late seventeenth century. While I have yet to uncover evidence of the movement of those fees in the sugar trade, in the tobacco trade the commission consignment merchants charged for selling tobacco fell from about 10 percent to about 2.5 percent over the seventeenth century. I would be surprised if commissions did not also decline in the equally competitive sugar business.[46] While the fees sugar merchants charged in the early to middle seventeenth century remain a mystery, by the end of the century those fees were about 2 percent, slightly below the rate charged by tobacco merchants. Indeed, the Royal African Company actually offered to waive commissions altogether in a desperate attempt to induce debtors to pay some of what they owed.[47]

Finally, interest rates fell in the late seventeenth century, from about 15 percent at midcentury to about 10 percent by century's end. Interest rates continued to fall over the eighteenth century; there are reports of interest rates as low as 5 percent in the islands on the eve of the American Revolution.[48] In so capital-intensive an enterprise as sugar this was a major saving. We can attribute the decline both to the successes of the Barbadian sugar industry, which made it at least seem a less risky investment, and to the general post-Restoration improvements in English capital markets, which lowered interest rates throughout the empire.[49]

As John McCusker and I noted some time ago, the evidence of substantial improvements in the productivity of the Barbadian sugar industry challenges the image of a backward, unenterprising, and conservative class of great planters unwilling to innovate, take risks, or try new methods. That image may accurately describe the great planters of the eighteenth century, but it certainly does not describe the behavior of the planters who created the sugar industry during the seventeenth century.[50]

We should not think of these seventeenth-century improvements in productivity as steady progress toward a more efficient system. It was more like movement up a slippery slope, for some of the changes that led to immediate gains in efficiency had unanticipated consequences that set the planters back. Two examples will illustrate the point. The conversion to windmills saved all sorts of costs related to livestock husbandry, but the elimination of animals also eliminated their manure, an important source of fertilizer in the planters' struggle to maintain soil fertility. So the conversion to wind probably also led to some decline in yields per acre.[51] Over the latter half of the seventeenth century sugar yields per acre fell from 1.35 tons per acre in 1649 to less than a ton per acre in 1690.[52] At least some of the decline in soil fertility can be attributed to the inability of planters to thoroughly manure their fields because of a shortage of animals following the change in how mills were powered. That planters were able to lower the price of their sugar in the face of such steep declines in the fertility of their soil is powerful testimony to their creativity in improving the overall productivity of their operations. The seriousness of the problem of soil exhaustion and the aggressive creativity with which planters attacked it is apparent in an effort to import some of the rich soils of Surinam to

Barbados, an experiment that had to be abandoned because of the damages that wood ants in the soil did to the ship.[53]

The drift toward sugar monoculture involved cutting down all the trees on the island, which forced planters to import wood to fuel their mills. Complaints about wood shortages appear as early as the 1650s.[54] For a time, Barbadians had to import wood for fuel, but they eventually discovered that milled cane trash, known as *burgasse,* would serve. Burgasse was a less efficient fuel than wood as it burned briefly and intensely at high temperatures instead of providing the less intense but longer and steadier heat, if slightly lower in temperature, that could be obtained from wood, but using cane trash was apparently more efficient than importing firewood. Destroying the forests also deprived the island's monkeys and raccoons of their habitat. The animals moved into the cane fields and did considerable damage to the crops until a bounty system created by the legislature led to their near-total destruction.[55]

Another of the unintended consequences of deforestation would have been welcomed by planters as a plus had they understood the connection. Cutting down the forests deprived runaway slaves of a place to hide and may have helped prevent the emergence of maroon communities on the island. Maroons seem not to have had much of a presence in colonial Barbados, probably because the island offered few places in which a maroon community could hide. In the 1640s, however, before the forests were destroyed, a visitor reported that hundreds of Africans were hiding in the woods.[56] This suggests that there was initially considerable potential for the development of maroon communities on the island. One hears less of runaways and little of maroons in Barbados after midcentury and the destruction of the forests. There is no evidence that planters saw the connection between deforestation and the absence of maroons, certainly none that they destroyed the forests to forestall the possibility of maroonage on a grand scale.[57] The only hint of maroonage that I have seen for eighteenth-century Barbados confirms its connection to the forest. In 1726 Thomas Wilkier told the bishop of London that it was still possible for Barbadian "Negroes to run away from their Masters into the woods for months together before they can be found out."[58]

Changes in the way slaves were fed made for another ambiguous development. Planters followed two broad strategies in providing food for their slaves. On the one hand, under what might be called the "allowance system," slaves were allowed rations out of plantation stores, stores either purchased from outside the plantation or produced by the slaves as part of their regular work requirements. On the other hand, under the slave-economy system slaves were allowed or required to feed themselves by "ceding them a portion of their time and access to gardens (sometimes called houseplots or yards) and provision grounds (sometimes called conucos, polinks, or Negro grounds). Such practices were not mutually exclusive, and they differed from place to place and they changed over time."[59] While the evidence is far from clear, my reading of it suggests that over time Barbadian planters shifted from an almost exclusive reliance on the allowance system, and on food purchased from outside the plantation, to a system in which slaves supplied a substantial portion of their own food. While this enabled planters to reduce cash outlays for imported food, it also required the diversion of some resources away from sugar and into food production. On the whole, however, planters probably came out ahead because it was a means of getting more work out of slaves, who saw the benefits of working harder to increase the quantity and variety of their food.[60]

Although the productivity gains were at times a mixed blessing, they did do their work. Retail sugar prices fell by about 50 percent on the London market during the latter half of the seventeenth century, while English consumption of sugar both widened, spreading from London and the major outports to the countryside, and deepened, going from a luxury reserved for the rich to become something the working poor regarded as a necessity. English imports of Barbadian sugar increased roughly fivefold from the 1750s to century's end.[61] The seventeenth century also witnessed a substantial increase in per capita consumption. According to estimates provided by Carole Shammas, annual consumption of sugar in England and Wales stood at just over 2 pounds per person in the 1660s; by the late 1680s it had reached just over 4 pounds per capita. If not yet an item of mass consumption, by century's end sugar had become a "constant presence in the lives of a significant number of English men and women."[62] British sugar consumption continued to rise over the eighteenth century, reaching 12 pounds per capita by the 1750s and 16.2 pounds per capita by the late 1660s.[63]

One can also trace the growth of sugar consumption in the expansion of England's refining industry. Evidence of the deepening of consumption is apparent in the increase in London's refineries, from five in 1615 to eight in 1650, thirty in 1670, and perhaps forty-five by 1700, while the widening of consumption is evident in the appearance of refineries in the major outports and many small industrial towns, as well as in Ireland and Scotland, by the end of the seventeenth century.[64] Clearly, the English were well on their way to developing the world's greatest sweet tooth as productivity gains in the colonial sugar industry made it possible to indulge themselves. Recently Shammas, echoing Eric Williams, reminded us of the central role played by tropical products in the creation of the great European commercial empires of the early modern era. Although her emphasis on growing European demand as the driving force in this process allows her to connect the rise of American plantations to some major new developments in European historiography, my sense is that she tells us only half the story. It is certainly central that Europeans wanted more plantation products and that they were willing to make sacrifices to get them, but it is equally important that productivity gains on American plantations lowered prices and thus brought tropical products within the budgets of growing numbers of potential consumers throughout the emerging Atlantic world.[65]

The evidence presented in this chapter has some implications for that hearty perennial concerning the character of the planter class. As Michael Mullin put the question, "Were planters capitalists or medieval seigneurs, that is, forward or backward looking?"[66] However hidebound and conservative they may have later become, the men who built the sugar industry in the seventeenth century were clearly willing to take risks and experiment when they thought it might improve their bottom line. Of course they had little choice. In the face of falling sugar prices planters had to either improve productivity or go under. In this context it is worth noting that the planters of seventeenth-century Brazil, often described as the most atavistic plantocracy in the Americas, who were subjected to the same pressures to reduce costs as their counterparts in the English Caribbean, exhibited the same risk-taking, experimental, and innovative approach to making sugar.[67] To be fair, we should note that Eugene Genovese, the leading advocate of the view that planters were backward looking, has protested that he did not call the planters of the Old South seigneurs. He did so label the planters of the English Caribbean, however, referring to them as "rentiers . . . who . . . gave little thought to the expansion of markets, to technological innovation, or to measures to overcome waste. In this respect they resembled planter classes of a decidedly seigneurial type."[68] I do not know where Genovese found such characters, but it certainly was not among the men who built the Barbadian sugar industry.

Another implication of the argument of this chapter is that the living standards of Barbadian planters did not decline with the seventeenth-century fall in sugar prices. While there is anecdotal evidence to support that proposition, I have as yet been unable to find any systematic quantitative evidence on the welfare of Barbadian planters over the seventeenth century. However, Nuala Zahedieh has assembled some data on the consumption of imported goods from London at the end of the century. These show that even when sugar prices were at their nadir Barbadians of European extraction lived well by the standards of colonial America.[69] John Oldmixon left a vivid description that supports the impression of prosperity conveyed by the data on the consumption of imported goods from London: "The masters merchants and Planters, live each like little Sovereigns in their Plantations; they have their Servants of the household, and those of the field; their Tables are spread every Day with Variety of nice dishes, and their Attendants are more numerous than many of the nobility in England; their Equipages are rich, their Liveries fine, their Coaches and Horses answerable; their Chairs, Chaises, and all the Conveniences for their traveling, magnificent, ... Their Dress, and that of their Ladies, is fashionable and courtly."[70]

Data on the performance of the Barbadian export sector, of which sugar and its by-products accounted for more than 90 percent, provide further evidence of sugar planters' success in increasing productivity in their industry. Over the latter half of the seventeenth century the value of exports from Barbados rose impressively, whether measured in absolute or per capita terms, despite the decline in sugar prices. In 1665–66 the annual value of Barbadian exports stood at £284.4 sterling. By 1698–1700 that figure had risen to £4,443.0 sterling. The increase in per capita exports was even more impressive, from £6.2 sterling in 1665–66 to £7.3 in 1699–1700. As David Eltis notes, these are extraordinary figures by the standards of the early modern world. By the 1660s Barbados had "already matched or exceeded average exports per person attained in the eighteenth- or nineteenth-century Caribbean." These figures also exceed by far those for any European country of the time and are probably much higher than those for any European colony in America before the American Revolution.[71]

One major consequence of the changes in the Barbadian sugar industry over the seventeenth century was a substantial increase in entry costs and the value of sugar plantations. In 1646, at the beginning of the sugar boom, a Barbadian reported that an investment of only £200 "might quickly gaine an estate by sugar, which thrives wonderfully."[72] The rise of the integrated plantation and the changes associated with it quickly brought an end to the era when a relatively modest investment would allow one to enter the sugar industry and set up as a sugar planter. Also in 1646, William Powrey, a Barbadian planter, explained to his uncle in England that for only £1,000 they could establish a sugar plantation that in only three years would generate an annual income of £2,000.[73] In 1690 Dalby Thomas placed the cost of establishing a sugar plantation at £5,625 sterling. In 1793 Bryan Edwards, the Jamaican planter-historian, estimated the cost of establishing a sugar plantation on that island at just under £30,000 sterling (see table A.10). And in 1732 Rev. Robert Robertson calculated that £11,700 sterling would be needed to establish the typical plantation on St. Kitts (see table A.6).

By the eve of the American Revolution, entry costs had risen even higher: the Jamaican planter-historian Edward Long included estimates of the cost of establishing three plantations of different sizes in his *History of Jamaica* (1774). The least expensive, which Long said would produce thirty to fifty hogsheads of sugar each year, cost £3,515 sterling; the most costly, capable of yielding three hundred hogsheads of sugar annually, was estimated to cost £28,039; and the middle-sized estate, capable of yielding one hundred hogsheads annually, was valued at £10,017 sterling by Long (see table A.7). The conclusion conveyed by these estimates that establishing a sugar plantation was an expensive proposition finds support in a document produced by the anonymous reviewer of *American Husbandry,* who claimed that it would take more than £24,000 Jamaican to start a plantation on that island in 1776 (see table A.1), and by the author of *American Husbandry* himself, who published several documents showing the high cost of building a sugar plantation in the early 1770s (see tables A.2, A.3, and A.4).

As Richard Sheridan has noted, in addition to the substantial expenditure needed to get started, a sugar planter needed a sizeable working capital to deal with recurring annual expenses and the cost of maintaining and replacing items on the plantation. The high mortality rate among slaves meant that maintaining the size of the workforce by purchasing new slaves was a major expense. The best estimates are that the West Indian slave population declined at a rate of about 5 percent per year during the eighteenth century, unless new slaves were bought to replace those who died. Planters did little to encourage reproductive increase, and most seem to have agreed with the Antiguan who told John Newton in 1751 "that it was cheaper to work slaves to the utmost, and by little fare and hard usage, to wear them out before they became useless, and unable to do service; and then to buy new ones, to fill up their places."[74] The Barbadian clergyman Morgan Godwyn, the only white resident of the West Indies in the seventeenth century with the humanity and courage to protest the way planters treated their slaves, seconded these opinions. Godwyn was outraged by the policy of deliberately overworking and underfeeding slaves so that they would die before they became superannuated and a loss to the plantation.[75]

Robert Robertson, the clergyman-planter from Nevis, provided a succinct summary of conventional wisdom regarding slave mortality in 1732: "The Loss in Slaves (not including those immediately from Guinea, of which about two fifths die in the Seasoning) may well, one year with another be reckoned at one in fifteen; in dry years when provisions of the country growth are scarce, I have known it one in seven on my plantations, and the same or worse in sickly seasons; and when the smallpox . . . happens to be imported, it is incredible what havock it makes among the Blacks." Given such high mortality, Robertson went on to explain, and the low birth rate because of hard usage and polygamy, combined with high rates of infant mortality, the loss of work of mothers, and the charges of raising children before they could be useful, the gain from reproduction "cannot be great," so planters did little to encourage births among their slaves.[76]

Such anecdotal evidence is confirmed by quantitative work on the Codrington estate, where 14 new slaves were required annually to maintain the workforce of 238 over the years 1712–48, indicating a mortality rate of about 6 percent.[77] In addition to replacement costs, slaves had to be clothed, provided with medical care, and fed, although the slave-economy system, discussed in chapter 5, shifted much of this responsibility to the slaves, thus keeping the planters' out-of-pocket expenditures for provisions at a minimum. Planters did not usually face expenditures for the construction and repair of slave housing. Slaves were expected to fend for themselves in this matter, building what shelter they could with whatever materials came to hand, which was often only Guinea grass and cane trash, although planters sometimes helped favored slaves, drivers or craftsmen, and might aid in rebuilding after an especially destructive storm. The result was that most slaves lived in crude wattle-and-daub huts with thatched roofs and dirt floors. Such houses required frequent repair, leaked when it rained, were drafty and cold in winter and hot in summer, and were especially vulnerable to fire.[78] In addition, the tools and equipment of the plantation needed frequent repair and replacement owing to hard usage, humidity, and frequent destructive hurricanes. Further, planters faced local taxes and wages for artisans and overseers, at least until they learned that slaves could perform much of the skilled and supervisory work of the plantation. As David Galenson has shown, by the late seventeenth century planters had learned that it was cheaper to train Africans and Afro-Barbadians to perform the skilled and supervisory tasks of the plantation than to continue to import indentured servants, who had controlled such positions earlier in the century.[79] Such expenses mounted; all told, a planter might need a working capital in the neighborhood of 10 percent of the total value of his plantation to keep the operation going.[80]

The documents reproduced in the appendix show why sugar plantations had become so expensive. All the estimates assumed that a sugar plantation required a large number of slaves, ranging from the 30 Edward Long recommended for a small plantation on Jamaica in 1774 to the 300 he recommended for a large operation on that island. On average, the several estimates reproduced in the appendix recommended that 171 slaves work sugar plantations. Such substantial workforces meant that slaves were regularly the most expensive item in these estimates, usually amounting to roughly 30 percent of the total cost of establishing a plantation, indicating that it was the shift to the integrated plantation that played the main role in driving entry costs up. Data presented by Stuart Schwartz for Brazil show that plantations organized under the dispersed system could get by with much smaller workforces, perhaps twenty to thirty slaves on average, a sharp contrast to the great integrated plantations of the British Caribbean.[81] Fixed-capital items—the sugar works, a distillery, mills, and other buildings—made up 20–30 percent of the value of sugar estates, meaning that increased processing also contributed to rising entry costs. Land and growing canes contributed another 25 percent, while livestock, chiefly cattle, horses, and mules, also accounted for about 25 percent.

Sugar plantations were large and expensive in comparison with plantations producing other crops. In 1755 Charles Woodmason estimated that a low-country rice plantation would require thirty slaves and could be established for £2,000 sterling (table A.8), while in 1770 the author of *American Husbandry* described a Chesapeake tobacco plantation with twenty-two slaves that could be established for £2,210 Virginia currency (table

A.9). This is clearly a high estimate, as in 1690 Dalby Thomas thought eight to nine hands adequate for tobacco, so that a tobacco plantation could clearly be operated entirely by family labor, with no slaves at all.[82] It is not just that sugar plantations were large in comparison with plantations producing other crops; indeed, they ranked among the largest economic organizations of the early modern world. The size of sugar plantations, combined with the extreme alienation of the workers, the heat, and the intensity and noise of the mill, led Sidney Mintz to call sugar plantations "factories in the field," and to suggest that historians of the beginnings of industrialization ought to pay as much attention to Caribbean sugar plantations as to the artisanal workshops of early modern Europe.[83]

Unfortunately, it is difficult to estimate the profitability of Caribbean sugar plantation with much confidence.[84] Contemporary estimates are often biased: Colonial promoters tended to exaggerate profits in the hope of attracting investors. One Jamaican warned against the practice of tempting investors with reports of exaggerated possibilities of high profits, noting the need for care in the management of estates and arguing that sugar estates returned a very comfortable maintenance to the planter who behaved with "constant circumspection and economy, and agreeable to the unerring counsel, which his annual state of accounts will present to his view."[85] Planters, on the other hand, often understated returns, hoping that pleas of poverty might prove useful in gaining political advantage. Even those who aimed for an unbiased estimate of rates of profit often used accounting procedures that might now be described as "inventive" at best. Given these difficulties, it is probably unlikely that we will be able to improve on Michael Craton's summary of the evidence: "It seems that far greater profits were made than the planters acknowledged. Sugar plantations as a whole probably made about 7.5% on capital (when realistically computed) in 1790, at least 10 percent between 1750 and 1775, and perhaps as much as 20 percent in the halcyon days before 1700. At no time before 1800—save perhaps temporarily during wartime or locally after devastating hurricanes—did annual profits represent less than 8 percent of the market value of the average plantation's slaves."[86] Small wonder, Craton concludes, that Adam Smith wrote in 1776 that "the profits of a sugar plantation in any of our West Indian colonies are generally much greater than those of any other cultivation that in known either in Europe or America."[87] Edmund and William Burke echoed Smith's opinion, claiming that there was no other place in the world in which great estates were made in so short a time as in the West Indies.[88]

David Eltis is troubled by such high estimates of profitability. Why, he asks, if sugar plantations were so profitable, and so much more profitable than the alternatives, did British investors put any of their funds into coal mines, canals, railroads, textile factories, and the like? While the estimates of returns on sugar plantations seem reliable, it is less certain that investment opportunities in England did not offer similar rewards.[89]

The assumption that sugar plantations earned substantial returns to scale is deeply embedded in the historical literature. As it turns out, this is a much more complicated issue than most historians admit. Contemporary opinion was divided. On the one hand, the governor of St. Vincent's, writing in the 1780s, reported that "a small estate is at a greater Expense in proportion to its produce than a large one, because the buildings, the stock and White servants necessary for one are sufficient for the other with very little additional expense."[90] On the other hand, Edward Long, in reporting rates of return on plantations with thirty, one hundred, and three hundred slaves, assumed that each plantation would earn 10 percent, implicitly contending that there were no returns to scale. Although most historians seem persuaded that profits on sugar estates did increase with size, David Ryden, one of the few scholars to have developed systematic evidence on the issue, thinks otherwise. Based on a census for St. Andrew's Parish, Jamaica, in 1753, Ryden concludes that beyond a certain minimum, probably the point at which it became possible to operate an integrated plantation, there were probably no economies of scale within the sugar industry. Ryden's conclusion is supported by the behavior of planters, who regularly divided their fields into several strips and their workers into three or more gangs, indicating that they saw no advantages to size. While Ryden is persuasive, it is not certain that the issue is settled. He measures productivity in terms of sugar produced per slave, but it may be that bigger planters improved more of their sugar and made more rum, so that if productivity were measured as income produced per slave rather than as sugar output, the data might yet yield evidence of economies of scale.[91]

Evidence of such handsome returns in sugar raises the specter of Eric Williams, who argued in his classic *Capitalism and Slavery* that profits earned in the slave trade and in the colonies helped finance British industrialization.[92] More fully, Williams argued that the large profits earned by Britons engaged in all colonial enterprises, but especially in the slave trade and the plantation colonies, provided the capital that funded British industrial development. The trade in slaves, along with plantation agriculture, Williams maintained, was central to colonial commerce and to the industrialization of the English economy. The slave trade was, in the words of one British mercantilist, "the spring and parent whence the others flow." "The first principle and foundation of all the rest," echoed another, "the mainspring of the machine which sets every wheel in motion. The slave trade kept the wheels of metropolitan industry turning; it stimulated navigation and shipbuilding and employed seamen; it raised fishing villages into flourishing cities; it gave sustenance to new industries based on the processing of raw materials; it yielded large profits which were ploughed back into metropolitan industry, and finally it gave rise to an unprecedented commerce in the West Indies and made the Caribbean territories among the most valuable the world has ever known."[93]

Not so, answer critics of the Williams thesis, at least not as directly as Williams would have it. The critics have the better of the argument, at least if one insists on reading Williams narrowly, more narrowly than his text warrants. The argument that profits from the slave trade were a major source of capital accumulation in Britain simply fails when tested against the evidence. The slave trade, it turns out, was not unusually profitable, at least not for European traders, and the revenues it generated were not big enough to have a major impact on British capital formation. Some men grew rich in the slave trade and put their profits into factories, but such activity was at best of minor importance in financing the industrial revolution.[94]

While many economic historians think of this debate as settled, it is clear that there are still some open questions concerning the role of slavery and plantation agriculture in British industrialization. Recently, Joseph Inikori, taking a cue from Jacob Price, has suggested another way of approaching the issue. Focusing on England's industrial heartland in the west Midlands, South Lancashire, and the West Riding of Yorkshire, Inikori identifies technological innovation in textiles and metallurgy as the driving force in industrialization. He goes on to note that those regions and industries were heavily engaged in exports, especially to the colonies. He argues that colonial demand, rather than spontaneous invention or rising domestic demand, caused the innovations.[95] In addition, Jacob Price and Paul Clemens have noted that colonial trades were important in nurturing large firms, firms big enough to supply the capital that manufacturers needed to provide customers with short-term commercial credits while still paying their workers and suppliers on time.[96] These considerations led Price to suggest that those sectors of the British economy oriented toward the colonies "may well have been the hot-house of the British economy, where progressive institutional innovations were forced decades or generations ahead of the times they 'normally' appeared elsewhere in the economy."[97]

The issue of plantation profitability is of considerable importance, for it intersects with several of the major debates in West Indian historiography. The debate over the consequences of absenteeism has often turned on the issue of whether the estates of absentee planters were less carefully managed and therefore less profitable than those of resident planters,[98] while the debate over the benefits of the sugar islands to the empire is closely related to the question of plantation profits.[99] Finally, the issue of profits is central to the arguments over the decline thesis, and through those to the debate over abolition.[100]

The initial, or "new," industry phase of the Barbadian sugar industry came to an end near the conclusion of the seventeenth century, when the industry entered a new era. London prices for West Indian muscavado sugar rose sharply in the late 1680s and remained high until the end of the century, apparently because of war-induced shortages. Since planters faced high freight and insurance costs and various difficulties getting their crops to market, they did not benefit much from these higher prices.[101] Prices fell slowly following the Peace of Utrecht, reaching their 1680 level by the early 1730s. Prices then rose rapidly, doubling by 1760 and then doubling again by the beginning of the American Revolution.

There is some disagreement concerning the performance of the Barbadian sugar industry in the eighteenth century. The usual argument is that these price increases did little for the planters of Barbados, for Barbadian sugar exports peaked at about thirteen thousand tons in 1698 and then stagnated for about thirty years before beginning a decline that lasted into the 1770s. The slack was taken up elsewhere, as first the Leewards and later Jamaica replaced Barbados as the leading sugar producer in the English Caribbean.

The problems with the Barbadian sugar industry seem clear in its declining share of West Indian output: in 1700–1704 Barbados produced 43 percent of the West Indian sugar shipped to England, a share that had fallen to 15 percent by the 1730s and to only 8 percent by the early 1770s.[102] This decline is usually attributed to soil exhaustion and a failure to innovate. The Barbadian sugar industry experienced a renaissance in the late eighteenth century as a result of improved cultivation techniques, the development of new cane varieties, and better processing technologies.[103]

John McCusker contends that this story of stagnation and decline is a myth, a myth fostered by changing hogshead sizes and increased processing, which create the illusion of an industry in trouble while production and income continued to rise, a myth encouraged by planters, who hoped to use tales of their difficulties to strengthen their case for various concessions from the metropolitan government.[104] The ploy was effective, and in 1739 Parliament relaxed the Navigation Acts to permit the direct shipment of sugar to southern Europe. In Barbados, as Edward Littleton explained, "we can get little by making sugar . . . except we improve it: that is purge it, and give it a colour. Others can live by making plaine sugar; we must live by the improved."[105] By the eve of the American Revolution the proportion of sugar that the planters of Barbados clayed approached 75 percent. Since such "improvement led to a substantial decrease in volume and a gain in value, the improving behavior of the planters persuaded those historians who focused exclusively on the volume of exports that the industry was in trouble."[106] But as McCusker notes, if we pay attention to the changing product mix, it becomes clear that the sugar industry in Barbados was fairly prosperous during most of the eighteenth century. "Improving" their sugar provided Barbadians with several benefits. First, and most important, improved sugars brought much higher prices in metropolitan markets; second, improving reduced the volume of the crop, thus saving freight charges; and third, improvement yielded more molasses, which could be distilled into rum and then sold at a profit throughout the Atlantic world. Finally, improvement, by reducing the volume of sugar exported created the illusion of an industry in trouble, when in fact the total value of the product of the Barbadian sugar industry rose impressively over the eighteenth century.[107]

5

Origins of the Barbadian Plantation Complex

THIS CHAPTER EXPLORES the histories of four institutions that would prove central to the organization of life and labor in the late colonial Caribbean: the integrated plantation, which brought together the production and processing of sugarcane in the hands of a single owner; the gang system of labor organization, in which slaves worked in closely supervised and tightly disciplined groups and were subjected to a regimentation designed to make them work as hard as possible; the slave-economy system, in which slaves were allocated time and land to grow much of their own food and were allowed to market whatever surpluses they might produce; and the commission system, whereby planters became entrepreneurs and sold their sugars in England on their own account and at their own risk through commission agents rather than on the island. All four systems, which together formed the Caribbean sugar complex from the early eighteenth century until abolition changed everything, developed in Barbados in the aftermath of the sugar boom. In much of the literature both the integrated plantation and the gang system are treated as if they had no history but simply emerged fully developed as soon as commercial sugar cultivation on a large scale appeared in Barbados.[1] Alternatively, some historians contend that the key components of the Barbadian plantation complex did have histories but that they developed well before the Barbadian sugar boom, in the Mediterranean and on the Atlantic islands, and were simply transferred to the island when planters there began to make sugar.[2] As we shall see, both the integrated plantation and the gang system did have a history, which must be attended to in order to understand the dynamics of the sugar boom. While I would agree that one can find some antecedents of the Barbadian plantation complex in the Mediterranean and on the Atlantic islands, the key institutions, the integrated plantation and the gang system, appeared first in Barbados as planters struggled to improve productivity in the face of falling prices.[3]

Before the Barbadian sugar boom of the seventeenth century, sugar production had always been organized according to what I have called the dispersed system, in which small farmers grew sugar for a big man's mill. Events in Barbados were to change that, with profound consequences for the subsequent history of the sugar industry, for Barbadians discovered that there were substantial efficiencies to be had by concentrating growing and milling in one owner's estate through what might be called the integrated system of production. How that change came about is a story worth exploring in some detail.[4]

It is useful to begin with the observation that the integrated plantation was not universal in Barbados throughout its history as a sugar producer. In the mid-seventeenth century, when sugar was taking root on the island, some Barbadian sugar estates were organized in the traditional dispersed fashion. Tenant farming was rare in Barbados in the early seventeenth century but clearly became more common after about 1650.[5] As long as land was cheap and readily available, especially for those willing to move away from the densely settled west coast into the interior or toward the northern and eastern regions of the island, few were willing to sign on as tenants. But as land prices jumped with the sugar boom, and as rich men began to assemble large holdings, recently freed servants who earlier might have acquired a small tract of their own found themselves squeezed out. Some became tenants to big planters and grew cane for their landlord's mill.[6]

It would be an error to assume an equivalency between tenant farming and the dispersed system. Tenants could grow crops other than sugar, such as cotton, tobacco, indigo, or provisions. Small landowners who could not afford a mill of their own could bring their sugar to a big man's mill and have it processed for a share of the crop. Just how many cane farmers there were and what proportion of the sugar crop they raised is impossible to say.

The history of Mt. Clapham plantation provides a window into the changing organization of the Barbadian sugar industry.[7] Thomas Noell acquired Mt. Clapham plantation, a 510-acre tract in St. Michael's and Christ Church parishes in 1650. Although we should not assume that all tenants grew cane, it seems likely that those at Mt. Clapham did so. Their rents seem too high to have been covered by the minor crops, and we do know that the landlord owned a sugar works.

Thomas Noell was a London merchant who, along with his brothers, Martin, Stephen, and James—the four were known locally as the "four brethren"—was among the leading investors in the Barbadian sugar boom.[8] In 1654 Mt. Clapham had a workforce of fifteen servants and twenty-nine slaves. At the optimum ratio of one worker for every two acres, this was barely enough for a small, 100-acre plantation, let alone one of Mt. Clapham's size.[9] Noell addressed the labor shortage by recruiting tenants. By June 1654 he had leased out 179 acres to twenty-four tenants for an annual rent of £362 Barbados currency. Ranging in size from 3.5 to 18 acres, often operated by two or three men in partnership, these leases ran from six to nine years at annual rents of £1.5 to £3 Barbados currency per acre.[10]

Mt. Clapham was not the only Barbadian sugar plantation with insufficient bound labor to operate as an integrated plantation. Indeed, Richard Dunn reports acreage and the number of servants and slaves for four Barbadian plantations ranging in size between 75 and 360 acres between 1640 and 1667. Only two of the four had enough servants and slaves to operate at the optimum level of 2 acres per worker as integrated plantations.[11] I have supplemented Dunn's list with about a dozen additional plantations reported elsewhere,[12] all of which were also understaffed. It appears that most midcentury Barbadian plantations were understaffed. Given the high and rising price of land, few planters could afford to leave much of their estate fallow. The temptation to follow Thomas Noell's lead and lease out some of the extra acreage must have been great. Keeping the entire plantation in cultivation was not the only goal of planters that led them to seek out tenants. They were also concerned to make sure that they had enough cane to keep their sugar works operating at full capacity.[13]

Neither labor shortages nor tenancy as a solution were unique to Barbados in the early stages of the sugar boom. There is evidence of similar developments on other islands during the conversion to sugar monoculture. Thus, when Christopher Jeafferson's effort to rebuild his St. Kitts estate in the aftermath of a devastating hurricane in 1681 stretched his labor force, he turned to share agreements with tenants in order to acquire sufficient cane for his mill and to keep his land fully cultivated.[14]

The rise of tenancy suggests a considerable contraction of opportunities for ex-servants in the early stages of the sugar boom, but renting offered better prospects than what came next, when many ex-servants found their prospects on the island so slim that they decided to leave in search of better chances elsewhere.[15] The issue of opportunity raises the question whether tenancy within the context of the dispersed plantation system served as an upward step on the agricultural ladder. For the Mt. Clapham tenants at least the evidence is that it did not, as none of them appeared as a landowner in the deeds registered in the island's court. While tenancy does not seem to have served as a springboard to acquiring land of one's own, growing cane on rented land was not without its rewards. The Mt. Clapham tenants, for example, were often able to marry and raise families and to participate in the public life of the island as members of juries, appraisers of estates, and witnesses to various transactions. Many were also able to accumulate modest personal estates.[16]

Integrated plantations were relatively rare in the early stages of the sugar boom. The first seems to have been operated by James Drax, whose two hundred slaves "working with sugar" were described as "quite a sight" by a French visitor in 1654.[17] By the 1670s, when Mt. Clapham was reorganized as a centralized plantation,[18] integrated plantations had become common, as more and more planters had acquired sufficient workers to pursue their advantages, which apparently lay in control over the supply of cane to the sugar works, as well as in the possibility of preventing small cane farmers from playing one mill owner off against another in search of a better deal. By 1680, as Dunn's analysis of the census of that year indicates, the integrated plantation had become a dominant institution in the island's sugar industry. According to the census of 1680, just over two hundred planters owned more than sixty slaves each, while another two hundred owned between twenty and sixty slaves. I suspect that the entire first group and at least some of the second were operating integrated plantations. In the 1680s the integrated plantation had become so common that "a plantation of about 200 acres, equipped with two or three sugar mills and a hundred slaves," doubtless operated as an integrated unit, "was considered the optimum size for efficient production."[19]

The dispersed system did not disappear with the rise of the integrated plantation; hundreds of small farmers remained on the island. The 1680 census reports just over one thousand small planters, those with more than ten acres of land and fewer than twenty slaves; and about twelve hundred "freemen" with less than ten acres of land.[20] Initially I assumed that those small operators were farmers who raised the minor staples or grew provisions, but David Eltis has recently shown that many of them exported small amounts of sugar and its by-products.[21] Since such plantations were probably too small to support their own mill, it is likely that some of these men took their cane to a big man's sugar works for processing, perhaps in exchange for a share of their crop.

In this context it is worth noting that some of the early developers of Jamaica also flirted briefly with the dispersed method of organizing sugar production. In the early 1670s Cary Helyar, in the process of organizing what would become Bybrook plantation, tried to persuade his brother William to provide the capital necessary to build a sugar mill by arguing that the mill would quickly pay for itself if they ground their neighbors' cane for a half-share of his crop.[22] While the integrated plantation was apparently more efficient, there were advantages to the dispersed system, which distributed costs and risks broadly, while greatly reducing entry costs. The case of Mt. Clapham suggests that we should focus on labor supply and demography to understand the changing organization of sugar production in Barbados.

If my reading of the admittedly limited evidence is correct, Barbadians flirted with the dispersed system of organizing their plantations in the early stages of the sugar boom, and it was not until the 1650s that the integrated plantation made its appearance and not until 1680 that it became clear that the integrated plantation would dominate the island. The size of the island's slave population suggests why this was the case (see table 5). Barbados has roughly 166 square miles, or 106,000 acres. Based on the conventional ratio of two acres per worker, island planters owned enough slaves to cultivate only a small portion of the island in 1640, but by 1680 the slave population had increased to a point where there were enough slaves to work most of the island in sugar. While planters did not have enough slaves to make much of a dent in the island's available land until the 1680s, potential tenants were available in abundance in the persons of recently freed indentured servants, who, once "out of their time," that is, once they had completed their term, found it increasingly difficult to acquire land as the sugar boom drove land prices up. Consequently, the island was well supplied with young men willing to sign on as tenant farmers raising cane for someone else's mill. By 1680 the number of slaves was adequate to cultivate most of the island, and the supply of willing tenants had started to dry up with the decline in indentured servitude. Faced with these new conditions, more and more planters decided to pursue the advantages offered by the integrated plantation.

One reason for the persistence of the dispersed system is that it perhaps took some time for planters to work out and implement what would eventually become the integrated plantation's hallmark and the major source of its productivity advantage over the dispersed system: gang labor, with its lockstep discipline and its liberal use of the whip to force slaves to work as hard as possible. While gangs were ubiquitous on integrated plantations in the late eighteenth century, there is little evidence that work was so organized in the seventeenth century. Mathew Mulcahy reports that the scattered probate inventories of the late seventeenth century in the Barbados National Archives show no evidence of gangs.[23]

The first clear evidence I have seen of gangs on sugar plantations dates from the 1740s on the Newton estates in Barbados,[24] although there is a reference to drivers, which may imply gangs, in an undated document at the Bodleian Library that David Eltis thinks is from the early 1690s.[25] In addition, Jerome Handler and Frederick Lange cite a passage from Richard Ligon as evidence that gangs appeared at the start of the sugar boom.[26] Ligon does discuss a workforce organized into several gangs ranging in size from ten to twenty workers; each gang was under the direction of a subordinate overseer and assigned a job according to the abilities of its members.[27] But Ligon does not discuss the matter of discipline, and it is not clear to me that the gangs Ligon discusses were subjected to the whip-driven, lockstep discipline characteristic of the fully developed gang system. Rather, I think Ligon's gangs were a way of seeing that each member of a large workforce had a job and that each job on a large plantation producing a complex crop had workers assigned to it. In short, I am inclined to read Ligon as describing a step along the way to a fully developed gang system. Even if one finds my reading of Ligon overly cautious, it is apparent that gang labor was not a regular feature of Barbadian plantations until sometime after 1740. As late as 1765 Samuel Martin, in his well-known "Essay upon Plantership," said nothing about the gang system in Antigua, although as Michael Craton, one of the few historians to probe the history of the gang system notes, it was by then well established in the more well developed colonies and on its way to becoming "rigorously standardized in all plantation colonies" as hard-pressed planters sought to increase productivity.[28] It is worth noting that the first pictorial representations of slave gangs that I am aware of date from the 1820s.[29]

As David Eltis has pointed out, it is of some interest to understand why gang labor first appeared in an English colony rather than in a colony of some other European nation. Eltis offers a cultural explanation: that the English were more willing to mistreat people of radically differing ethnicities than were other Europeans. I do not find this argument persuasive.[30] While England does seem to have been one of the most culturally integrated European nations of the early modern era, it was hardly a monolith; rather, it was marked by major variations in region, class, gender, and religious persuasion, variations so sharp that to speak of an English attitude toward anything, and certainly anything as complex as ethnicity or race, is at best severe overgeneralization, at worst a caricature.[31] I prefer a more materialist approach, although I recognize that a good deal more evidence is required before one can speak with authority on this issue.

It is not a puzzle why the integrated plantation first emerged in Barbados. The island possessed the key resource, access to the vast resources of the London capital market, which gave Barbadian planters means to purchase sufficient slaves to run integrated plantations. Barbadian planters were exceptionally "well friended," to use Richard Ligon's apt phrase.[32] Sugar was a capital-intensive crop no matter how production was organized. The integrated plantation made it even more capital intensive by greatly increasing the capital required to produce sugar. As a Spanish historian of the West Indies noted, "A large and well-equipped mill costs much money."[33] Operating a mill as part of an integrated plantation increased those costs substantially.

It is important to note that in addition to being closely connected to one of the world's largest capital markets, Barbadians, in contrast to Brazilians, worked within a legal system that was favorable to creditors.[34] While it is likely that the legal system in the English islands was usually more favorable to creditors than that of the Iberian colonies, there was an important change during the seventeenth century. Early in the century, as Richard Sheridan has pointed out, merchants and their factors were relatively powerful within Barbadian politics. They used this power to construct a legal system that protected their interests. The sugar boom was accompanied by an increase in the power of planter-debtors relative to that of merchant-creditors. When the planters acquired power, they began to change the legal system to protect their interests and those of debtors in general. As early as the mid-1660s one encounters complaints by merchants regarding the near impossibility of collecting debts on the island.[35] As we saw in chapter 4, during the seventeenth century sugar planters faced steadily falling prices and intense pressures to increase productivity.

Within this context, it is easy to imagine the development of the gang system as owners of integrated plantations with large numbers of slaves under their control began experimenting with new methods of organizing labor in order to increase productivity. As a result of gains in productivity, Barbadians acquired the reputation as the most capable planters in European America.[36] Slaves, who did the work, had their own perspective on the celebrated productivity of the island's agriculture. During questioning in connection with one of the several late-seventeenth-century slave conspiracies one slave is said to have declared, "The Devel was in the English-man, that he makes every thing work, he makes the Negro work, the Horse work, the wood work, the Water work, and the Winde work."[37]

In some of the literature on the organization of slave labor there is a tendency to naturalize the question, to argue that the decision whether to organize slaves into gangs or to have them work on tasks was more or less determined by the crop they produced. Some crops were suited to gang labor, others to tasking. As I hope the discussion so far demonstrates, this is a great oversimplification. To understand the organization of slave labor, we must be careful to historicize the issue, to approach it as a function of choices made by individuals within certain contexts. Given the importance of gang labor as a source of both high productivity and so much misery, the origin of the gang system is too important to treat as some sort of "natural" outcome of the labor requirement of a particular crop.[38]

By the late eighteenth century two major ways of organizing labor existed in the plantation colonies of British America, ganging and tasking. In the gang system, generally in use in the sugar colonies and along the tobacco coast, slaves worked from sunup to sundown and were closely supervised. They often worked in a line and were expected to keep pace with a leader, and close by was a driver, armed with a whip, who quickly disciplined those who failed to keep up. In the task system, most closely associated with the South Carolina and Georgia low country, slaves worked on their own on a particular task. Once the task was finished their time was their own. "Tasking and ganging were not hermetically sealed systems," Phillip Morgan cautions. "Rather we should think of them as two extremes, represented by individual tasking at one pole and large scale regimented ganging at the other. In between these two ideal types were various hybrids, most notably a system of collective tasking on the one hand, and small unsupervised gangs or squads on the other."[39] Historians have shown some interest in the origins of tasking but none in those of gangs. This is perhaps because gangs, since they were used on the great cotton plantations of the antebellum era, seemed normative, while tasking was the anomaly, requiring explanation.[40]

The slave-economy system in Barbados can be approached by reflecting on the consequences of the rise of the integrated plantation and the drift toward sugar monoculture described in chapter 4. At least in the short run these developments increased productivity in the island's sugar industry. The integrated plantation concentrated control of the whole process in one owner's hands and thus improved coordination, while monoculture focused all resources on the production of the most profitable available crop. But integrated plantations and monoculture also involved increasing the size of a hostile and angry slave population and thus exposed the planters to considerable risks, evident in the frequent slave conspiracies uncovered in the late seventeenth century.[41] By 1660 enslaved Africans accounted for about half of the island's population; by 1670 they made up 64 percent, and by 1700, 76 percent.[42] Sugar monoculture also made planters more vulnerable to the fortunes of a single crop, and it left them dependent on external sources for food. Doubtless it was more profitable to concentrate on sugar and purchase food abroad, but this did produce some anxious moments when the food ships were late and planters were left to contemplate what might happen if their large and angry slave population was also forced to endure hunger.

Richard Ligon tried to persuade everyone that the planters had things under control.[43] But I doubt that by the end of the seventeenth century, after evidence was uncovered of slave plots in 1675, 1683, 1686, and 1682,[44] even the most complacent of planters found Ligon fully persuasive. True, all of the plots were uncovered before they could be put into operation, but they still provided planters with all the evidence they needed of Africans' courage, defiance, and willingness to risk everything for their cause. One example will suffice to make my point. In the aftermath of the Coromantee plot of 1675 a slave named Tony was hauled before a judge in Speights Town and asked to reveal his coconspirators. When he remained silent, a member of the crowd that had gathered to watch the proceedings shouted, "Tony Sirrah, we shall see you fry bravely by and by," and Tony spat back contemptuously, "If you Roast me today, you cannot Roast me tomorrow."[45] The planters responded to a growing sense of crisis by scrambling, without much success, to recruit more whites to the island. Among the strategies the legislature pursued were the so-called deficiency laws, later widely copied, which imposed fines on planters who failed to keep in their employ a quota of Europeans for every African on their estates. The Assembly also reduced the usual term of servitude on the island and forbade the use of Africans in certain skilled trades, in the hope of persuading some former servants to remain on the island.[46] The legislature also worked, more successfully it appears, to create a sense of solidarity among the shrinking proportion of whites in Barbados.[47]

I also suspect that the rise of the slave-economy system can be understood as an effort to deal with the growing sense of crisis. In the middle decades of the seventeenth century, as Barbados drifted slowly toward sugar monoculture, the island seemed to be conforming to the rule laid out by Sidney Mintz and Douglas Hall in their classic article, by which flat or gently sloping islands such as Barbados or Antigua purchased food from abroad as planters devoted all their land to sugar production, whereas the slave-economy system was confined to islands with mountainous districts unsuitable to sugar, such as Jamaica.[48] There are reports that in the early stages of the sugar boom Barbadians were importing much of their food. Thus, in 1647 a colonist reported, "Provisions for the belly . . . at present is very scarce, because men are so intent upon sugar that they had rather buy food at very deare rates than produce it by labour, soe infinite is the profit of sugar workes after once accomplished."[49] Despite the profits, planters decided that they could not remain so dependent on outside sources for food. Whether planters turned to the slave-economy system because they were afraid of the prospect of hungry slaves or because they had discovered that despite the absence of mountains, not all of the soils on the island were suitable for growing sugar[50] is not clear. The possibility that fear of hungry slaves was important to the emergence of the slave-economy system in Barbados finds support in evidence that the first reported slave conspiracy on the island, that of 1649, was in part a response to food shortages. Indeed, one historian has gone so far as to compare that conspiracy to a food riot.[51]

For whatever reason, as early as the late 1660s there is evidence from contemporary observers and in the form of legislative efforts to regulate the marketing activities of slave women that some version of the slave-economy system was well established on the island.[52] Clearly, slaves were producing substantial food crops. Although it is possible that these food surpluses were produced by slaves in their gardens and house plots, the amount of legislative attention the produce generated suggests that planters had allocated more substantial acreages to their slaves for the purpose of growing foodstuffs. According to John Oldmixon, slaves in

Barbados had an "Allowance of Ground" or a "Plat of Ground allowed them, besides their little Gardens to each Cottage."[53] Masters offered an alternative explanation for the substantial surpluses slaves brought to market, claiming they had been stolen from plantation stocks.[54] There is evidence that slaves did not think taking food from plantation stores counted as stealing. According to George Pinckard, an expression commonly heard among slaves made the point clearly: "Me no tief him; me take him from Massa."[55] A proverb common throughout the islands makes a similar point: "For a thief to steal from a thief makes God laugh."[56]

While I suspect that fear of hungry slaves is a key explanation for the appearance of the slave-economy system in Barbados, it is also possible that the institution has West African origins. Traditionally, the literature on the comparative history of slavery has stressed the differences between the institution of slavery in Africa and in the Americas.[57] However, recent work by Judith Carney suggests that there might be reasons to think about similarities between the two institutions. Many of the people sold into the Atlantic slave trade had been slaves in West Africa. Not surprisingly, when they found themselves enslaved in the Americas, they tried to make their new situation conform as much as possible to their African experience. Carney offers the task system as one specific example of the way in which African slavery shaped slavery in the Americas. It seems likely that the slave-economy system is another such example.[58] It is common in the literature to explain the choice between the allowance and slave-economy systems in terms of the interests of the planters. However, as the Jamaican planter-historian Bryan Edwards noted in the 1790s, the slave-economy system was a "happy coalition of interests between the master and the slave."[59] The system permitted masters to reduce expenditures on food, while slaves were able to increase the quantity and variety of their food and perhaps to earn a bit of cash by selling surpluses. Given the possible benefits, it is not surprising that one encounters occasional reports that slaves initiated the process of growing some or all of their food. Thus, in 1789 Walter Byam, a St. Vincent's planter, told a parliamentary committee that his slaves "of their own accord offered to me that if I would give them the Saturday afternoon out of crop time, they would require nothing but salt provisions from me."[60]

Many planters also saw the late seventeenth century as the time to realize their "one consuming ambition," to escape the West Indies and go to England. Absenteeism was relatively rare in 1680, but the irony in the accomplishments of the great sugar magnates is that in building their

integrated plantations and converting to sugar monoculture, they transformed Barbados in ways that made it "almost uninhabitable" by their
standards. Once they acquired sufficient wealth, the exodus began. By the
early eighteenth century "absenteeism had become a permanent way of
life for many of the Barbados gentry."[61] While some of the unintended
consequences of the search for productivity gains may have terrified the
planters, others seem to have made the island safer. The drift to sugar
monoculture also involved cutting down all the trees on the island to
make way for the cane fields and to fuel the mills. This had profound consequences for life on the island; for example, as we have seen, deforestation limited the development of maroonage in Barbados.[62]

In contrast to the origins of the gang and the slave-economy system,
which remain shrouded in mystery, the origins of the commission system seem relatively clear. Like all the major institutional developments in
the sugar industry during the seventeenth century, it was rooted in the
changes that occurred on the island in the wake of the sugar boom.[63] During the first half of the seventeenth century trade between England and
Barbados was organized in several different ways. In the years immediately following the initial settlement by the English, colonists were forced
to depend on the chance arrival of a ship to find a market for their produce
and an opportunity to purchase the things they needed. However, once it
became clear that the settlement would survive and that the colonists
could pay, English merchants organized a more regular and dependable
trade and began to outfit ships for the island. Eventually, as this more
regular trade grew in volume, some merchants established factors on the
island, agents who could assemble cargos, sell trade goods, and collect
debts. In such a system, as Kenneth Davies noted, the merchant "made the
running, and could and no doubt did, exploit the initiative which he
held."[64]

There were advantages to the planter in such a method of organizing
trade. The planter got his pay immediately, without having to wait until
his crop was sold in Europe, and few early seventeenth century planters
were big enough to be able to afford the wait. Nor did planters have to take
the risks involved with getting the crop to market; if the ship sank or was
captured, if the crop was damaged during shipping, or if prices in Europe
suddenly collapsed, it was the merchant's loss, not the planters. There were
also costs. Richard Ligon explained them clearly. In the early 1650s a
planter could expect 3d. per pound of muscavado sugar sold on the island,

but if "you run the Hazards of the Seas as all Marchants doe and bring it to England," it would sell for 12d. a pound.[65] As sugar prices fell over the seventeenth century and each penny of income seemed more important, the incentive to hazard the risks of sea and sell in England increased.

As the incentive grew, so too did the means, for with the rise of the integrated plantation more and more Barbadian planters could afford to wait for their pay and to shoulder the risks involved. The rise of big planters was important in another way as well. Before the sugar boom few Barbadian planters produced crops big enough to merit the attention of a London agent.

With the rise of the integrated plantation there appeared in Barbados a class of planters whose business was large enough to warrant the attention of a busy London agent. At the same time, the growth of absenteeism meant the appearance in England of a group of men familiar with the sugar business and with the planters' needs from whom men might be recruited who could serve as planters' agents, to receive their sugars and arrange for their sale. At any rate, the convergence of all these factors meant that by the early 1670s the commission system was coming to dominate trade between England and Barbados. Under the commission system the planter shipped his sugar to England, usually to London, on his own account and at his own risk. The commission merchant received the sugar, paid the various charges related to shipping, freight, insurance, and wharfage, as well as the customs duties, and arranged for the sale of the sugar. The net proceeds from the sale were then sent to the planter, although, depending on instructions, the commission merchant might pay some outstanding debts or purchase various goods and hold some back on the planter's account, against which the planter could draw bills of exchange. In the beginnings of absenteeism and the commission system one can see the first glimmerings of what would emerge as a major institution of the empire in the eighteenth century: the West Indian lobby.[66]

By 1680 the elements of the Caribbean plantation complex were beginning to come together in Barbados. The integrated plantation was dominating sugar production, and the slave-economy and commission systems were well established. The remaining element, the gang system, was not yet in place, but the owners of the great integrated plantations were working out its details as they struggled to keep up with the productivity gains demanded by the highly competitive sugar industry. Once they worked out the most efficient way of organizing their workforce, the Barbadian plantation complex, which would dominate the industry from the early eighteenth century until abolition, would be in place.

Given that Philip Curtin has published an influential book on what he calls "the plantation complex," the type of society that developed in tropical colonies that specialized in agricultural production for sale at a distance, it is useful to conclude this chapter with a brief discussion of his concept in comparison with the idea of the Barbados plantation complex developed in this chapter. According to Curtin, "the 'mature' or 'full-blown plantation complex'" that emerged in the colonies of the greater Caribbean in the eighteenth century "had a number of features that set them off from other societies, and especially from contemporaneous Europe, their political master."[67] First, most of the productive labor was forced, and most people were slaves. Second, the population was not self-sustaining. Neither the European managerial staff nor the African work-force produced an excess of births over deaths. "Both groups had to be sustained by a constant stream of new population just to maintain their numbers—still more if the system were to grow." Third, "the agricultural enterprise was organized in large-scale capitalist plantations." Typically, these plantations had fifty to several hundred workers—a far larger scale than that of European agriculture of the time. The owner of the land and the capital equipment managed all steps of production through his agents. On the plantation itself, he gave orders for the conduct of all "agricultural operations," again a different pattern from anything in European agricul-ture. Fourth, although capitalist, these plantations had features that might be labeled feudal. The planter not only controlled the workforce during the workday but also had some form of legal jurisdiction. Fifth, the plan-tations were organized to supply a distant market with a specialized prod-uct. This meant that these societies depended on long-distance trade and metropolitan merchants to carry off the product and bring in supplies. Sixth and finally, political control over the system, while fragmented, "lay on another continent and in another kind of society."[68] Curtin's purpose differs from mine. He is concerned to identify the common characteristics of the plantation colonies as they emerged in the tropics during the early modern era, while I am concerned to describe the institutional mix that emerged in Barbados in the aftermath of the sugar boom and subse-quently spread to other islands in the British Caribbean. His complex is fairly general, mine more specific. While Barbados in the late seventeenth century seems to share the characteristics of Curtin's mature plantation complex, it is possible to be more specific in describing the institutional mix developed there following the sugar boom. In sum, I would argue that the Barbados plantation complex can be understood as a subset of Curtin's mature plantation complex. I also suspect that many of the other islands in the region, once examined closely, will reveal their own unique institutional mix. We ought to treat Curtin's mature plantation complex as a general theme on which the several plantation colonies played their own variation.

6

The Expansion of Barbados

ALTHOUGH I HAVE ARGUED that it is an error to say that sugar revolutionized Barbados, the rise of plantation agriculture and African slavery did change the island in ways that made it increasingly unattractive to those of European descent who lived there. The best evidence of this is the exodus that began in the aftermath of the export boom, the rise of sugar to dominance, and the triumph of the integrated plantation. Alfred Chandler estimates that thirty thousand people left Barbados in the years 1650–80. John Scott gives a figure of twelve thousand for the years 1645–77.[1] Richard Dunn thinks Chandler's estimate is a great exaggeration and suggests that ten thousand is closer to the mark.[2] Unfortunately, the available demographic evidence is not sufficient to permit one to choose among these estimates with much confidence, but if pressed, I would guess that Dunn is closest. Although the range in these estimates is large, the conclusion they point to is robust, and it is clear that the migration was substantial and an important event in early American history. Since the migrants carried with them ideas and institutions developed on the island during the sugar boom, the importance of the migration spread well beyond Barbados. Indeed, as we shall see, it was a rare corner of the emerging British Empire that escaped its impact. The exodus from Barbados in the aftermath of the sugar boom made the island a major "cultural hearth for the colonies of British America," according to Jack P. Greene, who defined cultural hearths as "sites for the creation of powerful local cultures, including social institutions and ways of manipulating a particular kind of environment, that are capable of recreation and, with appropriate modification, transferable to other areas in the Anglo-American world."[3]

While we do not know the destinations of all who left, we do have data on destinations of 593 travelers who left the island in 1679. I call them travelers rather than emigrants or out-migrants because we do not know the purpose or permanency of the departures. Some of these travelers may have gone out on business or for visits and returned to the islands once their purpose was accomplished. What we know about their destinations is summarized in table 16. These data are available because Barbadian officials, alarmed at the size of the exodus and concerned that some of those leaving might be indentured servants and that others might be escaping debts or family responsibilities by leaving behind dependents who would later become a public charge, began to require that all who left the island obtain a license. If we can assume that the destinations of these 593 travelers provide a rough guide to the destinations of the entire migrant group, then roughly a quarter went elsewhere in the Caribbean, where the chances of creating a new Barbados would seem most promising. Fully 40 percent of the travelers went to the mainland colonies, many to the Carolinas and Virginia, where efforts to build a plantation society might have seemed promising, but more than half of those headed to the mainland were bound for New England or New York, where the prospects of recreating Barbadian institutions must have seemed poor. About a third of the travelers were bound for England, most probably to tend to business affairs and return to the island, but some perhaps decided that they had had enough of life as colonists.

Thanks to the work of Richard Dunn, Peter Wood, Eugene Sirmans, and others, the impact of Barbadians on South Carolina is well established

TABLE 16
Destinations of 593 travelers leaving Barbados in 1679

Caribbean		North America		England		Other	
Antigua	65	Boston	68	London	51	Holland	1
Nevis	14	Rhode Island	3	Bristol	39		
Leeward Islands	15	New England	25	Other	15		
Jamaica	35	New York	34				
Other	25	Virginia	62				
Carolina	38						
Other	3						
Total	154	Total	233	Total	205	Total	1

Sources: Dunn, *Sugar and Slaves*, 111; Bridenbaugh and Bridenbaugh, *No Peace beyond the Line*, 230.

and familiar to most early Americanists.[4] Barbadians, both white and black, thoroughly dominated the early migration to South Carolina. More than half of the just over thirteen hundred settlers of European descent who moved to South Carolina between 1670 and 1690 were from Barbados. While most were recently freed servants or members of small-planter families, there were among them a number of men from middling families and a few members of the Barbadian planter elite, as well as several major merchants who were able to develop South Carolina in the image of Barbados. So influential were these Barbadians, and so closely was the new settlement tied to the island, that South Carolina is usefully thought of as a colony's colony.[5] While South Carolina's ties to Barbados are firmly established in the literature, it is less well known that South Carolina represents only the tip of what turns out to be a substantial iceberg. Table 16 suggests that nearly as many Barbadians went to Virginia as went to South Carolina. While it would be rash to argue that Barbadians in Virginia had the same importance as they did in the lower South, they did have some impact. Virginia would have become a plantation colony and a slave society with or without migrants from Barbados, but Barbadians played an important part in developing the trade connections to the island that would play a crucial role in the diversification of the regional economy and the rise of Norfolk.[6] Since many of the slaves who reached Virginia during the seventeenth century came by way of Barbados, migrants from the island doubtless played a major role in bringing slavery to Virginia.[7]

We must look to the Caribbean to find colonies where the impact of Barbadian migrants equaled that in South Carolina. In the aftermath of the exodus Antigua, Nevis, the Leeward Islands, and Jamaica soon followed Barbados down the path toward sugar monoculture and quickly acquired fully developed replicas of the Barbadian plantation complex. So successful were they in this journey that by the end of the seventeenth century they were beginning to compete with Barbados for supremacy in sugar production.[8] Part of the reason for the speed of their rise was doubtless the Barbadian exodus. Not all the migrants were impoverished exservants looking for a start; some were men of means who brought resources, including slaves, with them. Even those without means carried with them the idea of the integrated plantation and, in the form of contacts with London merchants, access to the capital to make that idea a reality. Barbadians were of particular importance in the development of Jamaica. Indeed, according to Richard Sheridan, "The real planting of Jamaica is said to have commenced in 1664 with the arrival of Sir Thomas

Modyford and some 700 experienced planters from Barbados."[9] The London merchant community, which had played so important a part in financing the Barbadian sugar boom, played a similar role in Jamaica. Martin Noell again took the lead. Noell acquired twenty thousand acres on the island in the 1650s and planned in partnership with Thomas Povey to put £20,000 sterling into the development of a plantation there.[10]

Even if the number of migrants to a particular colony was small, they sometimes had an influence far beyond their numbers. Many of them were determined, ambitious men with well-defined aspirations and some colonial experience. For example, none of the 179 travelers headed for Maryland, suggesting that few Barbadians migrated there, but those few included two future governors of Maryland (Thomas Notley and Jesse Wharton) and three men who became members of the Maryland Assembly (Benjamin Rozer, Wenlock Christon and Edward Pye).[11] These men were among the first to build big plantations on the Barbadian scale in their new home. Notley, for example, owned twenty-nine slaves when he died in 1679, his estate both pointing the way toward the great plantations that the Chesapeake gentry would build in the eighteenth century and demonstrating that the Chesapeake system of husbandry, previ-

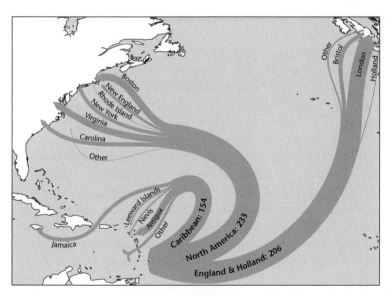

FIG. 9. Destinations of travelers leaving Barbados in 1679; based on Dunn, *Sugar and Slaves*, 111, and Bridenbaugh and Bridenbaugh, *No Peace beyond the Line*, 230. (Cartography Lab, University of Minnesota)

ously the domain of small planters, could be adapted to the large-scale, Barbadian-style plantation.[12] As David Galenson has pointed out, what might be called the Barbados demonstration effect, was important in persuading planters of the upper South that there were profits to be made in plantation agriculture based on slave labor.[13]

Rhode Island may represent another colony where Barbadians' influence far exceeded their numbers. Only three of the 1679 travelers indicated that they were headed for Rhode Island, although some of those destined for Boston or New England may have been headed there as well. By the early eighteenth century a group of a few dozen prominent families, now known as the Narragansett planters, whose fortunes were based on land and slaves organized into large units that echoed the great integrated plantations of Barbados, was firmly established on the western side of Narragansett Bay in Rhode Island. In 1748 about a third of the population of South Kingston, in the heart of the Narragansett district, was enslaved. Many of the slaves lived on plantations that would be considered large by mainland standards, if not by those of the islands.[14] While I have yet to establish that any of those families were descended from Barbadian émigrés, the connections between the Narragansett planters to the island were deep and intense. Initially, those families earned the bulk of their income from raising draught horses for the Barbados market, although they shifted to other exports—provisions, wood for fuel, building, and casks, and racing horses (the famous Narragansett pacers)—once Barbadians moved from animal-powered mills to mills powered by wind and water. They also acquired their slaves, at least those of African descent (many of the slaves in the region were Native Americans), at the great Bridgetown slave auctions.[15]

Not all of the émigrés' attempts to carry Barbadian institutions to other parts of the empire were successful. Perhaps their best-known failure was the settlement at Cape Fear, South Carolina, in which colonists from the island were heavily involved. Cape Fear was one of several mid-seventeenth-century enterprises in which the organizers hoped to establish a colony by tapping into the intercolonial migration stream or by recruiting settlers from established colonies. Cape Fear almost made it to the list of Barbadian success stories. By 1666, according to the best estimates, there were eight hundred colonists at the principal settlement, twenty to thirty miles upriver at Charles Town, and promoters, who had begun a subtle campaign to change the name of the colony's most prominent geographical feature to the less ominous Cape Faire, expected more arrivals shortly from both New England and Barbados. Unfortunately, this initial promise was soon undermined by a combination of bad luck, poor leadership, inadequate investment, intense resistance by local Native Americans, and, perhaps most important, the attractions of other Carolina sites at Albemarle and Port Royal and on the Ashley River. By 1667 the Cape Fear settlement had been abandoned, with most of the colonists returning to their colonies of origin, the rest to places unknown.[16] The Cape Fear enterprise may not have been a total loss, however, for there is reason to think that the promoters of the more successful settlement at Ashley River learned from mistakes made at Cape Fear.[17]

Barbadians also played a key role in the English colony at Surinam on the Spanish Main. Several hundred Barbadians migrated to the new colony. According to contemporary estimates, by the early 1660s Surinam was a settlement with some four thousand inhabitants living on five hundred plantations, forty to fifty of which had profitable sugar works. The major town, Toraica, had one hundred houses and a chapel.[18] The Barbadian émigrés might have made a success of the venture had not the English government pulled the rug out from under them by giving the colony to the Dutch in exchange for New Netherlands by the Treaty of Breda. By 1675 all but a handful of the English colonists at Surinam had left the Spanish mainland, most for Antigua and Jamaica.[19]

As table 16 suggests, a substantial number of Barbadians decided to follow their government's lead and exchange a Caribbean location for New York. The most prominent of them were the Morris brothers, Richard, a big Bridgetown merchant, and Lewis, once a colonel under Cromwell, later a rich sugar planter and member of the Barbados Council, who together purchased five hundred acres on the Harlem River then known as Bronk's Land, now called the Bronx.[20] Although the Barbadians did not manage to create a plantation gentry in New York, one wonders whether their vision had something to do with the appearance of great estates worked by slaves on Long Island and in the Hudson River valley. Finally, we can conclude this inventory of failures with New Barbados, New Jersey, which I regard as powerful testimony to the optimism of those who left the island in the aftermath of the sugar boom.[21]

The Barbados slave code of 1661 was the first comprehensive slave code created in British America and one of the most influential pieces of legislation passed by a colonial legislature. Four colonies—Antigua, Jamaica, South Carolina, and, indirectly, Georgia—adopted the entire code,[22] while bits and pieces of it appear in the laws of many other colonies.[23] So influential was the Barbadian slave code that Barry David Gaspar refers to the island as a "legal cultural hearth," borrowing D. W. Menig's definition of a cultural hearth as "an area wherein new basic cultural systems and configurations are developed and nurtured before spreading vigorously outward to alter the character of much larger areas."[24] As I hope this chapter demonstrates, Barbados was a cultural hearth for much more than the law.

Although since Barbados was the first English colony to write a comprehensive slave code, its code was especially influential, colonists did not confine their legal borrowing to Barbados but borrowed from other colonies as well. Indeed, I am convinced that not a single piece of legislation on the subject was unique to a particular colony.[25] Given such widespread borrowing, it is often impossible to establish an exact provenance for a specific law regulating the behavior of slaves or their owners. Despite this uncertainty, one often sees traces of the Barbadian codes. The Virginia slave code of 1705, for example, while not an exact copy of the Barbados code, does seem to borrow some of the provisions of the island legislation, as it requires that slaves have a written pass when away from their home plantation; calls for the severe punishment of those who aid fugitive slaves; and requires that masters whose slaves are executed for capital crimes be compensated by the public.[26] To cite another example, in the early 1660s, when the Maryland legislature, with the Barbadians Thomas Notley sitting in the speaker's chair and Jesse Wharton in the governor's seat, decided that it was time to address the colony's growing slave population, the laws it passed clearly reflected the influence of Barbados, even if Barbadian laws were revised slightly to address the Maryland legislature's perceptions of how the problem should be handled.[27]

This borrowing would seem to raise important questions for those historians who assume that legislation is especially revealing regarding attitudes toward race and slavery. Although it seems reasonable to assume that the initial Barbados code tells us a good deal about the attitudes of the island's emerging planter class, what are we to make of the same code when it reappears in Jamaica, passed by a legislature strong-armed by its governor, Thomas Modyford, who had come to Jamaica by way of Barbados?[28] And what do we do with the bits and pieces of the Barbadian code scattered throughout the colonies?

Clearly we must distinguish between laws that originate in a legislative assembly and those chosen, as it were, from a menu. The metaphor of legislators assembling a slave code by selecting from a menu may help account for some apparent anomalies in the laws regarding slavery and free blacks in the various colonies. For example, New Hampshire's legislature restricted the behavior of blacks in ways that are a puzzle at first glance, as the behavior prohibited could not have posed a serious problem, given the size of New Hampshire's black population.[29] One also sees echoes of the Barbadian slave code on Prince Edward Island, of all places.[30] One key feature of the Barbadian code that was universally followed in British America was the decision to classify slaves as "goods and Chattels," rather than provide them with special protection by classifying them as real estate attached to a particular plantation, in order to prevent creditors from dismantling plantations by stripping away their workforce in debt cases. This decision was not inevitable. Several colonies, including Barbados, considered classifying slaves as real property, but in the end the experiments were always abandoned, and the other colonies of British America followed the example of Barbados, although it took nearly fifty years to come to a decision. It is sometimes asserted that the question at issue in this debate was the protection of slaves against forced sales and removals. That is not true: the issue was the interests of debtors and creditors.[31] This decision had important consequences for the availability of credit, the supply of labor, and the organization of sugar production. Brazil and, indeed, most of Latin America did adopt the debtor-friendly strategy of classifying slaves as real estate, with the result that credit was harder to come by there, as lenders were not as assured of repayment.

These limitations on credit may explain why the integrated plantation, which required access to credit in order to acquire the necessary large labor force, was slower to develop in Latin America than in the creditor-friendly English colonies.[32] While the colonies of British America followed the creditor-friendly strategy developed in Barbados of classifying slaves as chattel, they also learned from the Barbadian example much about the ways in which a colony could protect debtors and put obstacles in the way of debt collection. Thus, one sees throughout British America echoes of strategies first developed on the island in the form of restrictions on interest rates, devaluations of currencies and paper money, and land-bank schemes.[33] The evidence suggests that mainlanders were good students and soon became masters in the business of harassing creditors, as the case of Micijah Perry III demonstrates. Perry, the greatest tobacco merchant of his age, was driven to the brink of bankruptcy and turned his assets over to his creditors in 1744, in large part because of frustrations over the collection of colonial debts. The merchants of course fought back, with Perry taking a leading role. In 1731 Perry joined with Richard Harris, a slave trader, and Humphrey Morice, a sugar merchant, in a petition to the king. They had great sums due them in the colonies, but "as the Laws now stand in some of the Colonies and Plantations in America, his Majesty's Subjects residing in Great Britain are left without any remedy for the recovery of their just debts, or have such remedy only as is very partiall and precarious." The Board of Trade responded in 1732 that while several of the colonial laws were unreasonable, many were of long standing, had not been questioned before, and should be allowed to stand for the present.[34]

Rebuffed by the Board of Trade, the merchants took their case to Parliament in the form of the Colonial Debts Act of 1732, an effort to tilt the playing field away from debtors and toward their creditors.[35] As Jacob Price explains, by the Colonial Debts Act of 1732 "British creditors could henceforth prove their claims in colonial courts by taking an oath before any chief magistrate in Great Britain; and the land, houses, chattels, and slaves of debtors in the American colonies became liable for the satisfaction of debts. . . . This appeared to mean that real estate and slaves in the colonies were liable for debts as if secured by bond or other specialty, even though they were not so secured."[36] The act raised a storm of protest from planters in Virginia and on the islands and provided a clear lesson of where power resided within the empire. While the legislation provided creditors with a valuable new tool, it did not end the struggle over debts between planters and merchants, which persisted until the revolution and beyond.[37]

If one is persuaded by Ira Berlin's notion of a "plantation revolution," the most important consequence of the Barbadian exodus was the spread of the integrated plantation beyond the island's limited territory, throughout the English Caribbean and eventually to the southern colonies of British mainland North America.[38] Even if one is skeptical about the idea of a plantation revolution, it is clear that plantations on the Barbadian scale eventually emerged as defining institutions in both the Chesapeake colonies and the lower South. Although the mainland planters would gradually put their own distinctive stamp on the great plantation, its roots in the Barbadian sugar boom of the mid-seventeenth century would remain clear. The Barbadian exodus also had an impact on the island. As figure 10 shows, the white population of Barbados, peaked at 30,000 in 1650, and then began a steady fall, reaching 15,000 in 1700. Given the sex ratio and mortality rates on the island, such a decline would have occurred with or without the exodus once the migrant stream to the island contracted, but the exodus clearly sped it up and made it steeper. While the white population was in decline, the African population grew rapidly as the great planters imported slaves by the thousands to build their integrated plantation. In 1660 Barbados had become the second English colony in America to have a black majority.[39] By 1700, 75 percent of the island's population was black and enslaved, making Barbados the most Africanized colony in European America.

Another Barbadian export during the exodus is arguably both the most important and the most difficult to pin down and describe with precision. Those colonists who scattered throughout British America during the exodus also carried some emerging ideas about race that would play a key role in the creation of the racial ideologies then being developed in the colonies. Barbadian racial ideology can be understood as a product of the demographic changes of the seventeenth century and of the sense of crisis those changes created among Barbadians of European decent. The planters knew that the rapid growth of a hostile and angry slave population exposed them to considerable risks. Richard Ligon tried to persuade everyone that the planters had things under control,[40] but I doubt that by the end of the century, evidence of planned uprisings by slaves in 1675, 1683, 1686, and 1682 having been uncovered, even the most complacent planters found Ligon fully persuasive.[41] True, all the plots were uncovered before they could be put into operation, but they still provided planters with ample evidence of Africans' courage, defiance, and

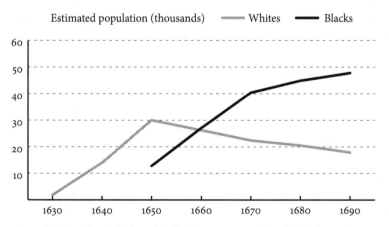

FIG. 10. Estimated population of Barbados, 1630–1690, from McCusker and Menard, *Economy of British America*, 153

willingness to risk everything for their cause, as the behavior of "Tony" following the Coromantee plot of the mid-1670s, cited in chapter 5, demonstrates.

The great planters responded to the growing sense of crisis by scrambling, without much success, to recruit more whites to the island and by working, apparently more successfully, to create a sense of solidarity among the shrinking proportion of whites in Barbados.[42] William, Lord Willoughby, identified the problem in a letter to Lord Clarendon written shortly after he arrived on the island in the early 1660s. After reporting on the decline of the white population, Willoughby noted, "I feare our negros will growe to hard for us," for a mere two thousand of the seven thousand men could be depended upon to fight if the enemy attacked. The remainder were small planters, freemen, and servants, who, "impoverished and disheartened, and without interest or hope of benefit here," would not expose themselves to danger.[43] Willoughby's message was clear: the great planters had to find some way of persuading the servants and small planters that they had reason to defend the island. The great planters decided to persuade these white men that there were advantages to being a white man in Barbados.[44]

One can follow this effort to create a white identity in the legislation passed at the time planters were uncovering evidence of slave conspiracies. The fear that haunted the great planters of Barbados was that their servants and slaves would band together, rise up, and turn the world they were creating during the sugar boom upside down. As Richard Ligon makes clear, this prospect was very much on the planters' minds as early as the late 1640s. In 1647, when Ligon arrived in Barbados, an islandwide servant rebellion had been revealed just in time. Eighteen of the alleged servant conspirators were executed. Ligon reported that the planters were building their houses "in the manner of Fortifications," equipped with bulwarks and bastions from which they could pour scalding water "on the attacking servants and slaves."[45] To forestall such a possibility, the great planters took steps to encourage servants to consider race rather than class when taking sides in the struggles under way on the island.

How the great planters attacked this problem is clear in the comprehensive codes governing the treatment of servants and slaves passed by the island legislature in 1661, one year after persons of African descent first became a majority of the population of Barbados. Lest anyone miss the point buried in the details of the laws governing servants and slaves, the legislature announced the differences between the two groups and the treatment they could expect on the island in the preambles to the respective laws. Africans were described as "an heathenish, brutish and an uncertaine, dangerous kind of people" who clearly could not be trusted with the rights of Englishmen.[46] Servants, by contrast, needed encouragement and what protection the law could provide, "whereas much of the interest and Substance of this Island consists in the Servants brought to, and disposed of in the same, and in their labour during the time they have to serve."[47]

The details of the two codes make clear the meaning of the different preambles. The new laws provided servants with several protections against cruel and arbitrary masters but left slaves to rely on their own resources to protect themselves. The law required masters to give slaves new clothing allotments each year but said nothing about food or working conditions and put few limits on the master's power to discipline slaves. The law established minimum allotments of food and clothing for servants, restricted how they could be disciplined, and permitted servants, but not slaves, to appeal to the courts if they were mistreated. Finally, servants and slaves accused of crimes were treated differently. Servants accused of felony were entitled to trial by jury, while slaves could be tried by the master for petty offences and by the master, two justices of the peace, and three freeholders for capital crimes. To make sure that the intended audience got the message, the legislature required that the acts be read in churches twice a year.[48]

Having distinguished between servants and slaves, the legislature turned in 1721 to the problem of the island's small free black population. In that year the Assembly denied those few free blacks that met the property qualification the right to vote and made suffrage the exclusive privilege of white men. The same law prohibited anyone of Negro ancestry from giving testimony in legal proceedings against whites: "No person whatsoever shall be admitted as a freeholder, or an evidence in any case whatsoever, whose extraction shall be proved to have been from a Negro, excepting only on the trial of Negroes and other slaves."[49] White solidarity was also promoted by rumors of what the several slave conspiracies intended. John Oldmixon provides a typical report: the Negroes planned to rise against their masters "and posess themselves of the island; all the Planters were to be killed, their Wives to be kept for the chief of the Conspirators, their children, and white Servants to be their Slaves."[50]

After differentiating servants from slaves, the Assembly turned to the business of providing privileges to free whites. In 1676 the Assembly excluded blacks from several skilled crafts in order to preserve those occupations for Christian artisans.[51] An act of 1682 denounced blacks, whose insolence was said to be driving poor whites off the island.[52] In the 1690s Governor Francis Russell, who understood the need to sacrifice class prerogatives in the interest of racial solidarity, proposed lowering the amount of property one had to own in order to vote from ten acres to two so that the big planters would treat the poor whites better in order to get their votes. Former servants, Russell explained, were "domineered over and used like dogs." Such treatment would drive away the commonality of white people. There were hundreds of such men on the island who had never tasted fresh meat or a dram of rum. If they could vote, candidates might offer them rum and fresh provisions in the hope of getting their votes. But the big planters in the Assembly insisted on keeping the ten-acre minimum so that "men of interest only may share in government."[53]

While the planters were unwilling to enlarge the franchise, they did what they could to keep Christianity the exclusive preserve of whites. In 1681 the Barbados Assembly explained to the governor that "we are ready to do anything for the encouragement of Christian servants . . . but as to making the Negroes Christians, their savage brutishness renders them wholly incapable. Many have endeavored it without success."[54] Having decided that Africans were incapable of becoming Christians, the Assembly went on to attack those who tried to convert them by levying severe fines on Quakers who brought their slaves to meeting. When the fines proved ineffective, the governor ordered the provost marshal to pull down all the seats and stalls in the Quaker meetinghouse in Bridgetown and nail the doors and windows shut.[55]

It was also in the 1660s that the great planters of Barbados took their first feeble steps to provide public education for the poor white children, but not the black children, of the island, thereby holding out the promise that the children of the white men of the island, however poor, would have the rudiments of literacy.[56] The island militia, in which all freemen aged sixteen to sixty were enrolled whether or not they owned property and whose major responsibility was the "regulation and policing of Negroes," was doubtless a key institution in building white identity both in Barbados and throughout the empire.[57]

Another privilege extended to whites in colonial Barbados was the right to beat on blacks with impunity. According to the 1661 slave code, whites who encountered blacks away from their home plantation without a pass were to "punish them by a moderate whipping." The slave who tried to defend herself from such moderation by offering "any Violence to any Christian" was to be severely whipped by the constable for the first such offence, while for the second such offence the slave was to be "severely whipped, his nose slit and be burned in the face."[58]

Attitudes toward work, sexuality, and gender were central to the process of creating an ideology of whiteness and building a white identity in Barbados. Exactly what happened, and when, remains obscure and only poorly documented, but some important developments are clear enough. Around the mid-seventeenth century it was not uncommon to see white women working side by side with Africans in the field. As the sugar boom developed and slaves came to dominate the workforce, white women gradually withdrew from field work. White men in colonial Barbados would be men whose female dependents were not degraded by working in the fields with blacks.

In the middle decades of the seventeenth century sexual relations between black men and white women did occur, although they could hardly be called common. By the end of the century, although Barbados, unlike most of the islands in the Caribbean, did not legislate against miscegenation, the liberal use of punishments such as castration and dismemberment against black men who had even consensual sex with white women effectively stopped that behavior and defined white women as the possession of white men. At the same time, the law permitted white men to rape black women with impunity.[59]

The great planters of Barbados did not immediately settle on "whiteness" as the means to assure that poor men on the island would support their rule. The legislation of the 1660s distinguished between Negroes and Christians, which may explain why the legislature became hysterical over Quaker efforts to convert Africans. Eventually the legislators came to understand that they were better off stressing physical rather than cultural differences between Africans and Barbadians of European ancestry. Oddly enough, the first reference I have seen to a Barbadian of European decent as white occurs in a tract published by George Fox in 1672.[60] That whiteness was a relatively new idea in the 1680s is suggested by Morgan Godwyn, who, writing in 1680, thought it necessary to tell his readers that in Barbados *white* was "the general name for Europeans."[61] By the 1680s the great planters had come to understand the utility of whiteness. An African could become Christian, but he could not become white. In the 1680s legislation began regularly to protect whites rather than Christians from the behavior of Negroes.[62] If John Oldmixon can be believed, there is evidence that the new ideology of whiteness was beginning to have the desired effect as early as the first decade of the eighteenth century. According to Oldmixon, "Every Freeholder, and white Servant, able to bear Arms is listed in the Militia of the Island, which consists now of about 1500 Foot, and about 1200 stout Horse; and these are as good or better than any regular Forces, for besides that the *Creoleons* are as brave Men as any in the World, they would certainly fight resolutely for so rich and so pleasant a Country."[63]

Although one might argue that the ideology of whiteness was created anew in the several plantation districts of British America, I find more persuasive the hypothesis that the ideology of whiteness, first built in Barbados, was gradually spread throughout the empire, often carried by Barbadian émigrés. The diffusion hypothesis finds some support in the appearance of aspects of the whiteness ideology in parts of the empire where blacks were too few to constitute a threat.[64] David Brion Davis, who makes a case for the diffusion hypothesis, tying together all of the colonies of European America, contends that the slave trade, which he describes as a "powerful agent of acculturation—one might almost say of Americanization," was the means by which ideologies were spread. This diffusion "tended to blur distinctions in custom and give a more uniform character to Negro slavery than would have been found among earlier forms of European serfdom."[65]

Disease, the most frightening Barbadian export to other colonies, seems to have moved on trade routes rather than with émigrés. By the late seventeenth century Barbados had become the hub of an emerging empirewide disease environment, in which it gathered various maladies, the most important being yellow fever and smallpox from Africa, and then dispersed them throughout the empire. Various other fevers my have reached the mainland colonies by way of Barbados, but their symptoms are not distinct enough to permit certainty. Yellow fever, popularly known in the mainland colonies as the "Barbados distemper" or the "plague of Barbados," was especially frightening because of its high mortality rate and the speed at which it moved through a population. Colonial port cities involved in the island trade were especially vulnerable. It is no accident that Charleston, probably the most deadly of the mainland cities, was also the port most heavily engaged in the island trade. Charleston suffered seven epidemics in the years 1699–75, while Philadelphia and New York experienced four each during the same period. Surprisingly, Boston, despite its deep engagement in island trade, escaped the disease. Whether it did so because the mosquitoes that carried the disease were less likely to survive the slightly longer voyage from Barbados to Boston or because of Boston's relatively strict quarantine policies is not clear.[66]

I will conclude this chapter with a brief mention of what were perhaps two of the more benign of the Barbadian exports. One was the commission system, in which planters became merchants and shipped their crops on their own account and at their own risk to a commission agent in England, who paid the various charges incurred in transport, freight, insurance, customs, and the like, sold the crop, and dispersed the proceeds of the sale according to the planter's instructions, all for a percentage of the proceeds of the sale. The other was the slave-economy system, by which slaves grew much of their own food. By the mid-eighteenth century the commission system, which originated in Barbados in the aftermath of the sugar boom, had become the dominant means or organizing trade in all the plantation colonies of British America except, surprisingly, in the South Carolina rice industry, where the characteristics of that crop and the strength of the Charleston merchant community led to different methods of organizing trade. While from the perspective of this chapter it would seem that the commission system was carried to other parts of the empire by Barbadians on the move, it is also possible that London merchants familiar with the system through the sugar trade were the agents who spread it throughout the empire.[67] By the mid-eighteenth century variations on the slave-economy system had appeared in all the plantation colonies of British America.[68]

I would be remiss if in this catalog of Barbadian influences on the history of the mainland colonies I did not at least mention the Salem witchcraft crisis. It is well known that several participants in that episode, most notably Samuel Paris and Tituba, had come from Barbados. While it would be an exaggeration to claim that Barbados was somehow responsible for the Salem outbreak, one wonders whether Tituba, who had been a slave on the island, had brought to Salem ideas about the supernatural that were developing in the island's emerging popular culture.[69]

Epilogue: Rethinking the
Sugar Revolution

THE CONCEPT OF A SUGAR REVOLUTION is perhaps the most important idea in Caribbean historiography.[1] Although the phrase *sugar revolution* did not appear in French, as "la revolution de la canne," until 1948 and in English until 1956,[2] the concept is much older. Most of the ideas were published by Richard Ligon in his *True and Exact History of Barbados* in 1657. Ligon pulled his analysis together under the category "the Sweet Negotiation of Sugar," which suggested the title of this book. John Scott picked up those elements of the concept not identified by Ligon in the 1650s. Although Scott did not put his ideas into print, the manuscript "The Description of Barbados," in the British Library, clearly suggests that he hoped to do so.[3] Despite Scott's failure to publish, his analysis of events in Barbados in the mid-seventeenth century proved very influential, as most modern historians of the island have consulted the manuscript and used some of its ideas in their work. Even Richard Dunn, who considers Scott a "notorious trickster,"[4] did not entirely escape his influence, as a close comparison of Dunn's and Scott's analyses of the rise of sugar cultivation in Barbados demonstrates.

Some time ago, K. G. Davies reviewed the notion of a sugar revolution and expressed some skepticism regarding its application to every place in the Caribbean except Barbados.[5] In the present book I have established that we ought to treat the notion of a sugar revolution in Barbados skeptically as well. Many of the ideas usually associated with the concept, such as the state of the Barbadian economy when sugar rose to prominence and the role of the Dutch in bringing sugar and slavery to the island, are quite simply wrong. Further, the core idea of the concept, the assertion that sugar transformed Barbados by introducing African slavery and large plantations to the island, misstates the relationship between sugar, slavery, and plantations. African slavery and big plantations were well on their way to Barbados in response to opportunities presented by the generalized export boom when sugar began to emerge as a major crop. Sugar did not bring slavery and plantation agriculture to Barbados; rather, it sped up and intensified a process already well under way. In the light of this evidence it would seem that the notion of a sugar revolution as traditionally understood has outlived its usefulness and ought to be abandoned.

While it is misleading to apply the notion of a sugar revolution to seventeenth-century Barbados, it is still possible that something revolutionary occurred on the island. If sugar did not revolutionize Barbados, perhaps one could contend that Barbados revolutionized the sugar industry by bringing to it the integrated plantation that would eventually emerge as the standard around which the industry was organized. Before the Barbadian sugar boom, sugar production had usually been organized around what might be called the dispersed system, in which several small producers raised sugarcane that was then processed at a big man's mill. The integrated system brought growing and processing together under the control of a single big planter who owned the workers who grew the cane as well as the mill that processed it.[6]

While the rise of the integrated plantation, which Philip Curtin calls one of the elements of the "mature plantation complex,"[7] certainly marked a major change in the industry, it might be an exaggeration to call its appearance in seventeenth-century Barbados a revolutionary event. For one thing, it took some time for the integrated method to rise to dominance, even in Barbados. It was not until the 1680s, nearly half a century after the start of the sugar boom, that the integrated plantation clearly dominated the island sugar industry. Perhaps one reason for the slowness of the integrated plantation's rise is that it took some time for planters to work out and implement what would eventually become one of the integrated plantation's hallmarks and the major source of its productivity advantage over the dispersed system, namely, gang labor, with its harsh discipline and frequent use of the whip to force slaves to work hard and fast. While gangs seem to have been ubiquitous on integrated plantations in the late eighteenth century, there is little evidence that work was organized to the same degree in the seventeenth century. It seems a stretch to call a change in the organization of production that took a century to complete a revolution. Instead of claiming that Barbados revolutionized the sugar industry, it would be more accurate to say that what happened on the island in the mid-seventeenth century put the industry on a path that would lead to a fairly thorough transformation. In sum, the sugar revolution ought to be classified with those events that Josephine Tey has labeled Tonypandy.[8]

Since a prominent historian of slavery in the Americas, Ira Berlin, has recently proposed a major expansion of the idea of the sugar revolution that includes its extension to the mainland under the guise of the "plantation revolution," it would be useful to conclude this brief discussion of the "sugar revolution" with some reflections on its conceptual limitations.[9] The idea of a socioeconomic revolution is an important part of the historian's set of analytic tools. While versions of the concept have often served the discipline effectively, primarily by highlighting an important set of changes and tying together several discrete events into a single process, the notion does have its conceptual downside, as should be apparent from the commentary on the sugar revolution provided in this book. For one thing, it tends to concentrate attention on the period of revolution, to the neglect of what came before. For another, it tends to encourage a before-and-after contrast that exaggerates differences, sometimes by distorting arrangements and structures in the immediate prerevolutionary era. In short, if the idea of a socioeconomic revolution is not used carefully, it can obscure as much as it illuminates.

One way of reading the evidence presented in this book might be to argue that we should replace the crop-specific notion of a sugar revolution with the more generalized idea of a plantation revolution in which the labor demands and opportunities associated with several crops transformed Barbados during the 1640s. This would have the advantage of being consistent with the evidence, but it would leave us with the general liabilities associated with the concept of socioeconomic revolutions. The Barbadian case examined here indicates the importance of two of these liabilities. First, the idea of a revolution focuses attention on the revolutionary era, to the neglect of what came before or after. Second, the notion of a revolution inclines one to exaggerate the contrasts between the pre- and postrevolutionary periods, often leading to a distorting exaggeration of differences. In the Barbadian case, for example, such exaggeration may explain the persistence of the belief that the Barbadian economy was depressed and a failure before the arrival of sugar, despite substantial evidence to the contrary. It might also explain the persistence of the myth that small planters disappeared from the island with the conversion to sugar, although it is clear that small planters were a prominent feature of

Barbados society well into the eighteenth century. Because of these limitations and liabilities, I suspect that Barbadian historiography would be better off abandoning the idea of a sugar revolution altogether rather than trying to revise it to accommodate the new evidence. The notion of a sugar boom, while not as dramatic as the idea of a sugar revolution, is consistent with the evidence and does not carry with it all the baggage that troubles the idea of a socioeconomic revolution.

Given all this, we ought to be skeptical of Berlin's effort to generalize the idea of a sugar revolution to other regions of British America under the rubric "plantation revolution." In the Chesapeake colonies, for example, while it is clear that the rise of plantation agriculture had a profound impact on all aspects of life, that impact is better described as gradual than revolutionary.[10] Even at the end of the colonial period a substantial portion of the tobacco exported from Virginia and Maryland was still grown on small family farms. One might think that Berlin has a stronger case in the low country. Certainly there the rise of the plantation economy, driven by the introduction of rice, was faster and more complete than in the upper South. However, South Carolina was not transformed by rice alone. Much like its parent colony, Barbados, the South Carolina low country was well on its way to becoming a plantation colony and a slave society before rice became its dominant export. Like sugar, rice quickened and intensified a process already under way.[11] If the notion of a sugar revolution is not abandoned, at the very least it ought to be classified with those other socioeconomic revolutions—the industrial revolution and the market revolution—that once were widely accepted by historians but have recently been reexamined and found by some to be more an obstacle than an aid to understanding the processes they were designed to illuminate.[12]

Appendix

*Estimates of the Cost of Establishing Plantations and
Farms in the Colonies of English America*

During the seventeenth and eighteenth centuries travelers, promoters of colonization, and commentators on the colonial scene often produced documents in which they presented lists of items needed to start a colonial farm or plantation and estimates of the cost of those items, along with estimates of the revenues one might expect from such an investment. I have discovered fourteen such estimates. Ten of them are estimates of the cost of establishing sugar plantations in the English Caribbean and are reproduced in this appendix. While the estimates of revenue, which I have not included in the transcriptions that follow, often strike me as somewhat fanciful celebrations of colonial agriculture, the estimates of costs seem more reliable. They summarize the opinions of informed observers of the costs of establishing colonial sugar plantations. As such, they provide useful guides to the overall cost of a sugar plantation, as well as to the way that cost was distributed. In addition to the estimates of the cost of establishing sugar plantations, which are printed below, I found six estimates of what it cost to establish rice and indigo plantations in the Carolina-Georgia low country.[1] I also found one each for Maryland-Virginia, Pennsylvania, New York, and Nova Scotia.[2] To provide context and facilitate comparison, I have included two estimates for mainland plantations, one for the low country (table A.8) and one for the Chesapeake colonies (table A.9).

One problem with these estimates is that it is not always clear which currency the author is using—sterling or the currency of the colony in question. Given the differences in the value of these currencies, this is an important issue, especially if one wishes to use these documents for comparative purposes. Fortunately for my purpose, it was possible to identify the currency with a fair degree of certainty for the ten estimates of the cost of establishing a sugar plantation. Given the detail these documents provide, it is surprising that they have not been more widely used by historians of early American agriculture and the colonial economy. Not that they have been entirely ignored, but they deserve more attention than they have so far received. I hope that reproducing those for the Caribbean in this appendix will encourage their more thorough exploration. Similar documents exist for plantations in the colonies of other European countries. Given the focus of this book on the English sugar industry, I have not included those documents here; however, it is worth noting that, as Ward Barrett has shown, there is much to be learned from cross-national comparisons of this type of evidence.[3]

Close readers of these documents will notice that they are plagued by errors of arithmetic. This is not surprising as the authors had to add long columns in English old-style currency without the benefit of a modern calculator. I have resisted the temptation to correct such errors in favor of reproducing the numbers as they appear in the sources on the theory that this would remind readers to approach these documents with caution.

			Jamaica Currency.
250 negroes, at £.70 each	—	—	17,500
80 Steers, at £.15	—	—	1,200
60 Mules, at £.28	—	—	1,680

Total in currency (equal to £.14,557 fterling) — £. 20,380

LET us now bring the whole into one point of view.

			Jamaica Currency.
LANDS,	—	—	14,100
BUILDINGS,	—	—	7,000
STOCK,	—	—	20,380
		Total in currency —	41,480

FIG. 11. Estimated cost of establishing a sugar plantation in Jamaica ca. 1793, by Bryan Edwards, from Edwards, *History, Civil and Commercial*, 2:251. (Courtesy James Ford Bell Library, Minneapolis)

TABLE A.1

Cost of establishing a plantation in Jamaica, on the north side of the island within a short distance of the sea, in 1776

Acres	R(od)s	P(erche)s	P(erche)s
225	0	10 land in canes	£4,506
248	0	0 land in pasture and provisions	3,428
453	1	30 wood land	813
		Mill, distilling house, curing ditto, and all other buildings and offices, complete	3,600
		Implements and utensils of all sorts in store, or in use	300
		146 negroes	1,760
		82 head of cattle (horned) old and young	943
		25 mules	1,050
		Total (in Jamaican currency)	£24,400

Source: Anonymous reviewer in *Monthly Review or Literary Journal* (London) 54 (1776), art. 7, reprinted in Carman, *American Husbandry,* xxii–xxiii.

Note: Figures are in Jamaican currency, which in 1776 exchanged with sterling at a rate of £140 Jamaican currency to £100 sterling. McCusker, *Money and Exchange,* 253. The exchange rate of 140 is for 1775, as McCusker does not report a 1776 rate.

TABLE A.2
Cost of establishing a considerable plantation in Jamaica ca. 1775

6,0000 acres of land purchased at £11 per acre	£6,600
Two windmills	1,000
Reservoir, &c	260
Boiling–house, coppers, &c	1,350
Curing house	460
The stove, &c	180
The still house, &c	180
Sheds	90
Stables, cattle pens, &c	230
Mansion and three other houses	1,600
Implements of all sorts exclusive of fixtures	500
10 negroes at an average of 120£	1,200
167 negroes at 50£	8,350
100 head cattle, 15£	1,500
100 head ditto at 10£	1,000
30 mules at 25£	750
100 swine, 15s	75
Total	£25,325

Source: Carmen, *American Husbandry,* 426–27.

Note: Currency is not specified, but probably, figures are in Jamaican currency. In 1775, the exchange rate was 140. That is, £140 Jamaican currency was worth £100 sterling. McCusker, *Money and Exchange,* 253.

TABLE A.3
Cost of establishing a small plantation on St. Kitts ca. 1770

110 acres of land, only part of which is fit for sugar, with a small mansion, one mill and a proportional set of buildings, coppers, &c	£3,200
For implements, &c	113
For 47 seasoned Negroes at 62£ per head	2,914
For cattle, &c	640
Total	£6,867

Source: Carman, *American Husbandry*, 446.
Note: Currency is not specified, but given the author's usual practice of using local currency, it is probably in the money of St. Christopher's, which in 1770 exchanged with sterling at a rate of £165 St. Christopher's currency to £100 sterling. McCusker, *Money and Exchange*, 267.

TABLE A.4
Cost of establishing a plantation in Grenada ca. 1770

Purchase of 350 acres of land for canes (200 cleared) and 95 of woodland in the hills for raising provisions, &c	£2,560
Mansion and one set of buildings	2,600
Utensils . . .	480
200 negroes at 56£ on average	11,200
Cattle	320
Total	£17,160

Source: Carman, *American Husbandry*, 461.
Note: Currency is not specified, but given the author's usual practice, figures are probably in Grenadan currency, which in 1770 exchanged with sterling at a rate of £160 Grenada currency to £100 sterling. McCusker, *Money and Exchange*, 274.

TABLE A.5

Dalby Thomas's estimate of the cost of establishing a plantation in Barbados in 1690

50 slaves	£1,250
7 white servants and 3 artisans	150
5 horses	125
8 bullocks	100
100 acres of land, houses, mills tools and other implements	4,000
Total . . .	£5,625

Source: Thomas, *Historical Account,* 18.

Note: Thomas does not specify the currency he is using, nor is the price of slaves much help in this case. Thomas implies a price of £25 per slave. According to David Galenson, in 1690 slaves cost £17.88 Barbados currency, or £16.27 sterling. Galenson, *Traders, Planters, and Slaves,* 65. Neither figure is close enough to the price Thomas used to support a firm conclusion. I suspect that Thomas used Barbados currency, as that was the form such data were available in. In 1690 the exchange rate was £110.38 Barbados to £100 sterling. McCusker, *Money and Exchange,* 241.

TABLE A.6

The Reverend Robert Robertson's estimate of the cost of establishing a plantation on St. Kitts in 1732

200 acres of land	£3,400
150 slaves	£3,300
A good substantial dwelling house, boiling-house, curing house, and still-house with the stables, and out-housing . . .	1,500
The coppers, Stills, and other implements and utensils for the boiling, curing, and still houses, and cattle mill	1,000
And if a windmill be thought needful (as indeed it is) on a plantation of 200 acres that would cost little less than	1,000
Then horses from the North-Continent, Mules from Porto-Rico, Curacao and the Spanish main, which are sold for 20 to 28£ sterling per head, Carts, cart-cattle, and other appendices too numerous to name	1,500
Total	£11,700

Source: Robertson, *Detection of the State and Situation of the Present Sugar Planters,* 42, reported in Sheridan, *Sugar and Slavery,* 265.

Note: Values are in sterling.

TABLE A.7
Edward Long's cost estimates for establishing plantations in Jamaica in 1774

To establish a plantation yielding 30 to 50 hogsheads of sugar annually

£300 acres of land and growing canes	1,567
Sugar works, other equipment and livestock	877
30 Negroes	1,071
Total	£3,515

To establish a plantation yielding 100 hogsheads of sugar annually

300 acres of land and growing canes	£2,970
sugar works and other equipment	2,463
60 head of cattle	1,014
100 Negroes	3,570
Total	£10,017

To establish a plantation yielding 300 hogsheads of sugar annually

900 acres of land and growing canes	£9,032
sugar works and other equipment	6,319
130 head of livestock	1,978
300 Negroes	10,710
Total	£28,039

Source: Long, *History of Jamaica*, 1:448–64. These documents are reproduced in Sheridan, *Sugar and Slavery*, 265.

Note: Values are in sterling.

TABLE A.8

Cost of purchasing a plantation in South Carolina, within 40 miles of Charles Town, in 1755

To 1,000 acres of land (one third of which ought to be good swamp, the rest oak and hickory, with some pine barrens)£4 per acre	£3,000
To a dwelling house, barn, stable, overseer's house, Negro huts, etc	10,000
To two valuable Negroes (a cooper and a carpenter) @£5000	1,000
To 26 other Negroes, (two-thirds men, and one-third women) @ £250 . . .	6,500
To two ordinary Negroes to look after the poultry, kine, hogs, etc . . .	400
To a waitingboy £200, a house wench £300	500
To 20 head of oxen, cows, etc at £10	200
To 2 stallions and 4 breeding mares at £40	240
To hogs, sheep, and poultry . . .	150
To plantation tools, a cart, plough, etc	150
To 2 riding horses for yourself, family overseer, etc., saddles, bridles,	250
To cloaths, provisions for the Negroes, feed vats, etc. for the first year	250
To contingencies, for nails, oil, etc	110
In all	£23,700
Currency, which is near £2,000 sterling.	

Source: C.W. (Charles Woodmason), in *Gentleman's Magazine* 25 (June 1755): 258–59, reprinted in Merrens, *Colonial South Carolina Scene,* 160–63.

TABLE A.9
Estimate of the cost of establishing a plantation in Maryland or Virginia ca. 1770

Freight and expenses of two persons from London	£50
Ditto of two others	25
20 negroes at £50	1,000
Two ditto women	100
An overseer	40
Patent fees and expenses of taking up 2,000 acres	40
House	100
Offices and tobacco house	100
Furniture	100
Implements of culture	50
A sloop and canoe	50
Arms ammunition and sundries . . .	10
Expenses of Negroes	60
Extra expenses on ditto	10
Housekeeping and family expenses	100
House servants wages	20
Livestock 10 horses at 4£	40
40 cows at 3£	120
50 young cattle	50
100 swine	25
100 sheep	25
poultry	5
sub-total livestock	265
expenses on orchard and garden	20
Incidental expenses	80
Total	£2,210

Source: Carman, *American Husbandry,* 168–69.

Note: The currency is not specified. While it is likely, given the author's practice, that these figures are in colonial currency rather than sterling, it is not clear whether Virginia or Maryland currency was employed. However, since in the text that surrounds this estimate the author shows more interest in Virginia than in Maryland, my best guess is that he used Virginia currency in estimating the costs. In 1770 the exchange rates were £151.03 Maryland currency to £100 sterling and £118 Virginia currency to £100 sterling. McCusker, *Money and Exchange,*198, 212.

TABLE A.10

Bryan Edwards's estimate of the cost of establishing a sugar plantation in Jamaica ca. 1793

Prime cost 600 acres at £14 currency	£8,400
Clearing 300 acres for canes at £12,100 acres provisions, 100 acres guinea grass at £7, enclosing at £700	5,700
Total Land	14,100
Watermill, windmill & animal mill, or two animal mills	1,400
Boiling house at £1,000, Curing house at £800, Distillery at £1600, Two trash houses at £300 each	4,000
Slave hospital	300
Overseer's dwelling house	600
Mule stable, sheds, tradesmen's shops outfitted	700
Total buildings	7,000
slaves at £70	17,500
80 steers at £15, 60 mules at £28	2,880
Total stock	*20,380*
Total capital	*£41,480 Jamaican currency, or £29,628 sterling.*

Source: Edwards, *History, Civil and Commercial,* 1:251. This document is also reprinted in Craton, *Sinews of Empire,* 133.

Note: Edwards reports figures in both Jamaican currency and sterling, using an exchange rate of £142 Jamaican currency to £100 sterling.

Notes

ABBREVIATIONS USED

BNA   Barbados National Archives, Lazaretto, St. Michael's
BL   British Library, London
PRO   Public Records Office, London

INTRODUCTION

1. Williams, *Capitalism and Slavery.* While many of Williams's arguments have been severely criticized, no one has challenged his point that slavery was central to Britain's American empire. I have reviewed recent scholarship on Williams in Menard, "Reckoning with Williams."

2. There is a substantial literature on the early Amerindian inhabitants of Barbados. Handler and Lange, *Plantation Slavery in Barbados,* 15, provides a brief summary and references to the scholarship.

3. The island's role as a source of slaves for the mainland is often misunderstood. Often it is argued that mainland planters acquired seasoned and partly acculturated slaves from the islands, when in fact they purchased newly arrived Africans at the great slave auctions at Bridgetown and Port Royal.

4. While there is a large literature on this subject, see esp. Price, "Economic Function and the Growth of American Port Towns."

5. Although the term *sugar revolution* apparently did not appear in print until the nineteenth century, Richard Ligon gathered the main ideas together under the rubric that suggested the title for this book in his *True and Exact History of Barbados,* 96.

6. For the literature on the sugar revolution and early Barbados, see McCusker and Menard, *Economy of British America,* 145–56. For a more recent review of the literature, see Higman, "Sugar Revolution."

7. Ligon, *True and Exact History of Barbados,* 96.

8. The best accounts of the transformation of Barbados are Dunn, *Sugar and Slaves;* and Beckles, *White Servitude and Black Slavery.* While my arguments occasionally differ from theirs, my debt to their pathbreaking scholarship should be obvious to anyone who knows their work. K. G. Davies stresses the power and intensity of the sugar revolution in Barbados in *North Atlantic World,* 180.

9. While this argument contradicts a long scholarly tradition, I am not the only scholar to suggest that historians have misunderstood the Barbadian economy in the presugar era. In "Why Sugar?" Robert C. Batie also describes the 1640s as a decade of prosperity for the island. While Alison Games does not directly contradict the older tradition, the evidence she presents of the substantial opportunities available to indentured servants who left London for the island in the 1630s, certainly suggests a buoyant economy. Games, *Migration*, 102–31.

10. Dunn, *Sugar and Slaves*, 46–83, provides the best summary of these changes. A brief summary is provided below, in the conclusion to chapter 3.

11. While most historians still seem to accept the traditional account, I am not alone in suggesting that the role of the Dutch has been exaggerated. See, e.g., Eltis, *Rise of African Slavery*, 214–18; Gragg, "To Procure Negroes"; and Emmer, "Jesus Christ was Good," 5.

12. Craton, *Empire, Enslavement and Freedom*, 30.

13. Schwartz, *Tropical Babylons*; Mintz, *Sweetness and Power*.

14. Readers familiar with the literature on the Chesapeake region will notice the similarities between the processes that drove the initial expansion of both the tobacco and sugar industries. See, e.g., Menard, "Tobacco Industry in the Chesapeake Colonies."

15. Mintz, *Sweetness and Power*, 19–73, provides an informed discussion of the ways in which the physical requirements of sugarcane constrained the organization of production.

16. Mintz and Hall, "Origins of the Jamaican Internal Marketing System."

17. Davies, "Origins of the Commission System."

18. Berlin, *Many Thousands Gone*, 95–111.

19. In this context, it is appropriate to note that my first foray into the history of Barbados was with a paper presented at a conference in honor of Lois Green Carr. See Menard, "Toward African Slavery in Barbados." As those who remember that paper will see, few of its ideas have made their way into this book. Other essays of mine have fared better in this project, and ideas published earlier appear here in much revised form. See McCusker and Menard, "Sugar Industry in the Seventeenth Century"; and Menard, "Law, Credit, and the Supply of Labour."

20. For the Chesapeake school, see Wood, "Century of Writing Early American History"; and the introduction to Menard, *Migrants, Servants and Slaves*.

21. The literature on this expansion is large, I have commented on it in Menard, "Reckoning with Williams." And in Menard, "Capitalism and Slavery."

22. An indispensable guide to colonial currency is McCusker, *Money and Exchange*. My comments on Barbados draw heavily on pp. 239–45.

23. If metropolitan sources are given short shrift in this book, that is because I suffered my stroke just after beginning my work in London. Indeed, I had just set off for the Public Records Office in Chancery Lane in pursuit of biographical detail on the London merchants who played an important role in financing the Barbadian sugar boom.

24. Bloch, *Historian's Craft*, 60–66.

25. The reconstruction of colonial social structure from nonintentional sources is one of the distinguishing practices of the Chesapeake school.

26. Tey, *Daughter of Time*, 105.

27. Ibid., 159. I am not so naïve as to believe that nonintentional sources never mislead. There is in fact a substantial literature on the correction of bias in probate records. See, e.g., Carr and Walsh, "Inventories."

28. Faulkner, *Absalom, Absalom!* 9.

29. This paragraph summarizes a large and complex literature with perhaps a bit more certainty than the underlying scholarship warrants. Davies, *North Atlantic World,* provides a brief summary of the debate over the Spanish failure to take the lead in developing an American sugar industry. There is a large literature on the early history of sugar. The place to start is Deerr, *History of Sugar.* On sugar in the Mediterranean, see Galoway, "Mediterranean Sugar Industry." On the role of the Arabs, see Watson, "Arab Agricultural Revolution."

1. THE EXPORT BOOM IN BARBADOS

1. Bridenbaugh and Bridenbaugh, *No Peace beyond the Line,* 93, 98.

2. On the importance of legal safeguards in persuading planters to invest in slaves, see Galenson, "Economic Aspects of the Growth of Slavery."

3. The 1661 code is discussed in chapter 6.

4. Quoted in Winthrop D. Jordan, *White over Black,* 64.

5. The 1661 code is reprinted in Engerman, Drescher, and Paquette, *Slavery,* 105–13.

6. Oldmixon, *British Empire in America,* 2:6.

7. On the Barbadian forest and the difficulty of clearing it, see Innes, "Pre-Sugar Era."

8. BL, Portland MSS, loan 29/27. The best guide through these conflicting stories is McCusker, "Rum Trade," 198–99, 280–83.

9. The most detailed description of sugar making is found in the relevant chapters of McCusker, "Rum Trade." See also Mintz, *Sweetness and Power,* chap. 2; Dunn, *Sugar and Slaves,* chap. 6; and Schwartz, *Sugar Plantations,* chap. 5.

10. Edwards, *History, Civil and Commercial,* 2:252.

11. Earle, "Staple Interpretation of Slavery and Free Labor."

12. Sheridan, *Sugar and Slavery,* 229–31.

13. David Ryden provides a good recent discussion of the issue of scale economies in "One of the Fertilest and Pleasantest Spots." I discuss the question in more detail in chapter 4.

14. Craton provides a good discussion of the literature on profitability in *Sinews of Empire,* 132–40. See also below, chapter 4.

15. Cary Helyar to William Helyar, 23 October 1671, quoted in Bennett, "Cary Helyar," 67.

16. Tyron, *Friendly Advice,* 301–2.

17. Littleton, *Groans of the Plantations,* 19–20.

18. Schwartz, *Sugar Plantations,* 199.

19. Mintz, *Sweetness and Power,* 36.

20. Wallerstein, *Modern World System,* 88.

21. McCusker, "Rum Trade," 198–99, 281–82. While some sugars were shipped

from Barbados to London in the 1630s (McCusker and Menard, *Economy of British America*, 149), I suspect that those sugars were Brazilian in origin, purchased from a ship that happened to stop in Barbados on its way to Europe. On this possibility, see Richard Batson's instructions to his factor to make such a purchase should the opportunity arise. Batson to Humfry Kent, 5 March 1641, Recopied Deed Books, RB 3/1, 47, BNA.

22. Ligon, *True and Exact History of Barbados*, 85–86.

23. Ibid., 86.

24. Ibid., 85–86. For the export of seventy chests of sugar in 1643, see Bennett, "English Caribbees," 372.

25. Ligon, *True and Exact History of Barbados*, 52. Slaves of African descent did much of the skilled and supervisory work on Brazilian sugar plantations in the early seventeenth century. Schwartz, *Sugar Plantations*, 149–52. It is also likely that Africans had earlier helped transfer the technology from Madeira and São Tomé to Brazil.

26. Emily Mechner constructed a table similar to table 1 out of deeds registered on the island; it shows essentially the same pattern. See Mechner, "Pirates and Planters," table 2.1.

27. Puckrein, *Little England*, 60; John Scott, "The Description of Barbados," BL, Sloane MS 3662.

28. Curtin, *Rise and Fall of the Plantation Complex*, 83. My estimate of the share of Barbadian land in sugar in the early 1660s is an interpolation: Curtin says 40 percent in 1645 and 80 percent in 1667.

29. Eltis, *Rise of African Slavery*, 196–99.

30. The quotation is from Price, *France and the Chesapeake*, 1:74. Menard, "Tobacco Industry in the Chesapeake Colonies," provides details on the industry's fluctuating fortunes in the 1630s and 1640s.

31. James Deering to Edward Deering, 20 July 1740, *Journal of the Barbados Historical and Museum Society* 27 (1960): 124–25. Recopied Deed Books, RB 3/1, 900, BNA; see also RB 3/1, 737.

32. See, e.g., Puckrein, *Little England*, 40, 53.

33. On the quality of Barbadian tobacco, see John Winthrop to Henry Winthrop, 30 January 1629, in *Winthrop Papers*, 2:67 ("verye ill conditioned, fowle, full of stakes, and evell coloured"); Archibald Hay to Peter Hay, 10 October 1637, Hay of Haystoun Papers, Scottish Records Office, Edinburgh ("your tobacco of Barbados of all that cometh to England is acompted the worst"); Samuel Atkins to John Cooks, undated, Recopied Deed Books, RB 3/1, 509, BNA ("the rottenest driest goods as ever I saw in my lyfe"); Ligon, *True and Exact History of Barbados*, 24 ("earthy and worthless").

34. John Winthrop to Henry Winthrop, 30 January 1629, in *Winthrop Papers*, 2:67.

35. Ligon, *True and Exact History of Barbados*, 24.

36. This paragraph builds on an important essay by Robert Batie, "Why Sugar?"

37. For the recovery of the industry as a whole, see Menard, "Tobacco Industry in the Chesapeake Colonies," 132–33. For Barbados prices, see Recopied Deed Books, RB 3/2, 123; RB 3/3, 44; and 4/4, 718, BNA.

38. Archibald Hay to Peter Hay, 10 October 1647, Hay of Haystoun Papers, Scottish Records Office.

39. John McCusker has provided me with some evidence from Amsterdam and London price currents for the mid-seventeenth century, which demonstrate that both products show considerable quality-related price differentials, suggesting that there were rewards to be earned by careful planters. If anything, the differentials were greater for tobacco than for cotton, which seems odd until we remember that quality in cotton was a function of several measurable characteristics—cleanliness, color, the length and strength of fibers—while quality in tobacco was almost entirely subjective, a function of tastes and consumer preferences. This suggests that cotton planters who took pains could be fairly certain that their efforts would be rewarded, while for tobacco planters considerable chance was involved. John McCusker, e-mail message to author, 1 July 2001.

40. The best account of the Barbadian cotton industry is Bridenbaugh and Bridenbaugh, *No Peace beyond the Line,* 55–61. For cotton prices on the island, see Recopied Deed Books, RB 3/1, 19, 291–99, 672, and RB 3/3, 718, BNA.

41. See below, chapter 3.

42. Henry Holt, quoted in Harlow, *Colonizing Expeditions,* 69.

43. Andrew White, "A Brief Relation of the Voyage unto Maryland by Father Andrew White, 1634," in Clayton Colman Hall, *Narratives of Early Maryland,* 35.

44. Bridenbaugh and Bridenbaugh, *No Peace beyond the Line,* 56. Note also the increasing plantation sizes reported in table 7.

45. Beckles, *White Servitude and Black Slavery,* 25; Bennett, "English Caribbees," 359–78.

46. My discussion of the cotton boom is based on a reading of the handful of sources discussed in the pathbreaking work of Beckles, Bridenbaugh and Bridenbaugh, and Bennett cited above in nn. 44 and 45. The often murky and sometimes mysterious history of the cotton gin is illuminated in an important recent dissertation by Angela Lakwete, "Cotton Ginning in America, 1780–1860."

47. Sloane, *Voyage to the Islands;* Dalby Thomas, *Historical Account.*

48. Bridenbaugh and Bridenbaugh reproduce Sloane's gin as plate 4 of *No Peace beyond the Line.*

49. Indigo was produced in many of the colonies of European America and as a consequence is the subject of a large literature, which is introduced in McCusker and Menard, *Economy of British America,* 186–87. Jelatis, "Tangled Up in Blue," discusses the more recent literature and has a good discussion of the crop's technical, labor, and capital requirements.

50. Ligon, *True and Exact History of Barbados,* 22.

51. Recopied Deed Books, RB 3/2, 116–17, BNA.

52. Dunn, *Sugar and Slaves,* 55.

53. Ibid., 56.

54. Games, *Migration,* 102–31. For later opportunities on the island, see below, chapter 4. And cf. Games's results with the experience of the tenants on Mt. Clapham in the 1650s, reported in chapter 4.

55. Games, *Migration,* 47.

56. John Scott, "An Account of Barbados and the Government thereof, with a Map of the Island," BL, Sloane MS 2441.

57. For what evidence there is, see Dunn, *Sugar and Slaves;* and Puckrein, *Little England,* esp. 181–94.

58. Puckrein, *Little England,* 181–94.

59. Foster, *Brief Relation of the Late Horrid Rebellion,* 3.

60. Gardyner, *Description of the New World,* 36–37.

61. Oldmixon, *British Empire in America,* 2:6.

62. Ligon, *True and Exact History of Barbados,* 96. For Drax, see Craton, "Reluctant Creoles," 331–32.

63. Games, "Opportunity and Mobility in Early Barbados."

64. Mechner, "Pirates and Planters," chap. 3, reports similar results.

65. See, e.g., Henry Holt, "The Voyage of Sir Henry Holt," in Harlow, *Colonizing Expeditions;* and Bizet, "Father Antoine Bizet's Visit to Barbados."

2. LAND AND LABOR DURING THE EXPORT BOOM

1. Williams, *Capitalism and Slavery,* 23.

2. I have commented on the general process of Africanization in the Americas in Menard, "Transitions to African Slavery in British America," and in Menard and Schwartz, "Why African Slavery?"

3. Eltis, "Free and Coerced Transatlantic Migrations," 278.

4. Davis, *Slavery and Human Progress,* 51.

5. Phillips, *Slavery from Roman Times to the Early Transatlantic Trade,* is an able survey of this complex subject.

6. Davis, *Slavery and Human Progress,* 51.

7. The most important work in this tradition is Winthrop D. Jordan, *White over Black.* For a recent effort to tie the growth of slavery to an emerging racial ideology, see Allen, *Invention of the White Race.* For a review of this debate, see Green, "Race and Slavery." For a recent work in this tradition, see Parent, *Foul Means.* Along with much of the work that attempts to use racism and ideology to explain the rise of African slavery, Parent seems to confuse cause and consequence.

8. The best discussion of slave imports to Barbados in the seventeenth century is found in Curtin, *Atlantic Slave Trade,* 52–60.

9. See table 10; and Curtin, *Atlantic Slave Trade,* 55.

10. Numerous descriptions of small estates appear in the Recopied Deed Books. See, e.g., RB 3/1, 61–62 (John Tawyer), 62–63 (Richard Goose), 105 (Henry Harford), 147–48 (Edward Cross), and 543–44 (William Price and Edmund Clarke), all in BNA. For inventories of larger estates in the early 1640s, see, e.g., Lancelot Pace's plantation, with 160 acres and 17 servants, appraised at roughly £1,700 Barbados currency; George Bulkey's plantation, with 10 servants, appraised at ca. £450 Barbados currency without the land; and Francis Skeete's plantation, with 20 servants, appraised at £550 Barbados currency, again without the land. Ibid., RB 3/1, 13–14, 15.

11. Here I am following the argument of Gemery and Hogendorn, "Atlantic Slave Trade."

12. The literature on indentured servitude in British America is reviewed in Kenneth Morgan, *Slavery and Servitude,* which contains a fairly comprehensive bibliography.

13. Records of Rappahannock County, 1664–1775, State Library of Virginia Richmond, VA, p. 23, quoted in Bruce, *Economic History of Virginia,* 1:2n.

14. Galenson, *White Servitude,* 7–8. Kussmaul, *Servants in Husbandry,* is the best analysis of this form of labor in England. There is a helpful discussion of the relation between various English labor systems and indentured servitude in Steinfeld, *Invention of Free Labor,* chap. 2.

15. Galenson, *White Servitude,* 7.

16. Ibid., 7–8.

17. Thomas Best, a servant writing in Virginia in 1623, quoted in Edmund S. Morgan, *American Slavery, American Freedom,* 128.

18. Galenson, *White Servitude,* 8.

19. Morris, *Government and Labor in Early America,* 390–401, surveys much of the colonial legislation governing customary servants. Unfortunately for my purposes, he was more interested in the mainland colonies than in the islands.

20. On differences between customary and contract servants, see Walsh, "Servitude and Opportunity"; and Menard, "British Migration," 126–27.

21. Recent studies of the redemptioner system include Grubb, "Immigrants and Servants"; and Wockeck, *Trade in Strangers.*

22. On convicts, see Ekrich, *Bound for America.*

23. Harlow, *History of Barbados;* Sheridan, *Sugar and Slavery,* 236.

24. For migration estimates, see Dunn, "Servants and Slaves," 159; and Menard, "British Migration," 121.

25. Allen, *Invention of the White Race,* 1:268–69.

26. Gary Nash, *Urban Crucible,* 111.

27. Horn, "Servant Migration," 92.

28. For the conditions servants faced in Barbados, see chapter 4. For conditions on the mainland, see McCusker and Menard, *Economy of British America,* and the literature cited there.

29. Galenson, *White Servitude,* 102–13.

30. For details on these statistical tests, see Menard "British Migration," 108, 118–19.

31. Menard, "Transitions to African Slavery in British America." This essay is reprinted, along with many of my other essays on servants and slaves, in Menard, *Migrants, Servants and Slaves.*

32. Work in this tradition includes Bean and Thomas, "Adoption of Slave Labor"; Green, "Supply vs. Demand"; and Beckles, "Economic Origins of Black Slavery."

33. Gemery, "Emigration from the British Isles." For similar efforts to estimate migration to the colonies, see Galenson, *White Servitude,* 212–18; Fogel et al., "Economics of Mortality in North America"; and Menard, "Migration, Ethnicity." For the degree of uncertainty underlying the estimates, compare Dunn, *Sugar and Slaves,* 334, which finds Barbados "a demographic disaster area," with Puckrein, *Little England,* 181–94, which considers Barbados one of the healthiest of England's

American colonies because the shortage of water on the island limited the growth of a mosquito population.

34. Wrigley and Schofield, *Population History of England,* 219. Users of the Wrigley-Schofield estimates will want to consider the powerful critique presented in Ruggles, "Migration, Marriage and Mortality."

35. Galenson, *White Servitude,* 218, provides a series of migration estimates to particular islands based on the indirect method. While these estimates describe a pattern similar to the pattern that emerges from table 9, they do not show as sharp a decline as that indicated by the lists of emigrants, which might suggest, as Puckrein argues, that historians have overestimated mortality rates on the islands.

36. Galenson, *White Servitude,* 218.

37. The evidence on terms and prices is summarized in Galenson, *White Servitude.*

38. "Petition of the President, Council, and Assembly of Barbados to his Majesty's Commissioners for Foreign Plantations," 1661, quoted in Beckles and Downes, "Economics of the Transition to the Black Labor System," 236–37.

39. See the parliamentary debate on this issue in Stock, *Proceedings and Debates of the British Parliament,* 1:253–59; and the discussion in Beckles, "English Parliamentary Debate." On the merchants and their connections, see below, chapter 3.

40. Beckles, *White Servitude and Black Slavery,* 46–52, 56–58; Dunn, *Sugar and Slaves,* 69.

41. Henry Whistler, "Extracts from Henry Whistler's Journal of the West India Expedition," in Venables, *Narrative of General Venables,* 146. See also Beckles, "Riotous and Unruly Lot."

42. Quoted in Stock, *Proceedings and Debates,* 1:150. For more on the island's bad reputation, see Greene, "Changing Identity in the British West Indies."

43. Martin Noell, quoted in Stock, *Proceedings and Debates,* 1:250.

44. Stock, *Proceedings and Debates,* 1:185–86.

45. Governor Sir Jonathan Atkins to the Lords of Trade and Plantations, 1680, PRO, CO 29/3, pp. 92–93. The deterioration of working conditions and opportunities in Barbados after 1650 is a commonplace in the literature. I agree with the consensus, except that I attribute it to the export boom and not exclusively to the rise of sugar.

46. Beckles, *White Servitude and Black Slavery,* 167.

47. Governor Aitkins to the Lords of Trade and Plantations, 26 October 1680, PRO, CO 29/3, pp. 92–93.

48. This migration is discussed in more detail below, in chapter 6.

49. The quotation is from John Scott, "The Description of Barbados," 40, BL, Sloane MS. 3662. For the volume of the slave trade, see Curtin, *Atlantic Slave Trade.* The role of the London merchants is discussed below, in chapter 3.

50. Curtin, *Atlantic Slave Trade,* 119, 126.

51. There is a large and growing literature on slave prices, to which Eltis, *Rise of African Slavery,* 293–97, is a good introduction.

52. Galenson, *Traders, Planters, and Slaves,* 64–69.

53. There have been several efforts to estimate the population of Barbados. While all tell roughly the same story, readers will not be surprised to learn that I

think the most reliable are those in McCusker and Menard, *Economy of British America,* 153.

54. Galenson, *White Servitude,* chap. 9.

55. Shammas, "Black Women's Work." While I find Shammas's argument persuasive, the process may have been more complex than Shammas allows, as there was an increase in the numbers of female servants late in the seventeenth century. Most of these young women seem to have done household work.

56. Berlin, *Generations of Captivity,* 79.

57. Finley, *Ancient Slavery and Modern Ideology,* 29. Curiously, after dismissing the "numbers game," Finley goes on to imply that in a slave society about one-third of the population was enslaved (80).

58. Berlin, *Many Thousands Gone,* 1–15; Thompson, *Making of the English Working Class.*

59. As demonstrated by Berlin's *Generations of Captivity* and *Many Thousands Gone,* the idea of a slave society does not always lead to a static conception of either the institution of slavery or the lives of slaves.

3. WHO FINANCED THE SUGAR BOOM?

1. The literature on credit and the sources of capital in early America is discussed in McCusker and Menard, *Economy of British America,* 234–37. In addition to the work cited below in this chapter, of particular importance on this subject are Price, *Capital and Credit in British Overseas Trade;* and Pares, "Merchants and Planters."

2. Menard, "Financing the Lowcountry Export Boom." This essay, along with much of my work on servitude and slavery, is reprinted in Menard, *Migrants, Servants and Slaves.*

3. How slavery and plantation development was financed is a question that needs study. Understanding the role of credit along the tobacco coast has been hindered by the ideological arguments of tobacco planters, especially Thomas Jefferson, which has misled scholars for three centuries. For a recent analysis of the issue of debt in the region that manages to escape the long reach of Jefferson, see Bernard, *Creole Gentlemen,* 61–101.

4. John Scott, "The Description of Barbados," 60, BL, Sloane MS 3662. See also Dalby Thomas, *Historical Account,* 13–14. Thomas echoes Scott's argument.

5. For details on this episode in Brazilian history, see Boxer, *Dutch in Brazil.*

6. Price, "Credit in the Slave Trade," 297.

7. Smith, *Inquiry into the Nature and Causes of the Wealth of Nations,* 554–55. Smith's opinion has often prevailed, and even his critics concede the central role of outside capital in financing the beginnings of the sugar boom. Thus, Pares states that "Adam Smith was wrong: the wealth of the British West Indies did not all proceed from the mother country: after some initial loans, in the earliest period which merely primed the pump, the wealth of the West Indies was created out of the profits of the West Indies themselves." "Merchants and Planters," 50.

8. Mill, *Principles of Political Economy,* 685–86.

9. Emmer, "Jesus Christ was Good," 212.

10. The myth of the Dutch is part of a more general golden-age ideology that has had considerable impact on our understanding of early American history. A thorough study of planters' reaction to the Navigation Acts and of the ideology they developed in their struggle against them represents a major opportunity for study of the intersection between economic and political history in early America.

11. Steensgaard, "The Growth and Composition of the Long Distance Trade"; Mazumdar, *Sugar and Society in China*.

12. Emmer, "Jesus Christ was Good," introduces the literature by Dutch historians on expansion.

13. The best-known example is Anthony Ashley Cooper, who in 1646 owned a 205-acre estate with twenty-one servants and nine slaves. Dunn, *Sugar and Slaves*, 68.

14. Nicholas Foster, writing in 1650, complained of a "generation of young Cavees lately come from England." *Brief Relation of the Late Horrid Rebellion*, 35. The best-known cases are Thomas Modyford and Henry Walrond. Modyford purchased a half-share of a working plantation of 500 acres, 102 slaves, and 28 servants for £7,000 Barbados currency shortly after arriving on the island in 1647, paying £1,000 down and the remainder in three equal installments over the next two years. Ligon, *True and Exact History of Barbados*, 22. As evidence developed in this chapter will make clear, it is no accident that Modyford's partners were Thomas Hilliard, a seasoned Barbadian planter, and William Kendall, a London merchant. Note also the example of Edgar Wildigos, who borrowed against an anticipated inheritance to set up a sugar plantation on 495 acres in 1647. Recopied Deed Books, RB, 3/2, 101–2, BNA.

15. Bowen, *Elites, Enterprise and the Making of the British Overseas Empire*, 92.

16. Brenner, *Merchants and Revolution*, has detail on many of these merchants and places the behavior of those who invested in Barbados in context.

17. Recopied Deed Books, RB 3/1, 3/2, 3/3, BNA.

18. Ibid., RB 3/2, 205. For the reference to the Noell brothers as the "four brethren," see RB 3/2, 202.

19. Ibid., RB 3/2, 152–56. The partners had high expectations of this enterprise, for a clause in the contract provided that Pead and Worsum would be paid an additional £200 if the Noells and Seaman cleared £1,000 in the next three years.

20. Ibid., RB 3/2, 202–5; RB 3/3, 467–69. Black Rock Plantation contained 150 acres when the brothers sold it in 1653. RB 3/3, 6–7.

21. Ibid., RB 3/2, 165–67, 201–2, 265.

22. In November 1747, Martin Noell entered into an agreement with Thomas Norton, another London merchant, and Ralph Wiatt, who lived in Barbados, to acquire land and develop a sugar plantation. The partnership eventually acquire a 125-acre tract in St. John's in March 1648. Ibid., RB 3/3, 549–50, 797–98.

23. For details on this early activity by London merchants, see Harlow, *History of Barbados*, chap. 1.

24. Price, "Credit in the Slave Trade," 296. I have explored some consequences of these differing legal systems in Menard, "Law, Credit, the Supply of Labour."

25. Davies, *Royal African Company*, 146.

26. These complex issues are ably discussed in Ernst, *Money and Politics in*

America. For detail on the Barbados paper currency act of 1706, see Nettels, *Money Supply,* 269–71.

27. Company of Royal Adventurers Trading to Africa, quoted in Davies, *Royal African Company,* 320.

28. On Modyford, see Campbell, *Some Early Barbadian History,* 133, 180.

29. Thomas Modyford, quoted in Galenson, *Traders, Planters, and Slaves,* 28.

30. Daniel Parke, quoted in Sheridan, *Sugar and Slavery,* 274.

31. Davies, *Royal African Company,* 323.

32. I am following the analysis in Galenson, *Traders, Planters, and Slaves.*

33. Dalby Thomas, *Historical Account,* 29.

34. Interest rates are discussed in chapter 4.

35. In March, 1,729 merchants (18 of whom are in my list of 62 investors) petitioned Parliament calling "for the dismantling of the landholding and political arrangements of the West Indian proprietorship and the creation of a favorable politico-legal environment for the commercial development they hoped to bring about." Brenner, *Merchants and Revolution,* 166. The petition is in Stock, *Proceedings and Debates,* 1:188–89.

36. Thompson is the central figure in Brenner's *Merchants and Revolution.*

37. On Noell and Spavin, see ibid., 522.

38. Barbadian politics of the mid-seventeenth century are complicated. My brief summary is based on Puckrein, *Little England.*

39. On the Navigation Acts, I am following Brenner, *Merchants and Revolution;* Andrews, *Colonial Period of American History,* vol. 4; and Farnell, "Navigation Act of 1651," 54.

40. On the western design and Jamaica, see Andrews, *Colonial Period of American History,* vol. 3, chap. 1.

41. See Sheridan, *Sugar and Slavery,* 92–95.

42. See the many references to horses (usually referred to as "draught nags") for the island during the 1650s in Sainsbury, *Calendar of State Papers, Colonial Series,* vol. 1.

43. See Beckles, *White Servitude and Black Slavery,* 53, 60.

44. Gragg, "To Procure Negroes." Gragg presents detailed evidence that merchants who invested in the island were heavily involved in the slave trade.

45. Boogaart and Emmer, "Dutch Participation in the Atlantic Slave Trade." Boogaart and Emmer's position on the relative role of the Dutch and English in the early Barbadian slave trade is supported by Postma, *Dutch in the Atlantic Slave Trade.*

46. David Eltis has begun this task: see his *Rise of African Slavery.*

47. Quoted in Davies, *Royal African Company,* 318.

48. See, e.g., Recopied Deed Books, RB 3/3, 460–67, 549–50, 751–52, 797–98, BNA.

49. For sugar prices, see John McCusker's forthcoming book *The Price of Sugar in the Early Modern Atlantic World* (in progress).

50. This group included Jonathan Andrews, Richard Batson, Thomas Frere, Walter Leere, and Luke Lucie.

51. This group included Thomas Applewhaite, Nicholas Black, John Colleton,

Samuel Farmer, Edward Keizer, Thomas Kendall, Thomas Pead, Henry Quintyne, Seth Rowley, and John Worsum.

52. Ligon, *True and Exact History of Barbados,* 43; Bennett, "Cary Helyar," 59.

53. Richard Vines to John Winthrop, 19 July 1647, in *Winthrop Papers,* 5:172.

54. Dunn, *Sugar and Slaves,* 57–58.

55. On the farm-building process and its relationship to the growth of slavery and plantation agriculture elsewhere, see Carr, Menard, and Walsh, *Robert Cole's World,* 160.

56. Thompson, who paid in bills of exchange drawn on his brother in London, appears as a factor for John Worsum in December 1644. Recopied Deed Books, RB 3/1, 680–68, BNA. I have no evidence that he was related to Maurice Thompson, the biggest colonial merchant of the time, but that is a possibility.

57. On Hilliard, see Campbell, *Some Early Barbadian History,* 91–94, 135–36. On his partnership with Farmer, see Recopied Deed Books, RB 3/2, 219–23, BNA.

58. Eltis, *Rise of African Slavery,* 251.

59. This quick summary of Barbados in 1680 is of course based on Dunn, *Sugar and Slaves,* 86–99.

60. On the issue of servile rebellions, see ibid., 256–58; and Beckles, *White Servitude and Black Slavery,* 110–14. The extensive notes in Gaspar, *Bondsmen and Rebels,* provide a guide to the larger literature.

61. On the developments of racial ideologies in the Chesapeake region, see Edmund S. Morgan, *American Slavery, American Freedom.* There is evidence that elite Barbadians understood the value of making whiteness a mark of privilege in order to encourage racial solidarity. In 1676 the island legislature prohibited slaves from entering skilled crafts "so as to preserve these occupations for Christian artisans." Fogel, *Without Consent or Contract,* 43. For more on the development of racial ideologies in Barbados, see below, chapter 6.

4. THE GROWTH OF THE BARBADIAN SUGAR INDUSTRY OVER THE SEVENTEENTH CENTURY

1. Curtin, *Rise and Fall of the Plantation Complex,* 83. Unfortunately, Professor Curtin does not explain the derivation of these estimates. While one might question the accuracy of any particular estimate, Curtin's main point, that Barbadians devoted a large and growing share of their resources to sugar, seems unassailable.

2. Eltis, *Rise of African Slavery,* 198.

3. Details on European sugar prices will appear in John McCusker's forthcoming book on the subject, *The Price of Sugar in the Early Modern Atlantic World* (in progress). I would like to thank Professor McCusker for giving me an advance look at his London and Amsterdam data.

4. McCusker and Menard, *Economy of British America,* 160–68.

5. Examples of this type of explanation abound in the literature; just one case out of many is Genovese and Genovese, *Fruits of Merchant Capital,* 45.

6. The planters' perspective is forcefully presented in Littleton, *Groans of the Plantations.*

7. Import taxes are summarized in Watts, *West Indies,* 263–64.

8. Sheridan, *Sugar and Slavery,* 36–53, is the best guide to the duties imposed on sugar and to the reexport trade.

9. Thornton, *West-India Policy under the Restoration,* 258–69.

10. Sheridan, *Sugar and Slavery,* 48–49.

11. There is a large literature on the processing of cane to make sugar. The best introduction to this complex subject is Mintz, *Sweetness and Power.*

12. For the debate over the scope of technology, see the essays in, McGraw, *Early American Technology.*

13. Dalby Thomas, *Historical Account,* 37.

14. Schwartz, *Sugar Plantations,* 98–159. In this context it is worth noting that even so well informed a historian of the industry as Richard Sheridan refers to sugar's "stable technological environment" during the seventeenth century. Sheridan, *Sugar and Slavery,* 108.

15. Schwartz, *Sugar Plantations,* 98.

16. On the differences between British and Latin America legal systems, see Price, "Credit in the Slave Trade."

17. Walsh, "Slave Society and Tobacco Production."

18. Beckles, *Natural Rebels,* 29.

19. On the Newton estates, see ibid.; and Handler and Lange, *Plantation Slavery in Barbados.* On Cardington, see Bennett, *Bondsmen and Bishops.* For more on the gender division of labor in the sugar industry, see Fogel, *Without Consent or Contract;* and Dunn, "Sugar Production and Slave Women in Jamaica," 49–72.

20. Eltis, *Rise of African Slavery,* 53. There is some disagreement in the literature about the role of shipping productivity in this price decline, with Eltis arguing that gains in shipping productivity were substantial in the slave trade. Eltis is supported by Gemery and Hogendorn, "Technological Change, Slavery, and the Slave Trade." The other side is taken by Richardson, "Costs of Survival."

21. Sheridan, *Sugar and Slavery,* 138–41.

22. Jonathan Atkins to Lords of Trade, 3 February 1675, quoted in Harlow, *History of Barbados,* 309.

23. Watts, "Origins of Barbadian Cane Hole Agriculture." See also Oldmixon, *British Empire in America,* 2:146.

24. See above, chapter 1; Curtin, *Rise and Fall of the Plantation Complex,* 85; and Starkey, *Economic Geography of Barbados,* 61.

25. Curtin, *Rise and Fall of the Plantation Complex,* 83.

26. Sheridan, *Sugar and Slavery,* 128.

27. Starkey, *Economic Geography of Barbados,* 81.

28. Oldmixon, *British Empire in America,* 2:118.

29. On changes in milling, see Starkey, *Economic Geography of Barbados,* 73, 89. The changes can be followed on the several maps of Barbados prepared during the colonial period that describe mills, especially those by Richard Ford (1674) and William Mayo (1722), housed in the John Carter Brown Library, Providence, RI.

30. Sheridan, *Sugar and Slavery,* 145–46, reports much useful detail on milling. On the cost of mills, see below, tables A.6 and A.12.

31. Schwartz, *Sugar Plantations,* 127. For the debate over the origin of the three-roller vertical mill, see Mintz, *Sweetness and Power,* 27.

32. The advantages of the three-roller mill are discussed in Schwartz, *Sugar Plantations*, 127–29.

33. Ibid., 432–33.

34. Ibid., 578.

35. McCusker, "Business of Distilling," 206.

36. Ibid., 119.

37. Schwartz, *Sugar Plantations*, 119.

38. The evidence regarding the production of clayed sugar in Barbados is reviewed in McCusker, *Rum and the American Revolution*, 1:201–7.

39. See the discussion and references in Eltis, *Rise of African Slavery*, 200–201.

40. On the difference between tariffs for clayed and for muscavado sugar, see Sheridan, *Sugar and Slavery*, 43.

41. The complexities of clayed sugar in Barbados are clearly explained in McCusker, "Rum Trade," 201–23.

42. Menard, "Transport Costs and Long Range Trade"; Shepherd and Walton, *Shipping, Maritime Trade*, 68–69.

43. Menard, "Transport Costs and Long Range Trade," 267.

44. Insurance rates are reported in Ward, "Profitability of Sugar Planting." See also Steele, *English Atlantic*, 225–27.

45. Eighteenth-century insurance rates are reported in Inikori, *Africans and the Industrial Revolution in England*, 350.

46. Menard, "Tobacco Industry in the Chesapeake Colonies." See also Price, "Transaction Costs."

47. Davies, *Royal African Company*, 323.

48. Carmen, *American Husbandry*, 447.

49. For interests rates in the islands, see Sheridan, *Sugar and Slavery*, 276–77. There is a large and growing literature on English capital markets, much of it focused on the public debt to the neglect of the private capital markets, which were more important to the financing of the sugar industry. A good place to start is Dickson, *Financial Revolution in England*.

50. McCusker and Menard, *Economy of British America*, 160. For the traditional view of planters, see Ragatz, *Fall of the Planter Class*. For evidence that even eighteenth-century planters did not stubbornly resist change, see Aufhauser, "Slavery and Technological Change"; and Sheridan, "Samuel Martin."

51. Otis Starkey suggests the connection between the supply of animals and soil fertility in *Economic Geography of Barbados*, 73–74.

52. Barrett, *Efficient Plantation*, 22.

53. Williams, *From Columbus to Castro*, 124.

54. Dunn, *Sugar and Slaves*, 67.

55. See Starkey, *Economic Geography of Barbados*, 72–79.

56. Plantagenet, *Description of the Province of New Albion*, 5.

57. There is a large literature on maroons in the Caribbean. Craton provides an excellent survey in *Testing the Chains*, 61–66.

58. Thomas Wilkier, quoted in Beckles and Watson, "Social Protest and Labour Bargaining." On runaways, see Beckles, "From Land to Sea."

59. Berlin and Morgan, *Cultivation and Culture*, 23. This is a complex subject

on which there is a large and growing literature. The topic is ably introduced in Berlin and Morgan's introduction.

60. The development of the provision-ground system is discussed in more detail in chapter 5. See also Higman, *Slave Populations*, 204–18.

61. On patterns of consumption in England, see Sheridan, *Sugar and Slavery*, part 2; and Mintz, *Sweetness and Power*.

62. Shammas, *Pre-Industrial Consumer*, 81–83, quotation on 82.

63. Austen and Smith, "Private Tooth Decay as Public Economic Virtue," 187.

64. McCusker, "Rum Trade," 42–44, traces the refining industry in Britain.

65. Shammas, "Revolutionary Impact."

66. Mullin, *Africa in America*, 115. This is an old debate, and there is of course a large literature, ably introduced in Kolchin, *American Slavery*, 278–82.

67. Schwartz, *Sugar Plantations*, 431–34.

68. Eugene Genovese, *World the Slaveholders Made*, 30.

69. Zahedieh, "Overseas Expansion and Trade in the Seventeenth Century," 410.

70. Oldmixon, *British Empire in America*, 2:127.

71. Eltis, *Rise of African Slavery*, 197–200, quotation on 199. See also idem, "Total Product of Barbados."

72. Rev. James Parker to Governor John Winthrop, 24 April 1646, quoted in Sheridan, *Sugar and Slavery*, 264.

73. William Hay and William Powrey to Archibald Hay, 8 October 1646, as reported in Dunn, *Sugar and Slaves*, 59. Although Dunn does not say, I suspect that these amounts are in sterling, as the nephews were trying to persuade their English uncle to invest and are likely to have given the amounts in the currency with which he was most familiar.

74. Quoted in Sheridan, *Sugar and Slavery*, 244. Sheridan provides an able summary of what we know about slave mortality.

75. Godwyn, *Negro's and Indian's Advocate*, 82–83.

76. Robertson, *Detection of the State and Situation of the Present Sugar Planters*, 42–44.

77. Bennett, *Bondsmen and Bishops*, 61.

78. Ibid., 22–33, 43, 101, 138; Handler and Lange, *Plantation Slavery in Barbados*, 51–54; Mullin, *Africa in America*, 96.

79. Galenson, *White Servitude*, 165.

80. Sheridan, *Sugar and Slavery*, 266–69, has an informed discussion of the issues raised in this and the preceding paragraphs.

81. Schwartz, *Sugar Plantations*, chaps. 5 and 6.

82. Dalby Thomas, *Historical Account*. For more on size, see Phillip D. Morgan, *Slave Counterpoint*, 35–36.

83. Mintz, *Sweetness and Power*, chap. 2.

84. There is a substantial literature on plantation profitability. In addition to the work cited below in this chapter and the essays by Ward Barrett cited in the appendix, important contributions include Douglas G. Hall, "Incalculability as a Feature of Sugar Production"; and Aufhauser, "Profitability of Slavery."

85. Carmen, *American Husbandry*, xvi–xxx.

86. Craton, *Sinews of Empire*, 138–39. There is also an excellent summary in Sheridan, *Sugar and Slavery*, 381–85.

87. Smith, *Inquiry into the Nature and Causes of the Wealth of Nations*, 366.

88. Burke and Burke, *Account of the European Settlements in America*, 125.

89. Eltis, *Rise of African Slavery*, 171–72.

90. Governor Seton, of St. Vincent's, to Lord Sidney, quoted in Sheridan, *Sugar and Slavery*, 264.

91. Ryden, "One of the Fertilest and Pleasantest Spots."

92. Williams, *Capitalism and Slavery*. There is a large literature on the several arguments advanced by Williams. A good starting point is Solow and Engerman, *British Capitalism and Caribbean Slavery*.

93. Williams, *From Columbus to Castro*, 148. The literature on this argument is reviewed in McCusker and Menard, *Economy of British America*, 19–45.

94. I am here summarizing a substantial literature. The key text is Engerman, "Slave Trade and British Capital Formation."

95. Inikori, *Africans and the Industrial Revolution in England*, esp. chap. 9. Kenneth Morgan, *Slavery, Atlantic Trade*, provides a review of the literature that is more skeptical of the Williams thesis than is Inikori.

96. Price and Clemens, "Revolution of Scale in Overseas Trade."

97. Price, "Colonial Trade and British Economic Development," quotation on 123.

98. There is a large literature on this issue. A good place to start is Douglas G. Hall, "Absentee-Proprietorship."

99. For this debate, see Sheridan, "Wealth of Jamaica in the Eighteenth Century"; R. P. Thomas, "Sugar Colonies of the Old Empire"; and Sheridan, "Wealth of Jamaica in the Eighteenth Century: A Rejoinder."

100. There is also a large literature on this question, for which good starting points include Ryden, "Does Decline Make Sense?" and Drescher, "Decline Thesis of British Slavery."

101. For sugar prices, see McCusker, "Rum Trade," 988–1188; and Sheridan, *Sugar and Slavery*, app. 5.

102. Engerman, "Europe, the Lesser Antilles, and Economic Expansion," table 8.3.

103. Higman, "Economic and Social Development." See also Beckles, *History of Barbados*. For sugar export by island, see Sheridan, *Sugar and Slavery*, app. 1.

104. McCusker, *Rum and the American Revolution*, 2:202–7. See also Pares, "London Sugar Market."

105. Littleton, *Groans of the Plantations*, 11–12.

106. McCusker, "Rum Trade," 201–3.

107. I am here following the argument of ibid., 200ff.

5. ORIGINS OF THE BARBADIAN PLANTATION COMPLEX

I published a preliminary exploration of some of the ideas advanced in this chapter in Menard, "Law, Credit, the Supply of Labour." This chapter grows out of and builds on that essay.

1. For a recent example, see Blackburn, *Making of New World Slavery,* 229–32. Readers will want to pay close attention to the evidence Blackburn introduces to support his arguments.

2. The strongest argument for this position is Craton, *Empire, Enslavement and Freedom,* chap. 1. As I read it, the evidence Craton presents tends to support my position rather than his.

3. On the organization of the sugar industry before its transformation in Barbados, see the essays in Schwartz, *Tropical Babylons.*

4. For the sugar industry before the Barbadian sugar boom, see Curtin, *Rise and Fall of the Plantation Complex.*

5. These observations regarding tenancy and leases are based on my work with the Recopied Deed Books in the BNA. See also Puckrein, *Little England,* 29, 62.

6. I found few leases in the Recopied Deed Books dating from the first half of the seventeenth century, but there are a considerable number dating from the early 1650s.

7. The description of Mt. Clapham offered here is based on a deed of sale from Thomas Noell to Governor Daniel Searle dated 6 June 1654 in Recopied Deed Books, RB 3/1, 109–13, BNA.

8. For more on the Noell brothers, see above, chapter 3.

9. The conventional ratio was one slave for every two acres. Dunn, *Sugar and Slaves,* 69.

10. Additional detail on the Mt. Clapham tenants is provided in Beckles, *White Servitude and Black Slavery,* 157.

11. Dunn, *Sugar and Slaves,* 69.

12. Menard, "Law, Credit, the Supply of Labour," 157.

13. This concern is evident in the papers of Christopher Jeafferson, of St. Kitts: Jeafferson, *Young Squire of the Seventeenth Century.* See also the contracts printed as an appendix to Pares, "Merchants and Planters."

14. Jeafferson, *Young Squire of the Seventeenth Century;* Sheridan, *Sugar and Slavery,* 153–254. For more on this hurricane and the problems it caused, see Mulcahy, "Melancholy and Fatal Calamities," chap. 3; see also idem, "Weathering the Storms."

15. Migration from the island is discussed in chapter 6.

16. This summary of the experience of the Mt. Clapham tenants rests on research carried out by three University of Minnesota undergraduates, David Goldman, Mary Parker, and Michael Menard, working under the supervision of David Ryden. I would like to thank those students for their effort and the university's Undergraduate Research Opportunities Program (UROP) for making this project possible.

17. Bizet, "Father Antoine Bizet's Visit to Barbados," 69.

18. Beckles, *White Servitude and Black Slavery,* 157.

19. Dunn, *Sugar and Slaves,* 96.

20. All comments about the 1680 census are from ibid., 91.

21. Ibid., 84–116; Eltis, *Rise of African Slavery,* 202–3.

22. On Bybrook and the Helyars, see Dunn, *Sugar and Slaves,* 219–22, 321–22; and Bennett, "Cary Helyar."

23. Mathew Mulcahy, e-mail message to author, July 2001. I would like to thank Professor Mulcahy for this information.

24. See the discussion in Beckles, *Natural Rebels*, 29.

25. Eltis, *Rise of African Slavery*, 202.

26. Handler and Lange, *Plantation Slavery in Barbados*, 72.

27. Ligon, *True and Exact History of Barbados*, 13–14.

28. Craton, *Sinews of Empire*, 121; Martin, *Essay on Plantership*. On Martin, see Sheridan, "Samuel Martin."

29. Clark, *Ten Views of Antigua*. Mintz reproduces some of Clark's illustrations in *Sweetness and Power*, following p. 78.

30. Eltis, *Rise of African Slavery*, passim.

31. For a survey of English culture on the eve of the invasion of the Americas stressing regional variations, see Fischer, *Albion's Seed*.

32. Ligon, *True and Exact History of Barbados*, 117.

33. Quoted in Davies, *North Atlantic World*, 179.

34. This is the central point explored in Menard, "Law, Credit, the Supply of Labour."

35. The story of the rise of the planter class in Barbados is ably told by Dunn, *Sugar and Slaves*. For Sheridan's argument, see *Sugar and Slavery*, 274. For details on debtor-creditor relations on the island, see above, chapter 3.

36. Jack P. Greene tracks the changing reputation of the island in "Changing Identity in the British West Indies."

37. *Great Newes from the Barbadoes*, 6–7.

38. On gang labor and productivity, see Fogel, *Without Consent or Contract*, chap. 2. Even so careful a student of the organization of slave labor as Phillip Morgan on occasion flirts with naturalistic explanations. See, e.g., Phillip D. Morgan, *Slave Counterpoint*, 179–203. In this context Fogel's tendency to assume that gangs were always used on plantations with large numbers of slaves is worth noting.

39. Phillip D. Morgan, "Task and Gang Systems," quotation on 190–91.

40. Phillip D. Morgan, "Task and Gang Systems," summarizes what we know about the origins of tasking. In addition to the work already cited, important studies of the organization of slave labor include Gray, *History of Agriculture*, 1:550–67; Schwartz, *Sugar Plantations*, 132–60; Phillip D. Morgan, "Work and Culture"; and Carney, *Black Rice*.

41. The best guide to reported slave conspiracies is Craton, *Testing the Chains*, 105–15.

42. Of the several series of Barbados population estimates, I relied on those in McCusker and Menard, *Economy of British America*, 153.

43. Ligon, *True and Exact History of Barbados*, 46.

44. See Craton's listing in *Testing the Chains*, 335.

45. This incident is described in detail in ibid., 109–10.

46. These efforts are detailed in Allen, *Invention of the White Race*, 2:228–30.

47. On efforts to recruit more whites, see Beckles, *White Servitude and Black Slavery*, 166–67. On the effort to build white solidarity, see below, chapter 6.

48. Mintz and Hall, "Origins of the Jamaican Internal Marketing System."

49. Quoted in Handler and Lange, *Plantation Slavery in Barbados*, 16.

50. See Starkey, *Economic Geography of Barbados*, 33–37.

51. Beckles, *History of Barbados*, 36.

52. For the report of a contemporary observer, see John Scott's comment in his 1667 "Description of Barbados," BL, Sloane MS 3662. Beckles reviews the legislation in *Natural Rebel*, 72–77.

53. Oldmixon, *British Empire in America*, 2:133, 134.

54. There is a useful discussion of slaves' surpluses in Handler and Lange, *Plantation Slavery in Barbados*, 86–92.

55. Pinckard, *Notes on the West Indies*, 2:118.

56. Quoted in Handler and Lange, *Plantation Slavery in Barbados*, 91.

57. There is a large and growing literature on slavery in Africa. The following are good places to start and provide guides to the literature: Manning, *Slavery and African Life*; Meyers and Kopytoff, *Slavery in Africa*; and Lovejoy, *Transformations in Slavery*.

58. Carney, *Black Rice*, 98–101, 155–59.

59. Edwards, *History, Civil and Commercial*, 1:123–24.

60. Byam is quoted in Woodville K. Marshall, "Provision Ground and Plantation Labor," 205.

61. The quotations are from Dunn, *Sugar and Slaves*, 116, 105. On absenteeism, see the discussion and references in McCusker and Menard, *Economy of British America*, 154–55.

62. On the connection between deforestation and maroonage, see chapter 4.

63. There is a substantial literature on the commission system. I have relied most heavily on the now-classic article by Kenneth Davies, "Origins of the Commission System." Other important contributions to this growing literature include Pares, *West India Fortune*; Hancock, "World of Business to Do"; and R. C. Nash, "Organization of Trade and Finance."

64. Davies, "Origins of the Commission System," 93.

65. Ligon, *True and Exact History of Barbados*, 95–96.

66. There is a substantial literature on West Indian interest groups in London. A good place to begin is the introduction to Ryden, *Promoters of the Slave Trade*.

67. Curtin, *Rise and Fall of the Plantation Complex*, 10, 11.

68. Ibid., 11–13.

6. THE EXPANSION OF BARBADOS

1. Chandler, "Expansion of Barbados," 106; John Scott, "The Description of Barbados," BL, Sloane MS 3662, 54–59.

2. Dunn, *Sugar and Slaves*, 112n.

3. Greene, "Colonial South Carolina," 68.

4. Dunn, "English Sugar Islands"; idem, *Sugar and Slaves*, 111–16; Peter H. Wood, *Black Majority*; Sirmans, *Colonial South Carolina*.

5. The substantial literature on the Barbados–South Carolina connection is ably summarized in Greene, "Colonial South Carolina."

6. The role of the Barbadians in Virginia is explored in Hatfield, *Atlantic Virginia*.

7. On the Caribbean origins of many of the slaves in early Virginia, see Berlin, *Many Thousands Gone*, 29–46.

8. Data on sugar production by island is available in Dunn, *Sugar and Slaves*, 203; and Thornton, "Some Statistics of West Indian Produce."

9. Sheridan, *Sugar and Slavery*, 95.

10. Ibid., 94–95.

11. Information on Notley, Wharton, and Rozer is scattered throughout David W. Jordan, *Foundations of Representative Government in Maryland*. See also the entries in Papenfuse et al., *Biographical Dictionary of the Maryland Legislature*.

12. There is a large literature on the Chesapeake system of husbandry. Carr, Menard, and Walsh, *Robert Cole's World*, is a good place to begin.

13. Galenson, "Economic Aspects of the Growth of Slavery."

14. Channing, *Narragansett Planters*, 10. Plantation sizes can be inferred from evidence on the size and composition of households available in the several Rhode Island census returns discussed in Wells, *Population of the British Colonies in America*.

15. We lack a modern study of the Narragansett planters. The best account is found in James, *Colonial Rhode Island*, 250–57. James's bibliography provides a fairly comprehensive guide to the meager literature on this group. The depth and intensity of the Narragansett planters' connection to Barbados is apparent in ibid. and in the manuscript sources James cites.

16. The best account of the Cape Fear settlement is in Craven, *Southern Colonies in the Seventeenth Century*, 29–33. Craven provides a thorough guide to the scanty documentation for this still rather obscure settlement.

17. Craven implies this in *Southern Colonies in the Seventeenth Century*.

18. Warren, *Impartial Description of Surinam*; Addis, *Letter Sent from Syrranam*.

19. Williamson, *English in Guiana and on the Amazon*; Bridenbaugh and Bridenbaugh, *No Peace beyond the Line*, 199–201.

20. Bridenbaugh and Bridenbaugh, *No Peace beyond the Line*, 212–13.

21. Relatively little is known about this settlement of Barbadians in New Jersey, but see the references in Wacker and Clemens, *Land Use in Early New Jersey*.

22. Nicholson, "Legal Borrowing," argued that all the major slave colonies except Maryland and Virginia accepted the Barbados slave code of 1661. I would argue that one could hear echoes of the Barbados code in the slave laws passed in the upper South.

23. On the influence and spread of the Barbados slave code of 1661, see Dunn, *Sugar and Slaves*, 238–39. Dunn calls this act "the most important surviving piece of legislation issued in the English islands during the seventeenth century" (239).

24. Gaspar, "Rigid and Inclement"; Menig, *Shaping of America*, 250–53.

25. Wiecek, "Statutory Law," is a valuable introduction to the subject and includes references to the various slave codes.

26. The Virginia code is in Henning, *Statutes at Large, Being a Collection of All the Laws of Virginia*, 3:460–61.

27. David W. Jordan, *Foundations of Representative Government in Maryland*,

102. On the law of slavery in the seventeenth century, see Johnson, "Origin and Nature of African Slavery in Maryland."

28. On the Barbados code in Jamaica, see Gaspar, "Rigid and Inclement," 78–96.

29. For examples of restrictions in New Hampshire, see Winthrop D. Jordan, *White over Black*, 104–5.

30. In 1781 the Prince Edward Island legislature mimicked the plantation colonies by ruling that baptism would have no effect on the status of slaves. See Ridell, "Baptism of Slaves in Prince Edward Island," 308.

31. Wiecek, "Statutory Law," 264. Some of the complex issues involved in these debates are explored in Ghachem, "Slave's Two Bodies."

32. Price, "Credit in the Slave Trade"; Menard, "Law, Credit, the Supply of Labour."

33. The large literature on these issues is ably introduced in McCusker, *Money and Exchange;* and Ernst, *Money and Politics in America.* The Barbados precedents are discussed above, in chapter 3.

34. The petition is discussed and quoted in Sheridan, *Sugar and Slavery,* 288.

35. Price, *Perry of London,* 82–89.

36. Ibid., 82.

37. The Colonial Debts Act of 1732 merits a detailed study. Although brief, the best available discussion is in ibid., 82–89.

38. Berlin, *Many Thousands Gone,* 109–11.

39. Providence Island was the first. Kupperman, *Providence Island,* xxx.

40. Ligon, *True and Exact History of Barbados,* 46.

41. See Michael Craton's listing of slave conspiracies in *Testing the Chains,* 335.

42. On the effort to recruit more whites, see Beckles, *White Servitude and Black Slavery,* 166–67.

43. Willoughby to Clarendon, 5 March 1664, Bodleian Library, Clarendon MSS 81, fol. 129.

44. In the large and growing literature in the field of whiteness studies the best place to start is Roediger, *Wages of Whiteness.* For a more recent statement that provides a guide to much of the recent literature, see Roediger's *Black on White.* I found Harris, "Whiteness as Property," especially helpful.

45. Ligon, *True and Exact History of Barbados,* 29, 46.

46. The 1661 slave code may be found in An Act for the Better Ordering and Governing of Negroes, Barbados, 1661, PRO, CO 30/2, pp. 16–26. It has been reprinted in full in Engerman, Drescher, and Paquette, *Slavery,* 105–13.

47. An Act for the Good Governing of Servants is in PRO, CO 30/2, pp. 23–28. Richard Dunn has an illuminating discussion of these two pieces of legislation in *Sugar and Slaves,* 238–46. My analysis builds on his insightful commentary.

48. An Act for the Better Ordering and Governing of Negroes, clause 23.

49. Handler and Sio, "Barbados," quotation on 230.

50. Oldmixon, *British Empire in America,* 2:42.

51. Fogel, *Without Consent or Contract,* 43.

52. Dunn, *Sugar and Slaves,* 243.

53. The issue of reducing the number of acres owned required of voters is discussed in ibid., 92–93; see also Allen, *Invention of the White Race*, 2:229.

54. Quoted in Winthrop D. Jordan, *White over Black*, 185.

55. Dunn, *Sugar and Slaves*, 104. See also Drake, *Quakers and Slavery*, 5–7.

56. These educational initiatives are described in Bridenbaugh and Bridenbaugh, *No Peace beyond the Line*, 395–99.

57. On the Barbadian militia, see Craton, *Empire, Enslavement and Freedom*, 82.

58. Barbados slave code of 1661, clauses 1 and 2.

59. On these issues, see Beckles, *Natural Rebels*; and idem, *Centering Women*. The latter book has a fairly comprehensive bibliography.

60. Fox, *To the Ministers, Teachers, and Priests*, 5.

61. Godwyn, *Negro's and Indian's Advocate*, 83.

62. See the discussion and the references in Dunn, *Sugar and Slaves*, 242.

63. Oldmixon, *British Empire in America*, 2, 126.

64. See the references to the restrictions on blacks in New Hampshire discussed above.

65. Davis, *Problem of Slavery in Western Culture*, 144. For an approach to the question that tends to see racism as invented anew in each colony, see Vaughan, *Roots of American Racism*.

66. Duffy, *Epidemics in Colonial America*, esp. chaps. 2, 3, and 4; Steele, *English Atlantic*, 254–58.

67. See, in addition to the discussion above, in chapter 5, R. C. Nash, "Organization of Trade and Finance." Nash provides a good guide to the literature on the organization of trade within the empire.

68. In addition to the literature cited above, in chapter 5, see Olwell, *Masters, Slaves and Subjects*, 145–58; and Phillip D. Morgan, *Slave Counterpoint*, 134–45.

69. For the Barbados connection of participants in the Salem episode, see Norton, *In the Devil's Snare*, 17, 229. See also Pierson, *Black Yankees*, 80–82.

EPILOGUE

1. Examples of recent scholarship that restively accepts the hypothesis include Kupperman, *Providence Island*, 112–13; Curtin, *Rise and Fall of the Plantation Complex*, 83–84; and Fogel, *Without Consent or Contract*, 22–23.

2. Higman, "Sugar Revolution," 214.

3. Scott, "The Description of Barbados," BL, Sloane MS 3662, 54–59.

4. Dunn, *Sugar and Slaves*, 75.

5. Davies, *North Atlantic World*, 180.

6. In my initial discussion of this issue, I contrasted the dispersed with the "centralized" method of organizing plantations. I have changed *centralized* to *integrated* on the grounds that the term *centralized* invites confusion with changes that occurred much later with the introduction of large, steam-powered mills. See Menard, "Law, Credit, the Supply of Labour."

7. Curtin, *Rise and Fall of the Plantation Complex*, 10–13.

8. Tey, *Daughter of Time*, 103.

9. Berlin, *Many Thousands Gone*, 109–11.

10. The rich literature on the Chesapeake region is introduced in McCusker and Menard, *Economy of British America,* chap. 6.

11. Menard, "Africanization of the Lowcountry Labor Force."

12. Recent literature on the Industrial Revolution is ably surveyed in the introduction to Mokyr, *British Industrial Revolution.* My perspective on the sugar revolution was shaped in part by Bushman's persuasive critique of the idea of a market revolution. See Bushman, "Markets and Composite Farms."

APPENDIX

1. For details, see Menard, "Financing the Lowcountry Export Boom," esp. 663n13.

2. These four maps appear in Carmen, *American Husbandry.*

3. Barrett, "Caribbean Sugar Production Standards"; idem, "Efficient Plantation." Barrett's essays provide a preliminary guide to these documents for French and Spanish colonies.

Bibliography

MANUSCRIPTS

Barbados
Barbados National Archives, Lazaretto, St. Michael's
Recopied Deed Books

Great Britain, British Library, London
Portland MSS
Sloane MS

Great Britain, Public Records Office, London
Colonial Office Papers, America and West Indies

United States of America
John Carter Brown Library, Brown University, Providence, Rhode Island
Maps of Barbados by Richard Ford (1674) and William Mayo (1722)

PRINTED PRIMARY SOURCES

Addis, Henry. *A Letter Sent from Syrranam*. London, 1664.
Bizet, Antoine. "Father Antoine Bizet's Visit to Barbados in 1654." Edited by Jerome Handler. *Journal of the Barbados Historical and Museum Society* 22 (1967): 56–76.
Carman, Harry J., ed. *American Husbandry*. New York, 1939. First published London, 1775.
Clark, W. *Ten Views of Antigua*. London, 1823.
Foster, Nicholas. *A Brief Relation of the Late Horrid Rebellion on the Island of Barbados*. London, 1650.
Fox, George. *To the Ministers, Teachers, and Priests in Barbados*. London, 1672.
Gardyner, George. *A Description of the New World, or, America Islands and Continent*. London, 1651.
Godwyn, Morgan. *The Negro's and Indian's Advocate, Suing for their Admission to the Church, etc.* London, 1680.
Great Newes from the Barbadoes. London, 1676.
Hall, Clayton Colman, ed. *Narratives of Early Maryland, 1633–1684*. New York, 1920.

Harlow, Vincent T., ed. *Colonizing Expeditions to the West Indies and Guiana.* London, 1925.

Henning, William Waller. *The Statutes at Large: Being a Collection of All the Laws of Virginia, from the First Session of the Legislature in the Year 1619.* 3 vols. Richmond, VA, 1809–23.

Jeafferson, John C. *A Young Squire of the Seventeenth Century: From the Papers of Christopher Jeafferson of Dulingham House, Cambridgshire.* London, 1878.

Ligon, Richard. *A True and Exact History of the Island of Barbados.* London, 1647.

Littleton, Edward. *The Groans of the Plantations: Or a True Account of their Grievous and Extreme Sufferings by the Heavy Impositions upon Sugar, and Other Hardships Relating more Particularly to the Island of Barbados.* London, 1689.

Long, Edward. *The History of Jamaica.* 3 vols. London, 1774.

Martin, Samuel. *An Essay on Plantership.* London, 1773.

Pinckard, George. *Notes on the West Indies.* 3 vols. London, 1806.

Plantagenet, Beuchamp. *A Description of the Province of New Albion.* London, 1648.

Robertson, Robert. *A Detection of the State and Situation of the Present Sugar Planters of Barbados and the Leeward Islands.* London, 1732.

Sainsbury, W. E., ed. *Calendar of State Papers, Colonial Series.* 39 vols. London, 1860–78.

Sloane, Hans. *A Voyage to the Islands Madera, Barbados, Neves, S. Christophers and Jamaica, etc.* 2 vols. London, 1707.

Stock, Leo F., ed. *Proceedings and Debates of the British Parliament Respecting North America, 1541–1739.* 3 vols. Washington, DC, 1924–41.

Thomas, Dalby. *A Historical Account of the Rise and Growth of the West Indies.* London, 1690.

Tyron, Thomas. *Friendly Advice to the Gentleman Planters of the East and West Indies. In three parts.* London, 1684.

Venables, General. *The Narrative of General Venables, with an Appendix of Papers Relating to the Expedition to the West Indies and the Conquest of Jamaica, 1654–1655.* Edited by Charles Firth. London, 1900.

Warren, George. *An Impartial Description of Surinam.* London, 1667.

Winthrop, John. *Winthrop Papers, 1498–1649.* Edited by Allyn B. Forbes. 5 vols. Boston, 1929–37.

SECONDARY SOURCES

Allen, Theodore W. *The Invention of the White Race.* 2 vols. London, 1994.

Andrews, Charles M. *The Colonial Period of American History.* 4 vols. New Haven, CT, 1934–38.

Aufhauser, R. K. "The Profitability of Slavery in the British Caribbean." *Journal of Interdisciplinary History* 5 (1974): 45–67.

———. "Slavery and Technological Change." *Journal of Economic History* 34 (1974): 36–50.

Austen, Ralph A., and Woodruff D. Smith. "Private Tooth Decay as Public Economic Virtue: The Slave Sugar Triangle, Consumerism, and European Industrialization." In Inikori and Engerman, *Atlantic Slave Trade,* 83–203.

Bailyn, Bernard, and Phillip D. Morgan, eds. *Strangers in the Realm: Cultural Margins of the British Empire.* Chapel Hill, NC, 1991.

Barrett, Ward. "Caribbean Sugar Production Standards in the Seventeenth and Eighteenth Centuries." In *Merchants and Scholars: Essays in the History of Exploration and Trade,* edited by John Parker. Minneapolis, 1930.

———. *The Efficient Plantation and the Inefficient Hacienda.* James Ford Bell Lecture 16. Minneapolis, 1979.

Batie, Robert C. "Why Sugar? Economic Cycles and the Changing of Staples in the English and French Antilles, 1624–1654." *Journal of Caribbean History* 8–9 (1976): 1–41.

Bean, Richard N., and Robert Paul Thomas. "The Adoption of Slave Labor in British America." In Gemery and Hogendorn, *Uncommon Market,* 377–98.

Beckles, Hilary M. *Centering Women: Gender Discourses in Caribbean Slave Societies.* Princeton, NJ, 1999.

———. "The Economic Origins of Black Slavery in the British West Indies, 1640–1660: A Tentative Economic Model." *Journal of Caribbean History* 16 (1982): 36–56.

———. "English Parliamentary Debate on White Slavery in Barbados, 1659." *Journal of the Barbados Historical and Museum Society* 37 (1982): 344–52.

———. "From Land to Sea: Runaway Barbadian Slaves and Servants, 1630–1700." *Slavery and Abolition* 6 (1985): 79–95.

———. *A History of Barbados: From Amerindian Settlement to Nation State.* Cambridge, 1990.

———. *Natural Rebels: A Social History of Enslaved Black Women in Barbados.* New Brunswick, NJ, 1989.

———. "A Riotous and Unruly Lot: Irish Indentured Servants in the English West Indies, 1644–1713." *William and Mary Quarterly,* 3rd ser., 47 (1990): 503–22.

———. *White Servitude and Black Slavery in Barbados, 1627–1715.* Knoxville, TN, 1989.

Beckles, Hilary M., and Andrew Downes. "The Economics of the Transition to the Black Labor System in Barbados, 1650–1680." *Journal of Interdisciplinary History* 18 (1988): 225–47.

Beckles, Hilary M., and Karl Watson. "Social Protest and Labour Bargaining: The Changing Nature of Slaves' Responses to Plantation Life in Eighteenth-Century Barbados." *Slavery and Abolition* 8 (1987): 272–93.

Bennett, J. Harry. *Bondsmen and Bishops: Slavery and Apprenticeship on the Codrington Plantations of Barbados, 2710–1838.* Berkeley and Los Angeles, 1958.

———. "Cary Helyar: Merchant and Planter of Seventeenth Century Jamaica." *William and Mary Quarterly,* 3rd ser., 21 (1964): 53–76.

―――. "The English Caribbees in the Period of the Civil War, 1642–1646." *William and Mary Quarterly*, 3rd ser., 24 (1967): 359–77.

Berlin, Ira. *Generations of Captivity: A History of Afro-American Slaves.* Cambridge, MA, 2003.

―――. *Many Thousands Gone: The First Two Centuries of Slavery in North America.* Cambridge, MA, 1998.

Berlin, Ira, and Phillip D. Morgan, eds. *Cultivation and Culture: Labor and the Shaping of Slave Life in the Americas.* Charlottesville, VA, 1993.

Bernard, Trevor. *Creole Gentlemen: The Maryland Elite, 1691–1776.* New York, 2002.

Binder, Wolfgang, ed. *Slavery in the Americas.* Würzburg, Germany, 1993.

Blackburn, Robin. *The Making of New World Slavery: From the Baroque to the Modern, 1492–1800.* London, 1997.

Bloch, Marc. *The Historian's Craft.* New York, 1953.

Boogaart, Ernst van den, and Pieter C. Emmer. "The Dutch Participation in the Atlantic Slave Trade, 1596–1650." In Gemery and Hogendorn, *Uncommon Market,* 353–75.

Bowen, H. V. *Elites, Enterprise and the Making of the British Overseas Empire, 1688–1775.* London, 1996.

Boxer, C. R. *The Dutch in Brazil.* Oxford, 1957.

Brenner, Robert. *Merchants and Revolution: Commercial Change, Political Conflict, and London's Overseas Traders, 1550–1653.* Princeton, NJ, 1993.

Bridenbaugh, Carl, and Roberta Bridenbaugh. *No Peace beyond the Line: The English in the Caribbean, 1624–1790.* New York, 1972.

Bruce, Phillip A. *Economic History of Virginia in the Seventeenth Century.* 2 vols. New York, 1895.

Burke, William, and Edmund Burke. *An Account of the European Settlements in America.* 2 vols. London, 1777.

Bushman, Richard L. "Markets and Composite Farms in Early America." *William and Mary Quarterly*, 3rd ser., 55 (1998): 351–74.

Campbell, P. F. *Some Early Barbadian History.* St. Michael, Barbados, 1993.

Canny, Nicholas, ed. *The Origins of Empire.* Vol. 1 of *The Oxford History of the British Empire.* New York, 1998.

Carney, Judith A. *Black Rice: The African Origins of Rice Cultivation in the Americas.* Cambridge, MA, 2001.

Carr, Lois Green, Russell R. Menard, and Lorena S. Walsh. *Robert Cole's World: Agriculture and Society in Early Maryland.* Chapel Hill, NC, 1991.

Carr, Lois Green, and Lorena S. Walsh. "Inventories and the Analysis of Wealth and Consumption Patterns in St. Mary's County, Maryland, 1658–1777." *Historical Methods* 13 (1980): 81–104.

Chandler, Alfred D. "The Expansion of Barbados." *Journal of the Barbados Historical and Museum Society* 1 (1946): 106–36.

Channing, Edward. *The Narragansett Planters: A Study of Causes.* Baltimore, 1886.

Cohen, David W., and Jack P. Greene, eds. *Neither Slave nor Free: The Freedmen of African Descent in the Slave Societies of the New World.* Baltimore, 1972.

Craton, Michael. *Empire, Enslavement and Freedom in the Caribbean*. Kingston, Jamaica, 1997.

———. "Reluctant Creoles: The Planters' World in the British West Indies." In Bailyn and Morgan, *Strangers in the Realm*, 314–62.

———. *Sinews of Empire: A Short History of British Slavery*. New York, 1974.

———. *Testing the Chains: Resistance to Slavery in the British West Indies*. Ithaca, NY, 1982.

Craven, Wesley Frank. *The Southern Colonies in the Seventeenth Century, 1607–1689*. Baton Rouge, LA, 1970.

Curtin, Phillip D. *The Atlantic Slave Trade: A Census*. Madison, WI, 1969.

———. *The Rise and Fall of the Plantation Complex: Essays in Atlantic History*. Cambridge, 1998.

Davies, K. G. *The North Atlantic World in the Seventeenth Century*. Minneapolis, 1974.

———. "The Origins of the Commission System in the West India Trade." *Royal Historical Society, Transactions* 12 (1952): 89–107.

———. *The Royal African Company*. London, 1957.

Davis, David Brion. *The Problem of Slavery in Western Culture*. New York, 1966.

———. *Slavery and Human Progress*. New York, 1984.

Deerr, Noel. *The History of Sugar*. 2 vols. London, 1949.

Dewey, C., and A. G. Hopkins, eds. *The Imperial Impact: Studies in the Economic History of Africa and Asia*. London, 1978.

Dickson, P. G. M. *The Financial Revolution in England: A Study in the Development of Public Credit, 1688–1756*. London, 1967.

Drake, Thomas. *Quakers and Slavery*. New Haven, CT, 1950.

Drescher, Seymour. "The Decline Thesis of British Slavery since Econocide." *Slavery and Abolition* 7 (1986): 3–23.

Duffy, John. *Epidemics in Colonial America*. Baton Rouge, LA, 1953.

Dunn, Richard S. "The English Sugar Islands and the Founding of South Carolina." *South Carolina Historical Magazine* 62 (1971): 81–93.

———. "Servants and Slaves: The Recruitment and Employment of Labor." In Greene and Pole, *Colonial British America*, 157–94.

———. *Sugar and Slaves: The Rise of the Planter Class in the English West Indies, 1624–1713*. Chapel Hill, NC, 1972.

———. "Sugar Production and Slave Women in Jamaica." In Berlin and Morgan, *Cultivation and Culture*, 49–72.

Earle, Carville. "A Staple Interpretation of Slavery and Free Labor." *Geographical Review* 68 (1978): 51–65.

Ernst, Joseph A. *Money and Politics in America, 1755–1775: A Study in the Currency Act of 1764 and the Political Economy of Revolution*. Chapel Hill, NC, 1973.

Edwards, Bryan. *The History, Civil and Commercial, of the British Colonies in the West Indies*. 2 vols. London, 1793.

Ekrich, Roger A. *Bound for America: The Transportation of British Convicts to the Colonies, 1718–1775*. New York, 1987.

Eltis, David. "Free and Coerced Transatlantic Migrations: Some Comparisons." *American Historical Review* 88 (1983): 251–80.

————. *The Rise of African Slavery in the Americas.* Cambridge, 2000.

————. "The Total Product of Barbados, 1664–1701." *Journal of Economic History* 55 (1995): 321–36.

Emmer, P. C. "Jesus Christ was Good, but Trade was Better: An Overview of the Transit Trade of the Dutch Antilles, 1734–1795." In Paquette and Engerman, *Lesser Antilles in the Age of European Expansion*, 206–22.

Engerman, Stanley L. "Europe, the Lesser Antilles and Economic Expansion, 1600–1900." In Paquette and Engerman, *Lesser Antilles in the Age of European Expansion*, 147–64.

————. "The Slave Trade and British Capital Formation in the Eighteenth Century." *Business History Review* 46 (1972): 430–43.

Engerman, Stanley L., Seymour Drescher, and Robert L. Paquette, eds. *Slavery.* New York, 2001.

Engerman, Stanley L., and Robert E. Gallman, eds. *The Cambridge Economic History of the United States.* Vol. 1, *The Colonial Era.* New York, 1996.

Farnell, J. E. "The Navigation Act of 1651, the First Dutch War, and the London Merchant Community." *Economic History Review,* 2nd ser., 16 (1964): 439–54.

Faulkner, William. *Absalom, Absalom!* New York, 1936.

Finley, M. I. *Ancient Slavery and Modern Ideology.* New York, 1983.

Fischer, David Hackett. *Albion's Seed: Four British Folkways in America.* New York, 1989.

Fogel, Robert William. *Without Consent or Contract: The Rise and Fall of American Slavery.* New York, 1989.

Fogel, Robert William, James Trussell, Roderick C. Floud, Clayne L. Pope, and Larry T. Wimmer. "The Economics of Mortality in North America, 1650–1910: A Description of a Research Project." *Historical Methods* 11 (1978): 75–108.

Galenson, David W. "Economic Aspects of the Growth of Slavery in the Seventeenth Century Chesapeake." In Solow, *Slavery and the Rise of the Atlantic System,* 365–92.

————. *Traders, Planters, and Slaves: Market Behavior in Early English America.* New York, 1986.

————. *White Servitude in Colonial America: An Economic Analysis.* New York, 1981.

Galoway, J. H. "The Mediterranean Sugar Industry." *Geographical Review* 67 (1977): 177–92.

Games, Alison F. *Migration and the Origins of the English Atlantic World.* Cambridge, MA, 1999.

————. "Opportunity and Mobility in Early Barbados." In Paquette and Engerman, *Lesser Antilles in the Age of European Expansion*, 165–81.

Gaspar, Barry David B. *Bondsmen and Rebels: A Study of Master Slave Relations in Antigua.* Baltimore, 1985.

————. "Rigid and Inclement: Origins of the Jamaican Slave Laws of the Seventeenth Century." In Tomlins and Mann, *Many Legalities of Early America,* 78–97.

Gemery, Henry A. "Emigration from the British Isles to the New World: Inferences from Colonial Populations." *Research in Economic History* 5 (1980): 179–231.

Gemery, Henry A., and Jan S. Hogendorn. "The Atlantic Slave Trade: a Tentative Economic Model." *Journal of African History* 15, no. 2 (1974): 223–46.

———. "Technological Change, Slavery, and the Slave Trade." In Dewey and Hopkins, *Imperial Impact*, 243–58.

———, eds. *The Uncommon Market: Essays in the Economic History of the Atlantic Slave Trade*. New York, 1979.

Genovese, Elizabeth Fox, and Eugene D. Genovese. *The Fruits of Merchant Capital: Slavery and Bourgeois Property in the Rise and Expansion of Capitalism*. New York, 1983.

Genovese, Eugene. *The World the Slaveholders Made: Two Essays in Interpretation*. Hanover, NH, 1988.

Ghachem, Malick W. "The Slave's Two Bodies: The Life of an American Legal Fiction." *William and Mary Quarterly*, 3rd ser., 40 (2003): 809–41.

Gragg, Larry. "To Procure Negroes: The English Slave Trade to Barbados, 1627–1660." *Slavery and Abolition* 16 (1999): 65–84.

Gray, Lewis C. *History of Agriculture in the Southern United States to 1860*. 2 vols. Washington, DC, 1932.

Green, William A. "Race and Slavery: Considerations on the Williams Thesis." In Solow and Engerman, *British Capitalism and Caribbean Slavery*, 25–49.

———. "Supply vs. Demand in the Caribbean Sugar Revolution." *Journal of Interdisciplinary History* 18 (1988): 403–18.

Greene, Jack P. "Changing Identity in the British West Indies in the Early Modern Era: Barbados as a Case Study." In Greene, *Imperatives, Behaviors, and Identities*, 13–68.

———. "Colonial South Carolina and the Caribbean Connection." In Greene, *Imperatives, Behaviors, and Identities*, 68–86.

———. *Imperatives, Behaviors, and Identities: Essays in Early American Cultural History*. Charlottesville, VA, 1992.

Greene, Jack P., Rosemary Brana-Shute, and Randy J. Sparks, eds. *Money, Trade, and Power: The Evolution of Colonial South Carolina's Plantation Society*. Columbia, SC, 2001.

Greene, Jack P., and J. R. Pole, eds. *Colonial British America: Essays in the New History of the Early Modern Era*. Baltimore, 1984.

Grubb, Farley. "Immigrants and Servants in the Colony and Commonwealth of Pennsylvania: A Quantitative and Economic Analysis." PhD diss., University of Chicago, 1984.

Hall, Douglas G. "Absentee-Proprietorship in the British West Indies." *Jamaican Historical Review* 4 (1964): 15–35.

———. "Incalculability as a Feature of Sugar Production during the Eighteenth Century." *Social and Economic Studies* 10 (1961): 340–52.

Hancock, David. *Citizens of the World: London Merchants and the Integration of the British Atlantic Community, 1735–1785*. Cambridge, 1995.

————. "A World of Business to Do: William Freeman and the Foundations of England's Commercial Empire, 1645–1707." *William and Mary Quarterly,* 3rd ser., 57 (2000): 1–34.

Handler, Jerome S., and Frederick W. Lange. *Plantation Slavery in Barbados: Archaeological and Historical Investigation.* Boston, 1978.

Handler, Jerome S., and Arnold A. Sio. "Barbados." In Cohen and Greene, *Neither Slave nor Free,* 214–57.

Harlow, Vincent T. *A History of Barbados, 1625–1685.* Oxford, 1926.

Harris, Cheryl. "Whiteness as Property." *Harvard Law Review* 106 (1993): 1701–91.

Hatfield, April Lee. *Atlantic Virginia: Seventeenth Century Intercolonial Relations.* Philadelphia, 2004.

Higman, Barry W. "Economic and Social Development of the British West Indies." In Engerman and Gallman, *Cambridge Economic History of the United States,* 297–336.

————. *Slave Populations of the British Caribbean, 1807–1834.* Baltimore, 1984.

————. "The Sugar Revolution." *Economic History Review,* 2nd ser., 53 (2000): 213–36.

Horn, James. "Servant Migration to the Chesapeake in the Seventeenth Century." In Tate and Ammerman, *Chesapeake in the Seventeenth Century,* 51–95.

Inikori, Joseph E. *Africans and the Industrial Revolution in England: A Study in International Trade and Economic Development.* Cambridge, 2002.

Inikori, Joseph E., and Stanley L. Engerman, eds. *The Atlantic Slave Trade: Effects on Economies, Societies and Peoples of Africa, the Americas, and Europe.* Durham, NC, 1992.

Innes, F. C. "The Pre-Sugar Era of European Settlement in Barbados." *Journal of Caribbean History* 1 (1970): 1–22.

James, Sydney V. *Colonial Rhode Island: A History.* New York, 1975.

Jelatis, Virginia. "Tangled Up in Blue: The Rise and Fall of the Indigo Industry in South Carolina." PhD diss., University of Minnesota, 1999.

Johnson, Worthington B. "The Origin and Nature of Slavery in Maryland." *Maryland Historical Magazine* 73 (1978): 136–45.

Jordan, David W. *Foundations of Representative Government in Maryland, 1632–1715.* Princeton, NJ, 1987.

Jordan, Winthrop D. *White over Black: American Attitudes toward the Negro, 1550–1812.* Chapel Hill, NC, 1968.

Jordan, Winthrop D., and Sheila Skemp, eds. *Race and Family in the Colonial South.* Jackson, MS, 1987.

Kolchin, Peter. *American Slavery, 1618–1877.* New York, 1993.

Kupperman, Karen Ordahl. *Providence Island, 1630–1641: The Other Puritan Colony.* New York, 1993.

Kussmaul, Ann. *Servants in Husbandry in Early Modern England.* Cambridge, 1981.

Lakwete, Angela. "Cotton Ginning in America, 1780–1860." PhD diss., University of Delaware, 1996.

Land, Aubrey C., Lois Green Carr, and Edward C. Papenfuse, eds. *Law, Society and Politics in Early Maryland.* Baltimore, 1977.

Lovejoy, Paul. *Transformations in Slavery: A History of Slavery in Africa.* New York, 1983.

Manning, Patrick. *Slavery and African Life: Occidental, Oriental and African Slave Trades.* New York, 1990.

Marshall, Woodville K. "Provision Ground and Plantation Labor in Four Windward Islands: Competition for Resources during Slavery." In Berlin and Morgan, *Cultivation and Culture,* 203–20.

Mazumdar, Sucheta. *Sugar and Society in China: Peasants, Technology, and the World Market.* Cambridge, MA, 1998.

McCusker, John J. "The Business of Distilling in the Old World and the New World during the Seventeenth and the Eighteenth Centuries: The Rise of a New Enterprise and its Connection with Colonial America." In McCusker and Morgan, *Early Modern Atlantic Economy,* 186–224.

————. *Money and Exchange in Europe and America, 1600–1775: A Handbook.* Chapel Hill, NC, 1973.

————. *Rum and the American Revolution: The Rum Trade and the Balance of Payments of the Thirteen Continental Colonies.* 2 vols. New York, 1989.

————. "The Rum Trade and the Balance of Payments of the Thirteen Continental Colonies, 1650–1775." PhD diss., University of Pittsburgh, 1970.

————, ed. *Lois Green Carr: The Chesapeake and Beyond—a Celebration.* Crownsville, MD, 1992.

McCusker, John J., and Russell R. Menard. *The Economy of British America, 1607–1789.* Chapel Hill, NC, 1985.

————. "The Sugar Industry in the Seventeenth Century: A New Perspective on the Barbadian Sugar Revolution." In Schwartz, *Tropical Babylons,* 289–330.

McCusker, John J., and Kenneth Morgan, eds. *The Early Modern Atlantic Economy.* Cambridge, 2000.

McGraw, Judith A., ed. *Early American Technology: Making and Doing Things from the Colonial Era to 1850.* Chapel Hill, NC, 1994.

Mechner, Emily. "Pirates and Planters: Trade and Development in the Caribbean, 1492–1680." PhD diss., Harvard University, 1990.

Menard, Russell R. "The Africanization of the Lowcountry Labor Force, 1670–1730." In Jordan and Skemp, *Race and Family in the Colonial South,* 81–110.

————. "British Migration to the Chesapeake Colonies in the Seventeenth Century." In *Colonial Chesapeake Society,* edited by Lois Green Carr, Philip D. Morgan, and Jean B. Russo, 99–132. Chapel Hill, NC, 1988.

————. "Capitalism and Slavery: Personal Reflections on Eric Williams and the Reconstruction of Early American History." In *The World Turned Upside Down,* edited by Michael Kennedy and William Shade, 321–33. Bethlehem, PA, 2001.

————. "Financing the Lowcountry Export Boom: Capital and Growth in Early South Carolina." *William and Mary Quarterly,* 3rd ser., 51 (1994): 659–76.

————. "Law, Credit, the Supply of Labour and the Organization of Sugar Production in the Greater Caribbean: A Comparison of Brazil and Barbados in the Seventeenth Century." In McCusker and Morgan, *Early Modern Atlantic Economy*, 154–62.

————. *Migrants, Servants and Slaves: Unfree Labour in Colonial British America.* London, 2001.

————. "Migration, Ethnicity, and the Rise of an Atlantic Economy: The Repeopling of British America." In *A Century of European Migrations*, edited by Rudolph J. Vecoli and Suzanne M. Sinke, 58–77. Urbana, IL, 1991.

————. "Reckoning with Williams: Capitalism and Slavery and the Reconstruction of Early American History." *Callaloo* 20 (1998): 791–99.

————. "The Tobacco Industry in the Chesapeake Colonies, 1617–1730: An Interpretation." *Research in Economic History* 5 (1980): 109–77.

————. "Toward African Slavery in Barbados: The Origins of a West Indian Plantation Regime." In McCusker, *Lois Green Carr*, 19–27.

————. "Transitions to African Slavery in British America, 1630–1730: Barbados, Virginia, and South Carolina." *Indian Historical Review* (New Delhi) 15 (1988–89): 33–49.

————. "Transport Costs and Long Range Trade, 1300–1800: Was There a European Transport Revolution in the Early Modern Era?" In Tracy, *Rise of Merchant Empires*, 118–275.

Menard, Russell R., and Stuart B. Schwartz. "Why African Slavery? Labor Force Transitions in Brazil, Mexico, and the Carolina Lowcountry." In Binder, *Slavery in the Americas*, 89–114.

Menig, D. W. *The Shaping of America: A Geographical Perspective on 500 years of History.* Vol. 1, *Atlantic America, 1492–1800.* New Haven, CT, 1960.

Merrens, H. Roy, ed. *The Colonial South Carolina Scene: Contemporary Views, 1697–1774.* Columbia, SC, 1977.

Meyers, Suzanne, and Igor Kopytoff, eds. *Slavery in Africa: Historical and Anthropological Perspectives.* Madison, WI, 1977.

Mill, John Stuart. *Principles of Political Economy.* New York, 1876.

Mintz, Sidney. *Sweetness and Power: The Place of Sugar in Modern History.* New York, 1985.

Mintz, Sidney, and Douglas Hall. "The Origins of the Jamaican Internal Marketing System." In *Papers in Caribbean Anthropology*, no. 57, pp. 3–26. New Haven, 1970.

Mokyr, Joel, ed. *The British Industrial Revolution: An Economic Perspective.* Boulder, CO, 1993

Morgan, Edmund S. *American Slavery, American Freedom: The Ordeal of Colonial Virginia.* New York, 1975.

Morgan, Kenneth. *Slavery and Servitude in Colonial North America.* New York, 2000.

————. *Slavery, Atlantic Trade and the British Economy.* Cambridge, 2000.

Morgan, Phillip D. *Slave Counterpoint: Black Culture in the Eighteenth Century Chesapeake and Lowcountry.* Chapel Hill, NC, 1998.

————. "Task and Gang Systems: The Organization of Labor on New World Plantations." In *Work and Labor in Early America*, edited by S. Innes, 189–222. Chapel Hill, NC, 1988.

———. "Work and Culture: The Task System and the World of Lowcountry Blacks, 1700–1880." *William and Mary Quarterly*, 3rd ser., 39 (1982): 563–99.

Morris, Richard B. *Government and Labor in Early America*. New York, 1946.

Mulcahy, Mathew. "Melancholy and Fatal Calamities: Natural Disasters in the Greater Caribbean, 1623–1781." PhD diss., 1999.

———. "Weathering the Storms: Hurricanes and Risk in the British Greater Caribbean." *Business History Review* 78 (2004): 635–63.

Mullin, Michael. *Africa in America: Slave Acculturation and Resistance in the American South and the British Caribbean, 1736–1831*. Urbana, IL, 1992.

Nash, Gary. *Urban Crucible: Social Change, Political Consciousness, and the Origins of the American Revolution*. Cambridge, 1979.

Nash, R. C. "The Organization of Trade and Finance in the Atlantic Economy: Britain and South Carolina, 1670–1775." In Greene, Brana-Shute, and Sparks, *Money, Trade, and Power*, 74–108.

Nettels, Curtis P. *The Money Supply of the American Colonies before 1720*. University of Wisconsin Studies in the Social Sciences and History, no. 20. Madison, WI, 1934.

Nicholson, Barry J. "Legal Borrowing and the Origins of Slave Law in the British Colonies." *American Journal of Legal History* 18 (1994): 38–54.

Norton, Mary Beth. *In the Devil's Snare: The Salem Witchcraft Crisis of 1692*. New York, 2003.

Oldmixon, John. *The British Empire in America: Containing the History of the Discovery, Settlement Progress and State of the Colonies on the Continent and Islands of America*. 2 vols. London, 1708.

Olwell, Robert. *Masters, Slaves and Subjects: The Culture of Power in the South Carolina Lowcountry, 1740–1790*. Ithaca, NY, 1998.

Papenfuse, Edward C., Alan F. Day, David W. Jordan, and Gregory A. Stiverson, eds. *A Biographical Dictionary of the Maryland Legislature, 1635–1789*. Baltimore, 1979.

Paquette, Robert L., and Stanley L. Engerman, eds. *The Lesser Antilles in the Age of European Expansion*. Gainesville, FL, 1996.

Parent, Anthony S., Jr. *Foul Means: The Formation of a Slave Society in Virginia, 1660–1740*. Chapel Hill, NC, 2003.

Pares, Richard. "The London Sugar Market, 1740–1769." *Economic History Review*, 2nd ser., 9 (1956): 254–70.

———. "Merchants and Planters." *Economic History Review*, suppl. no. 4 (2001).

———. *A West India Fortune*. London, 1950.

Phillips, William D., Jr. *Slavery from Roman Times to the Early Transatlantic Trade*. Minneapolis, 1985.

Pierson, William D. *Black Yankees: The Development of an Afro-American Subculture in Eighteenth-Century New England*. Amherst, MA, 1988.

Postma, Johannes. *The Dutch in the Atlantic Slave Trade, 1600–1815*. Cambridge, 1990.

Price, Jacob M. *Capital and Credit in British Overseas Trade: The View from the Chesapeake, 1700–1776*. Cambridge, MA, 1980.

———. "Colonial Trade and British Economic Development, 1660–1775." *Lex et Scienta* 14 (1978): 106–26.

———. "Credit in the Slave Trade and Plantation Economies." In Solow, *Slavery and the Rise of the Atlantic System,* 293–340.

———. "Economic Function and the Growth of American Port Towns in the Eighteenth Century." *Perspectives in American History* 8 (1974): 121–86.

———. *France and the Chesapeake: A History of the French Tobacco Monopoly, 1674–1791, and of Its Relationship to the British and American Tobacco Trades.* 2 vols. Ann Arbor, MI, 1973.

———. *Perry of London: A Family and Firm on the Atlantic Seaborne Frontier, 1615–1753.* Cambridge, MA, 1992.

———. "Transaction Costs: A Note on Merchant Credit and the Organization of Private Trade." In Tracy, *Rise of Merchant Empires,* 276–97.

Price, Jacob, and Paul G. E. Clemens. "A Revolution of Scale in Overseas Trade: British Firms in the Chesapeake Trade." *Journal of Economic History* 47 (1987): 1–43.

Puckrein, Gary A. *Little England: Plantation Society and Anglo-Barbadian Politics, 1627–1700.* New York, 1984.

Ragatz, Lowell J. *The Fall of the Planter Class in the British Caribbean, 1763–1833: A Study in Social and Economic History.* New York, 1928.

Richardson, David. "The Costs of Survival: The Transport of Slaves in the Middle Passage and the Profitability of the 18th Century British Slave Trade." *Explorations in Economic History* 24 (1987): 178–96.

Ridell, William R. "The Baptism of Slaves in Prince Edward Island." *Journal of Negro History* 4 (1921).

Rochefort, Charles de. *Histoire naturelle et mirale des Iles Antilles de l'Amerique.* Rotterdam, 1663.

Roediger, David R. *Black on White: Black Writers on What It Means to Be White.* New York, 1998.

———. *The Wages of Whiteness: Race and the Making of the American Working Class.* New York, 1991.

Ruggles, Steven. "Migration, Marriage and Mortality: Correcting Sources of Bias in Family Reconstitution." *Population Studies* 55 (1992): 507–22.

Ryden, David B. "Does Decline Make Sense? The West Indian Economy and the Abolition of the British Slave Trade." *Journal of Interdisciplinary History* 31 (2001): 347–74.

———. "One of the Fertilest and Pleasantest Spots: An Analysis of the Slave Economy in Jamaica's St. Andrew Parish, 1753." *Slavery and Abolition* 21 (2000): 32–55.

———. "Producing a Peculiar Commodity: Sugar Manufacturing, Slave Life, and Planter's Profits in Jamaica, 1750–1807." PhD diss., University of Minnesota, 1999.

———. *Promoters of the Slave Trade.* London, 2003.

———, ed. *The British Transatlantic Slave Trade.* Vol. 4, *The Abolitionist Struggle: Promoters of the Slave Trade.* London, 2003.

Sacks, David Harris. *The Widening Gate: Bristol and the Atlantic Economy, 1450–1700.* Berkeley and Los Angeles, 1991.

Schwartz, Stuart B. *Sugar Plantations in the Formation of Brazilian Society.* Cambridge, 1985.

———, ed. *Tropical Babylons: The Sugar Industry before the Seventeenth Century.* Chapel Hill, NC, 2004.

Shammas, Carole. "Black Women's Work and the Evolution of Plantation Society in Virginia." *Labor History* 26 (1985): 5–28.

———. *The Pre-Industrial Consumer in England and America.* Oxford, 1990.

———. "The Revolutionary Impact of European Demand for Tropical Goods." In McCusker and Morgan, *Early Modern Atlantic Economy,* 163–85.

Shepherd, James F., and Gary M. Walton. *Shipping, Maritime Trade and the Economic Development of Colonial North America.* Cambridge, 1972.

Sheridan, Richard B. "Samuel Martin, Innovating Sugar Planter of Antigua, 1750–1776." *Agricultural History* 24 (1960): 126–39.

———. *Sugar and Slavery: An Economic History of the English West Indies, 1623–1775.* Kingston, Jamaica, 1974.

———. "The Wealth of Jamaica in the Eighteenth Century." *Economic History Review,* 2nd ser., 18 (1965): 292–311.

———. "The Wealth of Jamaica in the Eighteenth Century: A Rejoinder." *Economic History Review,* 2nd ser., 21 (1968): 46–61.

Sirmans, Eugene M. *Colonial South Carolina: A Political History, 1663–1763.* Chapel Hill, NC, 1966.

Smith, Adam. *An Inquiry into the Nature and Causes of the Wealth of Nations.* New York, 1937. First published London, 1775.

Solow, Barbara L., ed. *Slavery and the Rise of the Atlantic System.* New York, 1991.

Solow, Barbara L., and Stanley L. Engerman, eds. *British Capitalism and Caribbean Slavery.* New York, 1987.

Starkey, Otis P. *The Economic Geography of Barbados.* New York, 1939.

Steele, Ian K. *The English Atlantic, 1675–1740: An Exploration of Communication and Community.* New York, 1986.

Steensgaard, Neils. "The Growth and Composition of the Long Distance Trade of England and the Dutch Republic in the Early Modern World." In Tracy, *Rise of Merchant Empires,* 102–52.

Steinfeld, Robert J. *The Invention of Free Labor: The Employment Relation in English and American Law and Culture, 1360–1870.* Chapel Hill, NC, 1991.

Tate, Thad W., and David Ammerman, eds. *The Chesapeake in the Seventeenth Century: Essays on Anglo-American Society and Politics.* Chapel Hill, NC, 1979.

Tey, Josephine. *The Daughter of Time.* London, 1979.

Thomas, R. P. "The Sugar Colonies of the Old Empire: Profit or Loss to Great Britain." *Economic History Review,* 2nd ser., 21 (1968): 30–45.

Thompson, Edward P. *The Making of the English Working Class.* London, 1965.

Thornton, Archibald P. "Some Statistics of West Indian Produce, Shipping and Revenue, 1660–1685." *Caribbean Historical Review* 4 (1954): 251–80.

———. *West-India Policy under the Restoration.* Oxford, 1936.

Tomlins, Christopher L., and Bruce Mann, eds. *The Many Legalities of Early America*. Chapel Hill, NC, 2001.

Tracy, James D., ed. *The Rise of Merchant Empires: Long-Distance Trade in the Early Modern World*. New York, 1990.

Vaughan, Alden T. *The Roots of American Racism*. New York, 1995.

Wacker, David O., and Paul G. E. Clemens. *Land Use in Early New Jersey: A Historical Geography*. Newark, NJ, 1964.

Wallerstein, Immanuel. *The Modern World System*. 3 vols. New York, 1974–78.

Walsh, Lorena S. "Servitude and Opportunity in Charles County, Maryland, 1658–1705." In Land, Carr, and Papenfuse, *Law, Society and Politics in Early Maryland*, 111–15.

———. "Slave Society and Tobacco Production in the Tidewater Chesapeake, 1620–1780." In Berlin and Morgan, *Cultivation and Culture*, 170–203.

Ward, J. R. "The Profitability of Sugar Planting in the British West Indies, 1650–1834." *Economic History Review*, 2nd ser., 31 (1978): 197–213.

Watson, A. M. "The Arab Agricultural Revolution and its Diffusion, 700–1100." *Journal of Economic History* 34 (1974): 8–35.

Watts, David. "Origins of Barbadian Cane Hole Agriculture." *Journal of the Barbados Historical and Museum Society* 42 (1987): 143–51.

———. *The West Indies: Patterns of Development, Culture and Environmental Change since 1492*. Cambridge, 1987.

Wells, Robert V. *The Population of the British Colonies in America before 1776: A Survey of Census Data*. Princeton, NJ, 1975.

Wiecek, William M. "The Statutory Law of Slavery and Race in the Thirteen Mainland Colonies of British America." *William and Mary Quarterly*, 3rd ser., 34 (1977): 258–80.

Williams, Eric. *Capitalism and Slavery*. Chapel Hill, NC, 1944.

———. *From Columbus to Castro: The History of the Caribbean*. New York, 1984.

Williamson, James A. *The English in Guiana and on the Amazon*. London, 1923.

Wockeck, Marianne S. *The Trade in Strangers: The Beginnings of Mass Migration to North America*. University Park, PA, 1999.

Wood, Gordon. "A Century of Writing Early American History: Then and Now Compared; or How Henry Adams Got It Wrong." *American Historical Review* 100 (1999): 697–716.

Wood, Peter H. *Black Majority: Negroes in South Carolina from 1670 through the Stono Rebellion*. New York, 1974.

Wrigley, E. A., and R. S. Schofield. *The Population History of England, 1541–1871: A Reconstruction*. Cambridge, 1989.

Zahedieh, Nuala. "Overseas Expansion and Trade in the Seventeenth Century." In Canny, *Origins of Empire*, 398–422.

Index